FANTASTIC
EARTH
FACTS

Miles
Kelly

First published in 2017 by Miles Kelly Publishing Ltd
Harding's Barn, Bardfield End Green, Thaxted, Essex, CM6 3PX, UK

Copyright © Miles Kelly Publishing Ltd 2017

This edition updated and printed 2020

6 8 10 9 7 5

Publishing Director Belinda Gallagher
Creative Director Jo Cowan
Editors Carly Blake, Fran Bromage, Rosie Neave, Sarah Parkin, Claire Philip
Editorial Assistant Lauren White
Designers Kayleigh Allen, John Christopher, Jo Cowan, Joe Jones, Sally Lace,
Simon Lee, Sophie Pelham, Andrea Slane, Elaine Wilkinson
Image Manager Liberty Newton
Production Elizabeth Collins, Jennifer Brunwin-Jones
Reprographics Stephan Davis
Assets Lorraine King

ISBN 978-1-78989-055-6

Printed in China

British Library Cataloguing-in-Publication Data
A catalogue record for this book is available from the British Library

Made with paper from a sustainable forest

www.mileskelly.net

Contents

PLANET EARTH.......................12-23

EXTREME EARTH.....................24-65

VOLCANOES.........................66-107

WEATHER..........................108-149

ROCKS AND MINERALS...........150-191

FOSSILS.............................192-233

POLAR LANDS.....................234-275

RAINFORESTS.......................276-317

OCEANS..............................318-331

DEEP OCEAN.......................332-373

INDEX...............................374

ACKNOWLEDGEMENTS.................383

PLANET EARTH

Planet Earth 12

Where did Earth come from?. . 14

In a spin 16

Massive mountains 18

Rivers and lakes 20

The planet of life 22

EXTREME EARTH

Extreme Earth 24

Climbing high. 26

Violent volcanoes 28

Hot springs and fountains 30

Rivers and waterfalls 32

Record-breaking lakes 34

Going underground. 36

Extreme earthquakes. 38

Terrifying tsunamis 40

Dry deserts 42

The ends of the Earth 44

Glaciers and icebergs. 46

Amazing oceans 48

Raining cats and dogs 50

Lightning strikes 52

Hammered by hail 54

Extreme snow and ice. 56

Twisting tornadoes 58

Howling hurricanes. 60

Water, water everywhere 62

Disastrous droughts. 64

VOLCANOES

Volcanoes. 66

Around the world 68

Plate boundaries 70

Parts of a volcano. 72

Eruptions 74

Lava. 76

Volcanic ash. 78

Gentle and explosive. 80

Volcanic features 82

Hazards of a volcano 84

Side effects 86

Using volcanoes 88

Volcano science 90

Fighting volcanoes 92

Mount St Helens. 94

Mount Pinatubo 96

Mount Vesuvius 98

Volcanoes at sea 100

The biggest volcanoes. 102

Past and future 104

Myths and legends 106

WEATHER

Weather 108

The four seasons 110

Fewer seasons 112

What a scorcher! 114

Our atmosphere 116

Clouds and rain 118

Not just fluffy 120

Flood warning 122

Deep freeze. 124

When the wind blows 126

Thunderbolts and lightning . . 128

Eye of the hurricane 130

Wild whirling winds 132

Pretty lights. 134

Made for weather. 136

Weather myths 138

Rain or shine? 140

Instruments and inventors . . . 142

World of weather 144

Weather watch. 146

Changing climate 148

ROCKS AND MINERALS

Rocks and minerals 150

The rock cycle 152

Formed in fire. 154

Incredible igneous 156

Lots of layers 158

Super sedimentary. 160

The rock that changes 162

Marvellous metamorphic. . . . 164

Space rocks. 166

Time capsules 168

The changing landscape 170

What are minerals? 172

Mineral detectives 174

Brilliant colours. 176

Metal minerals 178

Panning for gold 180

Special effects 182

A mineral meal. 184

Gems and jewels 186

Diamonds are forever 188

How to be a geologist. 190

FOSSILS

Fossils 192

What are fossils? 194

Fossils in myth and legend. . . 196

Fossils get scientific 198

How fossils form 200

Mould and cast fossils 202

Special preservation 204

Fossils from jelly 206

Fossils and time. 208

Working out dates 210

How many years ago? 212

Fossil-hunting takes off 214

Famous hot spots 216

Looking for fossils 218

At the dig 220

Cleaning up fossils 222

On display 224

Fossils come alive! 226

Trading, stealing, faking 228

Famous fossils 230

Looking to the future 232

POLAR LANDS

Polar lands 234

The ends of the Earth 236

Extreme seasons 238

Land around a frozen sea . . . 240

Sea around a frozen land . . . 242

Animals of Arctic lands 244

Realm of bears and wolves . . 246

Arctic seals 248

Whales of the far north 250

Summer visitors. 252
In the Southern Ocean 254
Antarctic waters 256
Antarctic birds 258
Sliding and diving. 260
Polar peoples 262

Living in the cold 264
Life of a herder. 266
On top of the world!. 268
Race to the South Pole. 270
Polar lands in peril 272
Protecting the poles. 274

RAINFORESTS

Rainforests 276
What is a rainforest?. 278
Not just jungles. 280
Where in the world? 282
Tree of life 284
Amazing Amazon. 286
People of the Amazon. 288
Forests of Oceania 290
Magical Madagascar 292
African adventures 294
Forests of the Far East. 296
Cloud forests. 298
Peculiar plants 300
On the move 302
Fantastic feathers 304

Kaleidoscope of colour 306
The key to survival. 308
The jungle's bounty 310
Paradise lost 312
Burning issues 314
Forests for the future 316

OCEANS

Oceans 318

Ocean features 320

Swimming machines 322

Shark! 324

Whales and dolphins 326

Ocean reptiles 328

Harvests from the sea 330

DEEP OCEAN

Deep ocean 332

The ocean zones 334

In deep water 336

The Light Zone 338

The Twilight Zone 340

Monster of the deep 342

The Dark Zone 344

The Abyssal Zone 346

Glass in the abyss 348

The Hadal Zone 350

Muds and oozes 352

Deep heat 354

Deep-sea coral 356

On the move 358

Breathing and diving 360

Glow in the dark 362

Deep-sea food 364

Anglerfish 366

Hide and seek 368

Searching the deep 370

Sea changes 372

PLANET EARTH

1 **The Earth is a huge ball of rock moving through space at nearly 3000 metres per second.** It weighs 6000 million, million, million tonnes. Up to two-thirds of the Earth's rocky surface is covered by water – this makes the seas and oceans. Rock that is not covered by water makes the land. Surrounding the Earth is a layer of gases called the atmosphere (air). This reaches about 700 kilometres from the Earth's surface – then space begins.

▶ Mercury, the planet nearest to the Sun, is small and hot. Venus and Earth are rocky and cooler.

Venus

Mercury

Sun

Where did Earth come from?

2 **The Earth came from a cloud in space.**
Scientists think the Earth formed from a huge
cloud of gas and dust around 4500 million
years ago. A star near the cloud exploded,
making the cloud spin. As the cloud spun
around, gases gathered at its centre and
formed the Sun. Dust whizzed around
the Sun and stuck together to form
lumps of rock. In time the rocks crashed
into each other to make the planets.
The Earth is one of these planets.

5. The Earth was made up
of one large piece of land,
now split into seven chunks
known as continents

1. Cloud starts to spin

▶ Clouds of gas and dust are made
by the remains of old stars that
have exploded or simply stopped
shining. It is here that new stars
and their planets form.

4. Volcanoes erupt,
releasing gases,
helping to form the
first atmosphere

3. The Earth begins to cool
and a hard shell forms

2. Dust gathers into lumps of
rock which form a small planet

3 At first the Earth was very
hot. As the rocks crashed together
they warmed each other up. Later, as
the Earth formed, the rocks inside it
melted. The new Earth was a ball
of liquid rock with a thin, solid shell.

4 Huge numbers of large rocks called meteorites crashed into the Earth. They made round hollows on the surface. These hollows are called craters. The Moon was hit with rocks at the same time. Look at the Moon with binoculars – you can see the craters that were made long ago.

► The Moon was also hit by rocks in space, and these made huge craters, and mountain ranges up to 5000 metres high.

▼ Erupting volcanoes and fierce storms helped form the atmosphere and oceans. These provided energy that was needed for life on Earth to begin.

5 The oceans and seas formed as the Earth cooled down. Volcanoes erupted, letting out steam, gases and rocks from inside the Earth. As the Earth cooled, the steam changed to water droplets and made clouds. As the Earth cooled further, rain fell from the clouds. It rained for millions of years to make the seas and oceans.

I DON'T BELIEVE IT!
Millions of rocks crash into Earth as it speeds through space. Some larger ones may reach the ground as meteorites.

In a spin

6 **The Earth is like a huge spinning top.** It continues to spin because it was formed from a spinning cloud of gas and dust. It does not spin straight up like a top but leans a little to one side. The Earth takes 24 hours to spin around once. We call this period of time a day.

Mid-day

Evening

7 **The Earth's spinning makes day and night.** Each part of the Earth spins towards the Sun, and then away from it every day. When a part of the Earth is facing the Sun it is day-time there. When that part is facing away from the Sun it is night-time. Is the Earth facing the Sun or facing away from it where you are?

◀ If you were in space and looked at the Earth from the side, it would appear to move from left to right. If you looked down on Earth from the North Pole, it would seem to be moving anticlockwise.

8 **The Earth spins around its Poles.** The Earth spins around two points on its surface. They are at opposite ends of the Earth. One is on top of the Earth. It is called the North Pole. The other is at the bottom of the Earth. It is called the South Pole. The North and South Poles are so cold, they are covered by ice and snow.

▲ The Earth moves around the Sun in a path called an orbit. It takes a year to make this journey. In that time it spins round 365 and a quarter times.

Morning

Night

▲ As one part of the Earth turns into sunlight, another part turns into darkness. It is morning when a part turns into sunlight, and evening when it turns into darkness.

MAKE A COMPASS

A compass is used to find the direction of the North and South Poles.

You will need:

a bowl of water   a piece of wood
a bar magnet   a real compass

Place the wood in the water with the magnet on top. Make sure they do not touch the sides. When the wood is still, check the direction the magnet is pointing in with your compass, by placing it on a flat surface. It will tell you the direction of the North and South Poles.

9 The spinning Earth acts like a magnet. At the centre of the Earth is liquid iron. As the Earth spins, it makes the iron behave like a magnet with a North and South Pole. These act on the magnet in a compass to make the needle point to the North and South Poles.

Massive mountains

10 **The youngest mountains on Earth are the highest.** Highest of all is Mount Everest, which formed 15 million years ago. Young mountains have jagged peaks because softer rocks on the mountain top are broken down by the weather. These pointy peaks are made from harder rocks that take longer to break down. In time, even these hard rocks are worn away. This makes an older mountain shorter and gives its top a rounded shape.

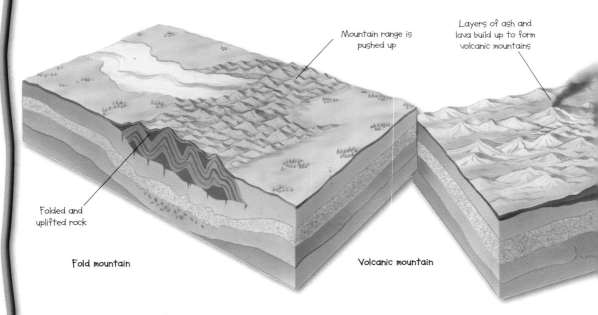

Mountain range is pushed up

Layers of ash and lava build up to form volcanic mountains

Folded and uplifted rock

Fold mountain

Volcanic mountain

11 When plates in the Earth's crust crash together, mountains are formed. When two continental plates crash together, the crust at the edge of the plates crumples and folds, pushing up ranges of mountains. The Himalayan Mountains in Asia formed in this way.

12 Some of the Earth's highest mountains are volcanoes. These are formed when molten rock (lava) erupts through the Earth's crust. As the lava cools, it forms a rocky layer. With each new eruption, another layer is added.

▲ Mountains are the tallest things on Earth. A good example of a young mountain range are the Himalayas, with their sharp, jagged peaks.

MAKE FOLD MOUNTAINS

Put a towel on a table top. Place one hand at either end of the towel. Push your hands together slowly and watch miniature fold mountains form.

Active volcano

Molten rock

Block forced up

Fault

Block mountain

Block forced down

13 **The movement of the Earth's crust can make blocks of rock pop up to make mountains.** When the plates in the crust push together, they make heat, which softens the rock, letting it fold. Farther away from this heat, cooler rock snaps when it is pushed. The snapped rock makes huge cracks called faults in the crust. When a block of rock between two faults is pushed by the rest of the crust, it rises to form a block mountain.

▲ It takes millions of years for mountains to form and the process is happening all the time. A group of mountains is called a range. The biggest ranges are the Alps in Europe, the Andes in South America, the Rockies in North America and the highest of all — the Himalayas in Asia.

Rivers and lakes

14 **A mighty river can start from a spring.** This is a place where water flows from the ground. Rain soaks into the ground, through the soil and rock, until it gushes out on the side of a hill. The trickle of water from a spring is called a stream. Many streams join together to make a river.

15 **Water wears rocks down to make a waterfall.** When a river flows off a layer of hard rock onto softer rock, it wears the softer rock away. The rocks and pebbles in the water grind the soft rock away to make a cliff face. At the bottom of the waterfall they make a deep pool called a plunge pool.

Oxbow lake

Meander

Delta

► High in the mountains, streams join to form the headwater of a river. From here the river flows through the mountains then more slowly across the plains to the sea.

16 **A river changes as it flows to the sea.** Rivers begin in hills and mountains. They are narrow and flow quickly there. When the river flows through flatter land it becomes wider and slow-moving. It makes loops called meanders which may separate and form oxbow lakes. Where the river meets the sea is the river mouth. It may be a wide channel called an estuary or a group of sandy islands called a delta.

◄ Waterfalls may only be a few centimetres high, or come crashing over a cliff with a massive drop. Angel Falls in Venezuela form the highest falls in the world. One of the drops is an amazing 807 metres.

Headwater

17 Lakes form in hollows in the ground. The hollows may be left when glaciers melt or when plates in the crust split open. Some lakes form when a landslide makes a dam across a river.

▲ A landslide has fallen into the river and blocked the flow of water to make a lake.

▼ A volcano can sometimes form in a lake inside a crater.

18 A lake can form in the crater of a volcano. A few crater lakes have formed in craters left by meteorites that hit Earth long ago.

▼ Most lakes are just blue but some are green, pink, red or even white. The Laguna Colorado in Chile is red due to tiny organisms (creatures) that live in the water.

19 Some lake water may be brightly coloured. The colours are made by tiny organisms called algae or by minerals dissolved in the water.

The planet of life

20 There are millions of different kinds of life forms on Earth. So far, life has not been found anywhere else. Living things survive here because it is warm, there is water and the air contains oxygen. If we discover other planets with these conditions, there may be life on them too.

21 Many living things on the Earth are tiny. They are so small that we cannot see them. A whale shark is the largest fish on the planet, yet it feeds on tiny shrimp-like creatures. These in turn feed on even smaller plant-like organisms called plankton,which make food from sunlight and sea water. Microscopic bacteria are found in the soil and even on your skin.

▲ Despite being the biggest fish in the oceans, the mighty whale shark feeds on tiny shrimplike creatures and plankton (right).

22 Animals cannot live without plants. A plant makes food from sunlight, water, air and minerals in the soil. Animals cannot make their own food so many of them eat plants. Others survive by eating the plant-eaters. If plants died out, all the animals would die too.

◄ This caterpillar eats as much plant-life as possible before beginning its change to a butterfly.

23 The air can be full of animals.
On a warm day, midges and gnats form
clouds close to the ground. In spring and
autumn flocks of birds fly to different parts
of the world to nest. On summer evenings
bats hunt for midges flying in the air.

24 The surface of the ground is home
to many small animals. Mice scurry
through the grass. Larger animals
such as deer hide in bushes. The
elephant is the largest land animal.
It does not need to hide because few
animals would attack it.

25 If you dig into the ground you
can find animals living there. The
earthworm is a common creature found in
the soil. It feeds on rotting plants that it
pulls into the soil. Earthworms are eaten
by moles that dig their way underground.

I DON'T BELIEVE IT!
The star-nosed mole has
feelers on the end
of its nose. It
uses them to
find food.

EXTREME EARTH

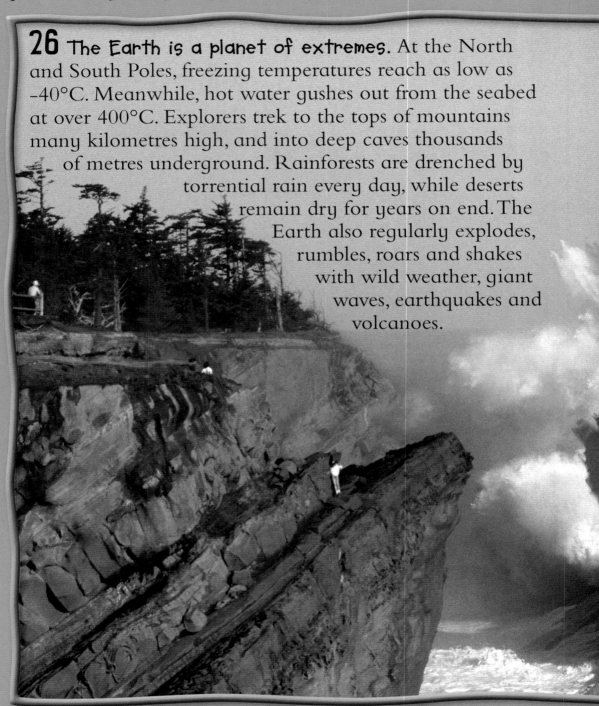

26 **The Earth is a planet of extremes.** At the North and South Poles, freezing temperatures reach as low as –40°C. Meanwhile, hot water gushes out from the seabed at over 400°C. Explorers trek to the tops of mountains many kilometres high, and into deep caves thousands of metres underground. Rainforests are drenched by torrential rain every day, while deserts remain dry for years on end. The Earth also regularly explodes, rumbles, roars and shakes with wild weather, giant waves, earthquakes and volcanoes.

▼ A wave crashes ashore on rocks at Cape Arago, Oregon, USA, throwing up a huge fountain of spray. Heavy waves can sink boats, smash buildings and sweep people off the shore.

Climbing high

27 **The Earth is covered with a thick layer of rock, or 'crust'.** In some places, sections of crust have squeezed together, forcing their way upwards to make mountains. Mountains often form in a long line or group, called a mountain range. High up, it is cold and windy. This means that the tops of mountains are very icy, snowy and stormy.

Mount Everest
8848 metres
(Asia)

Mount Kilimanjaro
5895 metres
(Africa)

Mount Cook 3754 metres (Oceania)

28 **Mount Everest is the world's highest mountain.** It's on the border between Nepal and China, in the Himalayas mountain range. It is about 8848 metres high. The first people to climb to the top of Everest were Edmund Hillary and Tenzing Norgay, on 29 May, 1953.

▼ Mount Everest is so high that climbers have to climb it over several days, stopping at camps along the way.

29 **The highest mountain on Earth isn't the hardest to climb.** Another peak, K2, is much tougher for mountaineers. At 8611 metres, it's the world's second-highest mountain. Its steep slopes and swirling storms make it incredibly dangerous. Fewer than 300 people have ever climbed it, and over 65 have died in the attempt.

▲ Edmund Hillary (left) and Tenzing Norgay, photographed in 1953, the year they became the first to climb Mount Everest. Hillary died in 2008.

Mount Aconcagua 6959 metres
(South America)

Mount McKinley
6194 metres
(North America)

Mount Blanc 4807 metres (Europe)

I DON'T BELIEVE IT!

Mountains seem big to us, but they're very small compared to the whole planet. If the world was shrunk to the size of a football, it would feel totally smooth.

◄ This diagram shows a height comparison of the highest mountains by continent.

30 Most mountains are shaped like big humps — but a cliff is a sheer drop. The east face of Great Trango, a mountain in Pakistan, is 1340 metres high, making it the tallest vertical cliff in the world. There's another giant cliff on Mount Thor in Canada, with a drop of 1250 metres. If a pebble fell off one of these cliffs, it would take more than 15 seconds to reach the bottom!

▼ The city of La Paz in Bolivia is situated in the Andes mountains. It has an altitude (height) of around 3600 metres.

31 Some people don't just climb to the tops of high mountains — they live there! The town of Wenzhuan in Tibet, China, is the highest in the world. It is in the Himalayas, 5100 metres up — that's over 5 kilometres above sea level! The highest capital city is La Paz, in the Andes in Bolivia, South America.

Violent volcanoes

32 **A volcano is a place where hot, liquid rock (magma) bursts out of the Earth.** At the Earth's surface, magma is called lava. Red-hot lava can be seen flowing or shooting out of a volcano. After a volcano erupts, the lava cools into solid rock. These rocky layers build the volcano higher and higher with each eruption.

33 **The biggest eruptions happen when pressure builds up underground.** The magma pushes up and up, but the crust on top stops it from escaping. The ground bulges and swells, until at last the magma bursts out in a huge explosion. This happened at Mount St Helens in Washington State, USA in 1980. The explosion was so huge, it blew away half the mountain!

▼ When first erupted, the temperature of lava is between 700 and 1300 degrees Centigrade.

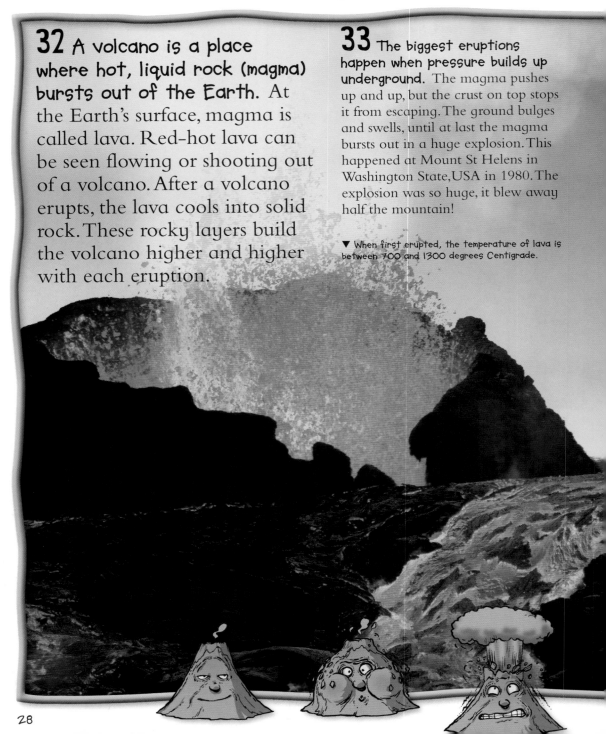

34 The biggest volcanic eruption ever recorded was the eruption of Mount Tambora in Indonesia in 1815. The eruption was heard on the island of Sumatra, over 2000 kilometres away. Ash from the eruption filled the sky and blocked out sunlight all around the Earth. It made the weather very cold, and people called 1816 'the year without a summer'.

▲ Mount Etna in Italy is a large, active volcano. It's fertile slopes are used by farmers to grow crops.

35 Volcanoes can be killers. Victims can be burned by hot lava, hit by flying rocks, suffocated under hot ash or poisoned by gas. After the eruption, ash can mix with rainwater to make fast-flowing mud that can drown whole towns. People are in danger from eruptions because there are many towns and farms close to volcanoes. This is partly because volcanic ash helps to make the land fertile for growing crops.

▲ The island of Surtsey today, more than 40 years after it appeared out of the sea.

36 A volcano can build a brand-new island! In 1963, smoke and steam began to billow out of the sea near Iceland. A volcano was erupting on the seabed. As the lava and ash piled up, it built a new island. The island was named Surtsey. Gradually, moss, grass and trees began to grow, and birds and insects began to live there.

VINEGAR VOLCANO MODEL

You will need:
Vinegar   Bicarbonate of soda   Red food colouring
Sand   Tray   Jug   Plastic bottle

Put a tablespoon of bicarbonate of soda in the plastic bottle. Stand the bottle on a tray and make a cone of sand around it. Put a few drops of red food colouring in half a cup of vinegar. Tip the vinegar into a jug then pour it into the bottle. In a few moments the volcano should erupt with red, frothy 'lava'.

Hot springs and fountains

37 There are natural hot baths and showers all over the world. You might think water outdoors is cold, but in some places, water meets hot rock under the ground and gets heated up. It sometimes even boils. The hot water can then make a lake or spring – or even shoot out of the ground like a fountain, forming a geyser.

38 Besides geysers, the Earth's hot water can form amazing thermal (hot) springs and pools. They often occur in places where there are lots of volcanoes, such as New Zealand and Japan. Some thermal pools are famous for their beautiful colours. These are caused by millions of bacteria (tiny living things) that live in the very hot water.

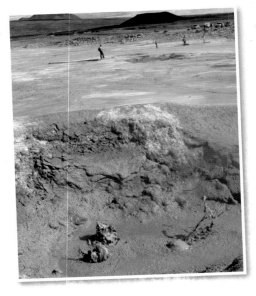

▲ A mudpot, like this one in Myvatn Geothermal Area in Iceland, is a pool of hot, bubbling mud. Some mudpots are boiling hot. Others bubble as hot gases burst up through them.

▲ The Prismatic Spring is the largest hot-water spring in the United States. Its amazing colour is due to bacteria that grow around the edge of the mineral-rich water.

39 You shouldn't stand too close to a geyser — even if nothing's happening! A geyser is a hole in the ground that suddenly shoots out hot water and steam. Under the hole there is a water-filled chamber. Hot rock beneath it heats the water until it rises back to the surface and erupts in a giant jet of water and steam.

40 Old Faithful is one of the world's most famous geysers. Found in Yellowstone National Park USA, it gets its name because it erupts on average once every 94 minutes. Its jet of steam and water can reach 55 metres high — as high as a 15-storey building.

▶ Strokkur (Icelandic for 'churn') is a geyser in Iceland. It erupts regularly, every 5-10 minutes, and can shoot water up to 25 metres in the air.

41 Soap helps geysers to erupt. People discovered this when they tried to use hot water pools and geysers to wash their clothes in. Soap disturbs the cold water in the chamber, helping the hot water to burst through.

I DON'T BELIEVE IT!

Japanese macaque monkeys use thermal springs as hot baths! They live in the mountains of Japan where winters are very cold. They climb into the natural hot pools to keep themselves warm.

▼ When rainwater seeps into the earth, it can be heated by hot rocks underground before rising back up to the surface as hot springs, pools and geysers.

Rainfall adds to groundwater

Geyser

Hot spring

Cold water travels down

Water is heated by hot rocks

Heated water starts to move upwards

Heat from Earth's interior

Rivers and waterfalls

42 **The Earth is laced with thousands of rivers.** Rivers are channels of water that flow towards the sea. They allow the rain that falls on the land to drain away. Rivers also provide people and animals with drinking water and a place to wash, swim and fish. A waterfall is a place where a river flows over a rocky ledge and pours down to a lower level.

43 **The world's longest river is the Nile, in Africa.** It starts in the area near Lake Victoria and flows north to Egypt, where it opens into the Mediterranean Sea. The journey covers nearly 6700 kilometres, and about 3470 cubic metres of water flows out of the Nile every second. The Nile provides water, a transport route, and fishing for millions of people. If it wasn't for the Nile, the civilization of ancient Egypt could not have existed.

44 **Although the Nile is the longest river, the Amazon is the biggest.** The Amazon flows from west to east across South America, and empties into the Atlantic Ocean. It carries 58 times as much water as the Nile, and about 200,000 cubic metres flow out of it each second. In some places, the Amazon is an amazing 60 kilometres wide.

◄ This aerial photo of the River Amazon shows how it twists and loops as it flows through the Amazon rainforest in South America.

▶ At Angel Falls, the world's highest waterfall, the water spreads out into a misty spray as it plunges down the cliff.

◀ Part of the Grand Canyon, with the Colorado River visible at the bottom of a deep gorge.

45 Angel Falls in Venezuela is the world's highest waterfall, spilling over a drop 979 metres high. It flows off the side of a very high, flat-topped mountain. Although it's the world's highest waterfall, it's not the biggest. Many waterfalls are much wider and carry more water – including Niagara Falls in North America and Victoria Falls in Africa.

46 Rivers can cut through solid rock. Over thousands of years, as a river flows, it wears away the rock around it. If the stone is quite soft, the river can carve a deep, steep-sided valley, or gorge. The Grand Canyon in Arizona, USA, is a massive gorge cut by the Colorado River. It is about 450 kilometres long, and in areas it is up to 29 kilometres wide and 1.8 kilometres deep.

Hard rock overhang

Fallen rocks

Plunge pool

Soft rock gets worn away

◀ A waterfall forms where a river flows from hard rock onto softer rock. The softer rock is worn away faster, while the overhanging ledge of hard rock gradually crumbles away. Over time, the waterfall retreats, or moves upstream.

33

Record-breaking lakes

47 The Caspian Sea in central Asia is actually the world's biggest lake! It covers 378,000 square kilometres. It isn't connected to true seas and oceans, but because it's so big, and is salty like the sea, some experts say it isn't a proper lake, either. The world's biggest freshwater (non-salty) lake is Lake Superior, in the USA and Canada.

▼ A picture of the Caspian Sea taken from space. Swirling clouds of sediment (sand and mud) and plankton (tiny plants and animals) can be seen.

Plankton and sediment

48 The Dead Sea in Israel is another lake that is referred to as a sea. At 400 metres below sea level, it is the lowest lake in the world. The Dead Sea is very salty because no rivers flow out of it. All the salts and minerals that are washed into it remain there as the water evaporates in the Sun's heat. In fact the Dead Sea is nine times saltier than the real sea. It gets its name because no fish or other animals can live in such salty water.

49 The world's deepest lake is Lake Baikal in Russia. At its deepest point, it's 1700 metres deep. Because of this, it contains far more water than any other lake in the world. Twenty percent of all the unfrozen freshwater on Earth is in Lake Baikal.

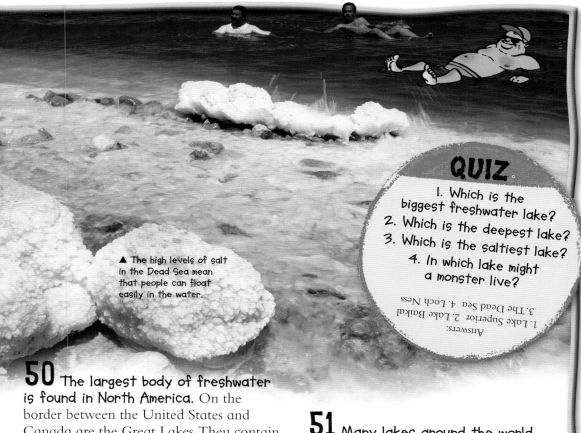

▲ The high levels of salt in the Dead Sea mean that people can float easily in the water.

QUIZ

1. Which is the biggest freshwater lake?
2. Which is the deepest lake?
3. Which is the saltiest lake?
4. In which lake might a monster live?

Answers:
1. Lake Superior 2. Lake Baikal 3. The Dead Sea 4. Loch Ness

50 **The largest body of freshwater is found in North America.** On the border between the United States and Canada are the Great Lakes. They contain one-fifth of the world's freshwater – a staggering 22.8 quadrillion litres!

51 **Many lakes around the world are believed to be home to mysterious monsters.** According to legend, a monster that looks similar to a plesiosaur lives in Loch Ness in Scotland, UK. Plesiosaurs were prehistoric water reptiles that lived at the same time as the dinosaurs. Scientists think they became extinct (died out) 65 million years ago. However some people believe they may still live in Loch Ness.

◄ The five Great Lakes are situated in the USA and Canada. The biggest is Lake Superior, followed by Huron, Michigan, Erie and Ontario.

Going underground

52 **Humans have climbed the world's highest mountains — but many underground caves are still unexplored.** Caves are usually formed by water flowing through cracks underground. The water slowly dissolves certain types of rock, such as limestone. Over thousands of years, it can hollow out deep shafts, tunnels and even huge underground chambers.

▼ Cavers explore one of the many interconnected passageways in Mammoth Cave in Kentucky, U.S.A.

53 **A cave in Malaysia contains the world's biggest single underground chamber.** The Sarawak chamber measures 600 metres long, 400 metres wide and at least 80 metres high. You could line up eight Boeing 747 aircraft, nose to tail, along its length — and still have space to spare.

54 **The world's longest cave system is Mammoth Cave in Kentucky, USA.** It has at least 570 kilometres of passageways — but explorers keep discovering more. Some experts think that only a small part of the whole cave has been explored.

▼ Caves form over thousands of years as water flows through cracks in underground rocks.

1. Rainwater seeps into cracks in rocks

2. Water dissolves rock, forming channels

3. Over time, large cave systems develop

◀ A view inside the Sarawak Chamber in Malaysia, the biggest cave chamber in the world.

55 In 2005, cave explorers broke a record, travelling more than 2 kilometres below the Earth's surface. They were exploring the Voronya Cave in Georgia, near Russia. It is the deepest cave in the world, with a maximum depth of 2140 metres.

56 Workers in a mine in Mexico discovered an amazing cave by accident in 2000. They were drilling a tunnel when they found a large chamber filled with enormous crystals. The crystals are made of the mineral gypsum. They look like giant swords, measuring 2 metres wide by up to 11 metres long. The chamber, which is around 300 metres deep, is now known as the Cave of Crystals.

▶ A geologist (a scientist who studies the Earth and its rocks) stands inside the amazing Cave of Crystals in Mexico.

‖ DON'T BELIEVE IT!

The cave salamander of central Europe is a type of amphibian. It spends its entire life in dark caves and its eyes have become blind as a result.

Extreme earthquakes

57 **An earthquake happens when the Earth's crust moves suddenly.** The crust trembles, cracks, or lurches up and down. Earthquakes can be disastrous. They make houses fall down, tear roads apart and destroy bridges. They can also cause tsunamis.

▶ Earthquakes often happen when two tectonic plates slip and grind against each other. The focus is the point where the plates suddenly move.

Fault line

Focus

Shock waves

58 **Earthquakes happen because the Earth's crust is like a jigsaw.** It is made up of several huge pieces called tectonic plates. The plates fit together quite neatly, covering the Earth. However they can squeeze and push against each other. Sometimes, this pushing makes the plates slip and move suddenly, causing an earthquake.

▼ Earthquakes waves travel through and across the ground in four different ways.

1. Primary waves stretch then squeeze the ground

2. Secondary waves shake the ground from side to side

3. Raleigh waves move in ripples up and down across the surface

4. Love waves travel across the surface moving the ground from side to side

▲ The San Andreas fault in California USA is a crack in the Earth's crust where two tectonic plates join. It has been the scene of several major earthquakes.

► Damage caused by an earthquake in Kobe, Japan, 1995. It measured 7.2 on the Richter Scale and killed more than 6000 people.

59 **Earthquakes can flatten whole cities and kill thousands.** One of the deadliest earthquakes ever hit the city of Tangshan, China in 1976. Most of the city's buildings were destroyed, and at least 240,000 people died. In 2003, an earthquake destroyed the ancient city of Bam in Iran. Over 70 percent of its buildings fell down and around 30,000 people were killed.

60 **Scientists measure earthquakes using the Richter scale.** It records the amount of energy that an earthquake releases. The biggest quakes are not always the most dangerous – it depends where they happen. In a big city, a quake measuring 4 or 5 on the scale could do more damage than a quake measuring 8 or 9 in the countryside.

I DON'T BELIEVE IT!

Since ancient times, people have noticed animals behaving strangely just before earthquakes. Dogs and cats can get agitated, and herds of cattle have been known to run away.

61 **There are things you can do to stay safer during an earthquake.** For example, if you are outside, you should keep away from buildings and power lines. If you are indoors, you should shelter under a strong table. Some places also have quake-proof buildings.

▼ As there are a lot of earthquakes in Japan, school children regularly practise what to do if an earthquake strikes.

Terrifying tsunamis

62 A tsunami is a giant wave, or series of waves. Tsunamis form when a large amount of water in a sea or lake is moved suddenly. This sets up a circular wave, a bit like the ripples you see when you throw a pebble into a pond. The wave then zooms outwards until it hits land.

► A tsunami begins as fast-travelling waves far out at sea. As they approach land, the waves slow down, but become much taller.

As the tall tsunami reaches shallow water, it surges forward onto the shore

63 When a tsunami hits, it can smash the coast to smithereens. Out in the ocean, tsunami waves are very long, low and fast-moving. However as a tsunami moves into shallow water, the wave slows down. All the water in it piles up, forming a powerful wall of water, often between 10 and 30 metres high. As it crashes onto the shore, it can flood towns, tear up trees and sweep away cars, buildings and people.

▼ A tsunami wave crashes onto the promenade on Ao Nang Beach, Thailand in 2004. The power and speed of a tsunami can easily sweep away cars and even entire buildings.

Decreasing depth slows speed but increases wave height

Upward wave

An earthquake beneath the sea floor causes a sudden movement of a massive column of water

65 **The tallest tsunami was higher than a skyscraper.** It occurred at Lituya Bay, in Alaska, USA, in 1958. An earthquake triggered a landslide, and rock and soil plunged into the sea. A giant tsunami, over 500 metres high, zoomed down the bay. Luckily, there were no towns there, but the wave stripped the coast of trees. A giant tsunami such as this is sometimes called a mega tsunami.

64 **Most tsunamis are caused by earthquakes under the sea.** A section of seabed shifts suddenly and the water above it is jolted upwards. Tsunamis can also happen when a landslide or volcanic eruption throws a large amount of rock into the sea, pushing the water aside. This happened when Krakatau, a volcano in Indonesia, erupted in 1883. The tsunamis it caused killed 36,000 people.

66 **A tsunami in the Indian Ocean in 2004 was the deadliest ever recorded.** It was caused by a huge undersea earthquake near the coast of Indonesia. Tsunami waves spread across the ocean and swamped coasts in Indonesia, Thailand, Sri Lanka, India and the Maldive Islands. Around 230,000 people were killed.

▼ The town of Kalutara in Sri Lanka, shown in satellite images before (left) and after (right) being swamped by the deadly 2004 tsunami.

Dry deserts

67 **Deserts occur in places where it's hard for rain to reach.** Most rain comes from clouds that form over the sea and blow onto the land. If there's a big mountain range, the clouds never reach the other side. An area called a rainshadow desert forms. Deserts also form in the middle of continents. The land there is so far from the sea, rainclouds rarely reach it.

▲ The Namib Desert in the southwest of Africa contains some of the biggest sand dunes in the world.

QUIZ

Which of these things would be useful if you were lost in the desert?

1. Mirror
2. Woolly blanket
3. Swimming costume
4. Umbrella

Answers:
1, 2 and 4.
You should not wear swimming gear in case of sunburn

68 **The world's biggest desert used to be a swamp!** The Sahara takes up most of northern Africa. It is made up of 9 million square kilometres of dry sand, pebbles and boulders. There are some oases too, where freshwater springs flow out of the ground. Animal bones and objects left by ancient peoples show that around 6000 years ago, the Sahara was green and swampy. Lots of hippos, crocodiles and humans lived there.

▼ These sand piles show the relative sizes of the world's biggest deserts.

Kalahari Desert
520,000 km²

Gobi Desert
1,040,000 km²

Arabian Desert
1,300,000 km²

Australian deserts
3,800,000 km²

Sahara
9,269,000 km²

70 Deserts aren't always hot. The hottest temperature ever recorded was 57.8°C in Libya. However, deserts can be cold, too. The average temperature in the Atacama Desert, South America is only about 10°C. In the Gobi Desert in Asia, winter temperatures can drop to −40°C. All deserts can be cold at night, as there are no clouds to stop heat escaping.

▲ Desert roses aren't plants. They occur when desert minerals, such as gypsum, combine with sand to form crystals.

▶ Sand dunes form in different shapes and patterns, depending on the type of wind and sand in the desert. The blue arrows indicate the wind direction.

Barchan dune

Parabolic dune

Star dune

Seif dune

Transverse dune

69 The world's driest desert is the Aatacama Desert in Chile, South America. This desert is right next to the sea! It formed because in South America, rainclouds blow from east to west. They drop their rain on the Amazon rainforest, but cannot get past the Andes mountains. On the other side of the Andes, next to the Pacific Ocean, is the Atacama Desert. It is so dry that people who died there 9000 years ago have been preserved as mummies.

71 Even in dry deserts, there is water if you know where to look. Desert plants, such as cactuses store water in their stems, leaves or spines. When rain does fall, it seeps into the ground and stays there. Desert people and animals chew desert plants or dig into the ground to find enough water.

▶ An oasis is a freshwater spring in a desert. Oases form when water stored deep underground meets a barrier of rock that it can't soak through, and rises to the desert surface.

43

The ends of the Earth

72 **The Earth is round, but it has two 'ends' – the North Pole and the South Pole.** The Earth is constantly spinning around an imaginary line called the axis. At the ends of this axis are the poles. Here, it is always cold, because the poles are so far from the Sun.

▲ The position of the poles means they receive little heat from the Sun.

73 **At the North Pole, the average temperature is –20°C.** At the South pole, it's much colder – about –50°C. It's hard for humans to survive in this cold. Water droplets in your breath would freeze on your face. If you were to touch something made of metal with your bare hand, it would freeze onto your skin and stick there.

74 **The area around the North Pole is called the Arctic.** Parts of Europe, Asia and North America reach into the Arctic, but most of it is actually the Arctic Ocean. Many animals live in the Arctic. Polar bears and seals live on the ice and Arctic foxes, Arctic hares and snowy owls live on the land. The sea around the pole is mainly frozen. Scientists have found the ice is melting because of global warming. This is happening because pollution in the air is trapping heat close to the Earth, making it warm up.

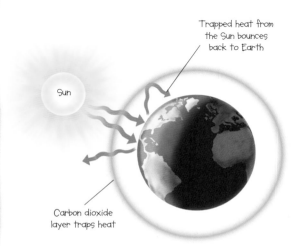

Trapped heat from the Sun bounces back to Earth

Sun

Carbon dioxide layer traps heat

◄ Pollution in the form of carbon dioxide gas traps heat from the Sun, making the Earth warm up. This is one reason that the polar ice is melting.

▲ There are several different species (types) of penguins living in Antarctica. These emperor penguins and their chicks are the largest species.

75 The Antarctic is mostly made up of a huge continent, called Antarctica. Much of it is covered in a layer of solid ice up to 4.7 kilometres thick. The Antarctic is colder than the Arctic because its thick ice and mountains make it very high, and the air is colder higher up. Because Antarctica is so big, the seas around it cannot warm it very much. Little wildlife lives here, but it is home to lots of penguins.

76 Explorers didn't make it to the poles until the 20th century. US explorer Robert Peary and his team reached the North Pole in 1909. Soon afterwards, two explorers raced to reach the South Pole. Norwegian Roald Amundsen arrived first, in December 1911. British explorer Robert Scott arrived one month later – but he and his men died on their way home.

◄ There are no towns or cities in Antarctica as it's so cold, but people do go there to explore and to study nature. They sometimes use snowmobiles to travel around on the snow and ice.

Glaciers and icebergs

77 About two percent of the water in the world is permanently frozen as ice. The ice is found at the chilly polar regions, and on high mountains where the air is freezing cold. On steep slopes, the ice creeps downhill, like a very slow river. This kind of ice 'river' is called a glacier. On high mountains, glaciers flow downhill until they reach warmer air and start to melt. At the poles, many glaciers flow into the sea.

▶ A glacier develops deep cracks called crevasses as it moves downhill. The lower end of a glacier is called the 'snout'.

Snout

Crevasse

▼ Instead of melting on the way down a mountain, this glacier in Prince William Sound, Alaska is flowing into a fjord.

78 One of the world's biggest glaciers, not including the ice at the poles, is the Siachen Glacier in the Himalayas. It is 78 kilometres long and, in places, its ice is over 100 metres thick. India and Pakistan have been fighting a war over who the glacier belongs to since 1984. It has been home to hundreds of soldiers for more than 20 years.

79 Glaciers have shaped the Earth.

As a glacier flows down a mountain, the heavy ice pushes and scrapes at the soil and rocks. This carves a huge, U-shaped valley, known as a glacial valley. 20,000 years ago, when the Earth was in an Ice Age, glaciers covered much more of the land than they do now. Since then, many have melted, revealing their glacial valleys.

81 Icebergs exist because of glaciers.

At the poles, glaciers flow downhill to the sea. There, the ice is slowly pushed out into the water, where it starts to float. Every so often, a large chunk of the glacier breaks off and floats away into the sea. This is an iceberg and it drifts until it melts.

80 Icebergs are a problem for ships.

As an iceberg floats, only about one-tenth of it sticks up out of the sea. The rest is below the surface. Many icebergs have odd, lumpy shapes. This means that a ship can bump into the underwater part of an iceberg, even if the part above water looks far away. Icebergs have damaged and sunk many ships, including the famous ocean liner *Titanic* in 1912.

▼ These penguins are on an iceberg in the Southern Ocean, close to Antarctica. A huge mass of ice can be seen below the water's surface.

MAKE AN ICEBERG

You will need:
Plastic container   Clear bowl   Water

1. Fill the container with water and put it in the freezer.
2. When frozen, remove your 'iceberg' from the container.
3. Fill the clear bowl with water and place your iceberg in it.
4. Look through the side to see how much of your iceberg is underwater, and what shape it makes.

Amazing oceans

82 About 70 percent of the Earth's surface is covered by ocean. The oceans cover about 361 million square kilometres and they are all connected. The average depth of the ocean is 3750 metres. Over 90 percent of the Earth's species (types) of living things live in the oceans.

▶ The *Trieste*, which made the deepest deep-sea dive ever in 1960, was made of a large tank full of gasoline to give buoyancy, with a small round passenger chamber fixed underneath.

83 The deepest point in all the world's oceans is called Challenger Deep. It is in the Mariana Trench in the Pacific Ocean and is 10,923 metres deep – almost 11 kilometres. A tower of 3500 elephants, one on top of the next, could stand in it without touching the surface. In 1960, two explorers, Jacques Piccard and Don Walsh, visited the bottom of Challenger Deep in a diving vessel called *Trieste*.

84 If you were sitting at the bottom of the deep ocean, you'd be squashed flat. At great depths, the weight of all the water above presses from all sides. At the bottom of Challenger Deep, the water pressure is more than 1000 times stronger than at the surface. It's cold, too – only just above freezing point. People can only go there inside specially built diving machines with thick walls that can resist the pressure and cold.

Oceanic crust

Deep-sea trench

Ocean ridge

Underwater volcano

94 Long ago, people used to think lightning was a punishment sent by their gods. However, from the 1500s, scientists began learning about electricity and how it worked. Around 1750, US scientist Benjamin Franklin found that lightning was a kind of electricity. He invented the lightning conductor to protect buildings from lightning damage. It is a metal pole that can be fixed to tall buildings. If lightning strikes, the electrical charge runs down the pole and down a metal wire, then flows safely into the ground.

95 It is quite rare for lightning to strike people, and most of those who are struck, survive. However, lightning does kill over 2000 people around the world each year.

▼ Fulgarites occur when lightning strikes sand. The high temperature makes the sand melt. It eventually cools into hollow tubes.

◀ You can clearly see the lightning conductor on the spire of this cathedral in Liverpool, UK.

96 Lightning can make glass. Glass is made by heating up sand. When lightning strikes in a sandy desert or on a sandy beach, this happens naturally. At the place where the lightning hits the ground, it creates a tubelike tunnel of glass in the sand. These natural glass tubes are called fulgurites.

Hammered by hail

97 **Hail doesn't happen often — but it can be one of the scariest kinds of weather.** When it hails, balls of hard, heavy ice fall out of the sky. Hailstones are usually small, about the size of peas. However, they can be bigger — marble-sized, egg-sized or even tennis-ball-sized. Sometimes they're big enough to crush crops, smash car windows or even kill people.

▼ A man shows off scars on his back — the result of being hit by hailstones while riding a bicycle.

Droplets freeze, circulate and grow bigger

Hail falls from cloud

Water droplets sucked upwards

▲ Hailstones only form inside thunderclouds. Eventually they become too heavy, and fall to the ground as lumps of ice.

98 A hailstone needs a seed. Hailstones form inside thunderclouds when very cold water droplets freeze onto a tiny object — the 'seed'. It could be a speck of dust or a plant seed carried into the sky by the wind. The tiny hailstone is then tossed around by strong winds inside the cloud. More and more layers of ice build up around it, until it is so heavy that it falls to the ground.

99 **The biggest hailstone ever recorded was the size of a melon!** This giant hailstone fell in Aurora, Nebraska, USA in 2003. It measured 18 centimetres across. The biggest hailstones are usually 'aggregate' hailstones. They are made of smaller hailstones that have clumped together before falling to the ground.

I DON'T BELIEVE IT!
Hail usually only falls for a few minutes. However, a hailstorm in Kansas, USA in 1959 went on for over an hour. It covered the ground with a layer of hailstones 46 centimetres deep!

▲ The largest hailstone on record is shown here at actual size. It fell in Nebraska, USA in 2003.

101 **The world's worst hailstorms happen in Northern India and Bangladesh.** Hailstones often destroy crops, and people are regularly injured and killed. In 1888, a hailstorm in India killed around 250 people and more than 1000 sheep and goats.

100 **Sometimes a hailstone forms around a living thing.** A farmer in Quebec, Canada reported finding a frog inside a hailstone in 1864. In 1894, a hailstone with a turtle inside was reported to have fallen on Bovina, Mississippi, USA. Smaller creatures such as spiders and flies are often trapped inside hailstones.

▶ People in Mexico City, Mexico, shovel hailstones after a huge hailstorm on 3 August, 2006.

Extreme snow and ice

102 **An ice storm isn't stormy — but it is dangerous.** Cold rain falls onto freezing cold surfaces. The rain freezes solid, forming a thick layer of ice on the ground, trees and other objects. Ice storms cause 'black ice'— invisible ice on roads that causes accidents. Ice-laden trees fall down, breaking power lines and cutting off roads.

◄ Overburdened by the weight of ice from an ice storm, this tree has collapsed across a road.

▲ An avalanche thunders downhill in Silverton, Colorado, USA. This avalanche was started deliberately by dropping explosives, in order to make the mountains safer for visitors.

103 **An avalanche is a massive pile of snow crashing down a mountainside.** Avalanches can happen whenever lots of snow piles up at the top of a slope. They can be deadly if the snow lands on top of mountain walkers or skiers. Sometimes, big avalanches bury whole houses or even whole villages.

104 **A blizzard, or snowstorm, is even more dangerous than an ice storm.** If you get caught outdoors in a blizzard, it's very easy to get lost. Falling snow fills the air, making it impossible to see. Thick snowdrifts build up, making it hard to walk or drive. People have lost their way and died in blizzards, just a short distance from safety.

▲ Ice can form beautiful crystal patterns as it freezes across a window or car windscreen.

105 **If you get stuck in a blizzard or avalanche, a hole in the snow can keep you warm.** Snow is a great insulator. as heat does not flow through it very well. If you curl up inside a hole dug in the snow, it traps the heat from your body and keeps it close to you. Many people have survived blizzards by making snow holes.

▼ A man uses a reindeer sledge to collect remains of a woolly mammoth discovered buried in ice.

106 **We put food in a freezer to keep it fresh – and the same thing happens in nature.** Snow and ice can stop dead bodies from rotting away. Woolly mammoths that lived 10,000 years ago have been dug out of the ice in northern Russia, perfectly preserved. In 1991, the body of a 5000-year-old man was found in the ice in mountains in Austria. He was nicknamed Ötzi the Iceman.

Twisting tornadoes

107 **Tornadoes are also called twisters.**
A tornado is an incredibly powerful windstorm that twists around in a swirling 'vortex' shape. It forms a narrow funnel or tube, stretching from the clouds to the ground. Tornadoes often look dark because of all the dirt, dust and broken objects that they pick up as they travel across the land.

108 **You can sometimes tell when a tornado is coming, because the sky turns green.** Tornadoes usually develop from thunderclouds. Scientists are not sure exactly how they form. They think that as warm, damp air rises, drier, colder air is pulled in and begins to swirl around it. This creates a spinning tube of wind that moves along the ground. A tornado can travel at up to 80 kilometres an hour.

109 **Tornadoes contain some of the fastest winds on the planet.** Wind inside a tornado can move at up to 500 kilometres an hour. This powerful wind can cause terrible damage. Tornadoes smash buildings, tear off roofs, make bridges collapse, and suck out doors and windows. They can pick up people, animals and cars, and carry them through the air. In 2006, a tornado in Missouri, USA picked up 19-year-old Matt Suter and carried him nearly 400 metres. He survived with only cuts and bruises.

Cold front

Warm front

◀ Tornadoes often form where a front, or mass, of cold air meets warm air. They spin around each other and form a funnel shape.

▲ A large, terrifying tornado snakes down to the ground from the base of a big thundercloud.

Minneapolis

Sioux Falls

Chicago

Denver

Kansas City

St Louis

Wichita

USA

Amarillo

Oklahoma City

Dallas

New Orleans

Houston

MEXICO

110 Damaging tornadoes happen most often in Tornado Alley. This is an area which stretches across the middle of the USA, between the states of Texas and Illinois. Tornadoes are most common there in the tornado season, from April to August. The Great Tri-State Tornado of 1925 was one of the worst ever. It roared through Missouri, Illionois and Indiana, travelling 350 kilometres. It destroyed 15,000 homes and killed 695 people.

◄ The shaded area on this map shows the part of the USA known as Tornado Alley, where tornadoes are most common.

111 Sometimes, tornadoes occur in deserts, or over the sea. In sandy deserts, small tornadoes pick up sand and carry it along in a whirling tower. They are called sand devils or dust devils. Tornadoes over the sea can suck up water in the same way, and carry it for long distances. They are known as waterspouts.

Howling hurricanes

112 **A hurricane is a huge, swirling mass of stormclouds.** Hurricanes form over the ocean, but often travel onto land where they cause floods and destroy whole towns. A typical hurricane is about 500 kilometres wide. In the middle is a small, circular area with no clouds in it, about 70 kilometres wide. This is called the 'eye' of the hurricane.

▲ A man struggles through the high winds of Hurricane Andrew that hit the USA in 1992. Only Hurricane Katrina in 2005 has been more destructive.

114 **The word 'hurricane' is only used to describe storms in the Atlantic Ocean.** The scientific name for this type of storm is a tropical cyclone. The same type of storm in the Indian Ocean is known as a cyclone, and in the Pacific Ocean it is called a typhoon.

113 **Hurricanes begin in the tropics where the ocean is warm.** The ocean surface has to be about 27°C or warmer for a hurricane to start. Warm, wet air rises, forming rainclouds. These begin to swirl in a spiral, caused by the spinning Earth. If the winds reach 118 kilometres an hour, the storm is called a hurricane. Hurricane winds can be as fast as 240 kilometres an hour.

I DON'T BELIEVE IT!

Surrounding the eye of the hurricane is the eyewall. This is a mass of severe thunderstorms where most of the worst weather occurs.

115 Most hurricanes rage harmlessly over the ocean. If they hit land, less powerful, slow-moving hurricanes can cause more damage than stronger hurricanes, which die out more quickly.

116 Hurricanes and other tropical cyclones can cause terrible disasters. When Hurricane Katrina struck the southern coast of the USA in August 2005, it damaged many cities on the coasts of Mississippi and Louisiana. In New Orleans, huge waves broke through the flood barriers and more than 80 percent of the city was flooded. The hurricane killed over 1800 people and caused damage costing over $80 billion. The Bhola cyclone, which hit Bangladesh in 1970, killed over 300,000 people.

▲ A satellite view from space showing a hurricane swirling across the Gulf of Mexico.

117 Scientists think hurricanes are getting worse. Global warming means that the Earth's temperature is rising, so the seas are getting warmer. This means that more hurricanes are likely. Hurricanes are also becoming bigger and more powerful, as there is more heat energy to fuel them.

▼ These buildings near Lake Pontchartrain, Louisiana, USA, were destroyed by Hurricane Katrina in 2005.

Water, water everywhere

118 A flood happens when water overflows and covers what is normally land. Floods can be caused by rivers overflowing their banks after heavy rain. The sea can also flood the land with large waves or tsunamis. Floods can be useful – some rivers flood every year in the rainy season, bringing water and mud that make farmland moist and fertile. However, most floods are bad news.

▲ A satellite image of the River Nile in Egypt flowing into the Mediterranean Sea. The green triangular area is the Nile Delta. The Nile used to flood each summer, spreading fertile silt across the land. These floods are now controlled by the Aswan Dam in southern Egypt.

▼ A woman carries a precious pot of clean drinking water through dirty floodwaters during a flood in Bangladesh in 1998.

119 Floods can cause death and destruction. When floodwater flows into houses, it fills them with mud, rubbish and sewage (smelly waste from drains and toilets). It ruins electrical appliances, carpets and furniture. After a flood, homes have to be completely cleaned out and repaired – costing huge amounts of money. Even worse, fast-flowing floodwater can sweep away people, cars and even buildings.

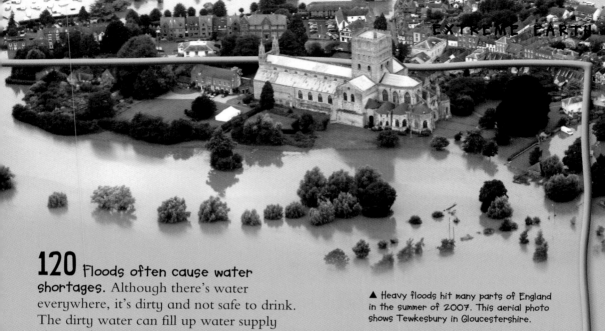

120 Floods often cause water shortages. Although there's water everywhere, it's dirty and not safe to drink. The dirty water can fill up water supply pipes and water treatment works. They can't supply clean water, and the taps have to be switched off. During bad floods, the emergency services have to deliver water in bottles or tanks, so that people have enough clean water to drink.

▲ Heavy floods hit many parts of England in the summer of 2007. This aerial photo shows Tewkesbury in Gloucestershire.

I DON'T BELIEVE IT!

The Bible tells of a great flood that covered the world in water. Some scientists think flood stories may be based on flooding that happened around 10,000 years ago, as sea levels rose when ice melted after the last Ice Age.

121 More floods are coming. Because of global warming, the Earth is heating up. In some areas, this means more water will evaporate into the air, causing more clouds and more rain. Global warming also means higher sea levels, so more areas of land are at risk of being flooded.

▼ This car was caught in a flash flood (a sudden, unexpected flood) in Texas, USA. Flash floods can wash entire towns away.

Disastrous droughts

122 **A drought is a shortage of rainfall that leaves the land dry.** Deserts hardly ever get rain, and are dry and dusty all the time. A drought happens when a place gets much less rain than usual. Scientists don't always know why weather patterns change. However, this can be caused by changes in the oceans. Every few years, a change in sea temperatures in the Pacific, called El Niño, affects weather around the world and causes droughts.

▲ During drought conditions, water is precious. Without it people, animals and plants will die.

SOUTH AMERICA

Equator

Warm water

PACIFIC OCEAN

AUSTRALIA

Cold water

▲ El Niño is a warming of surface ocean waters in the eastern Pacific that can lead to flooding and drought around the world.

123 **Droughts are disastrous for people, animals and plants.** A shortage of rain means crops can't grow properly, and herds of animals can't get enough drinking water. So people face food and water shortages. Dried-out grass and trees can easily catch fire, and loose dust can blow up into blinding dust storms. Droughts can also cause wars, when people are forced to leave their lands and flock into other areas.

125 Droughts have always happened. They are mentioned in many ancient books, such as the Bible and the writings of the ancient Mesopotamians, who lived in the area around what is now Iraq. However, scientists think that today, global warming is making some droughts worse. As the world gets warmer, weather patterns are changing. Some areas, such as eastern Australia, are now having worse droughts than they used to.

▲ Part of the Murray River in southern Australia, usually flowing with water, lies empty during a drought.

124 The 'Dust Bowl' was a great drought disaster that hit the USA in the 1930s. Several years of drought dried out farm soil in the central states of the USA, such as Oklahoma and Kansas. It blew away in huge dust storms, and farmers could not grow their crops. Hundreds of thousands of people had to leave the area. Many trekked west in search of new lives and jobs.

TRUE OR FALSE?

1. Droughts make forest fires more likely.
2. The Dust Bowl is a volcano in the USA.
3. El Niño is a temperature change in the Indian Ocean.

Answers:
1. True. Droughts make forests drier so they burn more easily 2. False. The Dust Bowl was a drought 3. False. El Niño is in the Pacific Ocean

◀ A massive dust storm about to engulf a farm during the Dust Bowl years. Caused by drought conditions, these storms devastated the American prairies.

VOLCANOES

126 **A volcano is an opening on the Earth's surface where molten (liquid) rock emerges from underground.** When a volcano erupts, magma (molten rock below the Earth's surface) is expelled. Sometimes it is spewed out as lava – in flowing rivers or as spectacular lava fountains, or sometimes towering clouds of ash are blasted into the air. As lava solidifies and ash is compressed, new rock may form. Volcanoes have shaped much of the Earth's surface.

▼ This is Karymsky, a volcano in eastern Russia. Its perfect cone has been built up from layers of erupted ash and lava.

Around the world

127 **Volcanoes happen because the Earth is hot inside.** The surface is cool, but it gets hotter the deeper you go into the Earth. Under the crust, magma is under so much pressure that it is almost solid. Sometimes the pressure is released by the shifting of the crust and the magma melts. Then it can bubble up through the cracks in the crust as volcanoes.

300 million years ago

200 million years ago

65 million years ago

▶ Scientists know that the continents were once joined because matching rocks and fossils are found in places that are now separated by vast oceans.

128 The Earth's crust is cracked into giant pieces called tectonic plates. There are about 60 plates, and the seven largest are thousands of kilometres across. Tectonic plates move slowly across the Earth's surface. This movement, called continental drift, has caused the continents to move apart over millions of years.

A few kilometres below the crust, magma becomes liquid when the pressure on it is released

Crust

Mantle
500–4500°C

Outer core
4000–5000°C

Inner core
5000–7000°C

◀ The internal structure of the Earth. The centre of the Earth – the inner core – is solid even though it is intensely hot. This is because it is under extreme pressure.

I DON'T BELIEVE IT!

Tectonic plates move at about the same speed as your fingernails grow. That is just a few centimetres each year.

129 About 250 million years ago there was just one continent, known as Pangaea. The movement of tectonics plates broke Pangaea apart and moved the land around to form the continents we recognize today.

130 Most volcanoes erupt along plate boundaries. These are the cracks separating tectonic plates. On a world map of plate boundaries (below) you can see there are often rows of volcanoes along boundaries.

131 Volcanoes also happen at 'hot spots'. These are places where especially hot magma being driven upwards in the mantle, burns through the middle of a plate to form volcanoes. The most famous hot-spot volcanoes are those of the Hawaiian islands.

▼ Most active volcanoes occur along the 'Ring of Fire' (tinted red). Five volcanoes from around the world are highlighted on the map below.

Mount Bromo, Asia

Hawaii, Pacific Ocean

Mount Rainier, North America

EURASIAN PLATE

RING OF FIRE

NORTH AMERICAN PLATE

AFRICAN PLATE

PACIFIC PLATE

INDO AUSTRALIAN PLATE

SOUTH AMERICAN PLATE

ANTARCTIC PLATE

Mount Kilimanjaro, Africa

Arenal, South America

Plate boundaries

132 **Tectonic plates meet at plate boundaries.** The plates on either side of a boundary are moving at different speeds and in different directions. There are three types of plate boundary – constructive, destructive and transform.

133 **In some places, tectonic plates move away from each other.** The boundaries between these plates are known as constructive boundaries. As the plates move apart, magma moves up from below into the gap and cools, forming new crust.

▶ At Thingvellir in Iceland, giant cracks in the landscape show the position of a constructive plate boundary.

Plates move apart

Mantle

Magma erupts through the gap

▲ Constructive boundaries often occur in the middle of oceans, forming ocean ridges.

134 **Some volcanoes occur along constructive boundaries.** Most constructive boundaries are under the ocean, so volcanic activity here usually goes unnoticed. The Mid–Atlantic Ridge is an undersea constructive boundary and the volcanic islands of the Azores, off Portugal, have formed over it.

135 In other places tectonic plates move towards each other. The boundaries between these plates are called destructive boundaries. One of the plates often dips below the other and is destroyed as it moves into the mantle below. This is called subduction.

▼ Here, an oceanic plate dips below a continental plate. The thinner oceanic plate is pushed down into the mantle.

Plates move together

Subducted plate melts into mantle

A volcano has formed along the edge of the overlying plate

136 Some volcanoes form on destructive plate boundaries. As one plate is forced down, magma may force its way up through the plate above. If it melts through the surface, it erupts as a violent volcano. The volcanoes of the Andes, South America, have formed over a subduction zone.

I DON'T BELIEVE IT!
The Mid-Atlantic Ridge stretches 14,000 kilometres along the sea floor under the Atlantic Ocean.

▲ The Aleutian Islands, off Alaska, are volcanic islands, formed along a destructive plate boundary.

Parts of a volcano

137 Material erupted from a volcano can build up to form a mountain. Beneath the surface is a system of pipes and chambers that supply the volcano with magma from below the crust.

139 A magma chamber is a store of molten rock under a volcano. As magma moves through cracks in the Earth's crust, it collects in huge reservoirs underground. Magma chambers are usually 1–10 kilometres underground. Some volcanoes have several magma chambers.

138 Magma rises up through a conduit. This is a giant pipe that leads from the magma chamber to the surface. Usually there is one main conduit that leads to the summit of a volcano. The hole at the top of the conduit is called a vent. There are often side vents on a volcano's slopes that have branched off the main conduit.

Vent

Side vent

Conduit

Upper magma chamber

◄ The mountain on the surface is only the tip of a volcano. Chambers and pipes deep underground store and feed magma to the volcano.

Deep magma chamber

Mantle

A composite volcano (also known as a stratovolcano) has steep sides built up of layers of lava and ash.

A shield volcano has a low, wide shape, with gently sloping sides.

▶ Volcanoes come in different shapes and sizes. Here are three common examples.

A caldera is a huge crater left after an old eruption. New cones often grow again inside.

140 A crater can form around the vent of a volcano.

As magma is blasted out during an eruption, the material forms a rim around the top of the vent. Sometimes several vents may be erupting into the same crater. A crater can fill with lava during an eruption. When this forms a pool it is known as a lava lake.

▼ Crater Lake in Oregon, USA. It formed in the caldera of Mount Mazama and is around 9 kilometres across.

141 Lakes can form in the craters of dormant (inactive) volcanoes.

When a volcano stops erupting and cools down, its crater can slowly fill with rain water, creating a lake. Crater lakes also form in calderas – huge craters that form when a volcano collapses into its empty magma chamber.

QUIZ
Which of these are parts of a volcano?
1. Conduit
2. Bed chamber
3. Side vent
4. Ventricle
5. Crater

Answers:
Only 1, 3 and 5 are parts of a volcano

73

Eruptions

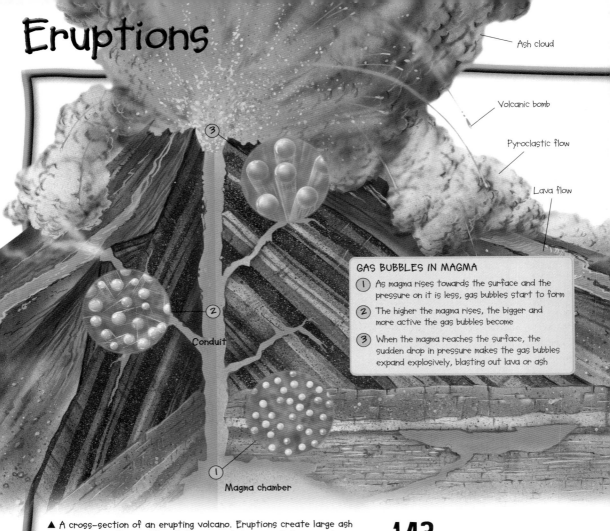

Ash cloud

Volcanic bomb

Pyroclastic flow

Lava flow

3

2

Conduit

GAS BUBBLES IN MAGMA

1 As magma rises towards the surface and the pressure on it is less, gas bubbles start to form

2 The higher the magma rises, the bigger and more active the gas bubbles become

3 When the magma reaches the surface, the sudden drop in pressure makes the gas bubbles expand explosively, blasting out lava or ash

1

Magma chamber

▲ A cross-section of an erupting volcano. Eruptions create large ash clouds and lava flows, although these rarely happen at the same time.

142 At any time, about 20 volcanoes are erupting around the world. On average, 60 volcanoes erupt each year. Eruptions can go on for just a few days or for years on end. A single eruption can spew out millions of tonnes of material.

143 An eruption happens when magma swells beneath the Earth's surface. Magma is a mixture of molten rock and other materials, including dissolved water and gases. As magma rises, the pressure on it lessens. This allows the dissolved gas and water to form bubbles. This makes the magma swell quickly, causing an eruption.

▲ The island of Stromboli, Italy, is an active volcano that erupts almost continuously.

144 As well as lava and hot gases, explosive eruptions throw out pieces of solid magma. As the volcano erupts, the pieces of rock are blasted into billions of fragments called pyroclasts. These fragments mainly form vast clouds of ash during an eruption.

145 A volcano can be active or dormant. An active volcano is one that is erupting now or seems likely to erupt. Some scientists define an active volcano as one that has erupted in the last 10,000 years. A dormant volcano is one that is not active at the moment, but might become so in the future.

146 Volcanoes that seem unlikely to erupt again are described as extinct. Some say that a volcano that has not erupted in the last 10,000 years is extinct. But experts cannot always be sure that a volcano will never erupt again.

GASES IN MAGMA

You will need:
bottle of fizzy drink

Shake the bottle of fizzy drink a little, but not too much, and put it in the sink. As you gradually open the cap, watch the drink in the bottle closely. Bubbles of gas will form, rush upwards and force the drink out of the bottle. The gas stays dissolved in the drink until the pressure on the drink is released. This is the same as what happens when the pressure on magma is released.

▶ Sugar Loaf Mountain in Brazil is a volcanic plug — the solidified core of an extinct volcano.

Lava

◄ A slow-moving lava flow engulfs a road. A person could walk away from a lava flow like this without any danger.

148 A lava flow is a river of lava. Thin, runny lava can flow downhill at speeds up to 100 kilometres an hour. Lava flows follow the natural contours of the land. They can reach many kilometres from the volcano before the lava cools and stops. Lava often spreads out to form lava fields.

147 Lava is liquid rock ejected from a volcano. Some lava is very runny and flows downhill quickly. Another type is thick and gooey and flows very slowly. The temperature, consistency and thickness of lava affect the way it is erupted.

▼ Sometimes lava keeps flowing below the surface through a 'lava tunnel', under a solidified crust.

TRUE OR FALSE?

1. Aa lava is fast flowing.
2. Igneous rock is made when lava cools down.
3. A shortcrust bomb is made from lava.

Answers:
1. True – aa lava is thick, slow-moving lava
2. True – all igneous rocks are formed when magma, lava or ash cools
3. False – but a breadcrust bomb is

149 When lava or magma cools, it forms rock. This kind of rock is called igneous rock. Basalt — a dark-coloured rock — is one common type of igneous rock. Over time, lava flows build up on top of each other forming deep layers of igneous rock.

The front of the lava flow is steep

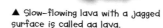
▲ Slow-flowing lava with a jagged surface is called aa lava.

150 Pahoehoe and aa are the two main types of lava. Thick lava that flows slowly cools to form jagged blocks. This is called aa (say ah) lava. Fast-flowing, runny lava cools to form rock with a smooth surface. This is called pahoehoe (say pa-hoey-hoey) lava.

Lava has a smooth, folded surface

▲ Fast-flowing lava, called pahoehoe lava, cools to form smooth, rope-like rock.

▶ Pele's tears are tiny lava bombs often produced in Hawaiian eruptions.

Pele's tears

Breadcrust bomb

Spindle bomb

Cowpat bomb

Ribbon bomb

151 A volcanic bomb is a flying lump of lava. Lumps of lava, usually bigger than the size of a fist, are thrown upwards by jets of gas from the vent during an eruption. Sometimes the outside of a bomb solidifies while it is in the air and splits open when it lands. This is called a breadcrust bomb. If the bomb is still soft when it lands, the bomb splats like a cowpat.

◀ Lumps of lava blasted into the air by a volcano form different shapes in the air.

Volcanic ash

152 Volcanic ash is made up of tiny bits of rock. Close up, pieces of ash look like tiny shards of glass. Sometimes, frothy lumps of lava are blasted out with the ash. They cool to form pumice rock, which looks like honeycomb.

▶ Pumice rock is full of holes making it very light.

153 Towering clouds of ash form during explosive eruptions. Hot gases rush out of a volcano's vent at hundreds of metres a second, firing ash thousands of metres into the air. It billows upwards and outwards in an eruption column. These towering ash clouds can reach more than 50 kilometres into the sky.

MAKE A MODEL VOLCANO

You will need:

vinegar   plastic bottle   bicarbonate of soda   jug   red food colouring   tray   sand

Put a tablespoon of bicarbonate of soda in the bottle. Stand the bottle on a tray and make a cone of sand around it. Put a few drops of red food colouring in half a cup of vinegar. Use the jug to pour the vinegar into the bottle. The volcano should erupt with red frothy lava!

▶ Ash is blasted into the sky from the crater of Mount St Helens, USA.

▶ When the wind blows an ash column sideways, it creates an ash plume that can can stretch for kilometres.

154 Volcanic ash can travel thousands of kilometres. Ash that is carried high into the atmosphere can be blown great distances before it finally falls. Near the volcano, the fallen ash builds up in layers and over time compresses to form a type of rock called tuff.

156 Pyroclastic flows can travel long distances. They can reach speeds up to 700 kilometres an hour and they can even flow up and over hills that are in their way. Their super-heated gases and swirling ash destroy everything in their path.

155 Ash sometimes forms red-hot avalanches. If part of an eruption column collapses, it turns into an avalanche of ash, rock and hot gases, which flows down the side of a volcano. This kind of avalanche is called a pyroclastic flow. Pyroclastic flows can also be set off when the side of a steep volcano collapses.

Part of the eruption column collapses

Pyroclastic flow

Lighter ash particles are thrown up in a cloud above the pyroclastic flow

▶ A pyroclastic flow is a mixture of ash, pumice and hot gases, which flows down the side of a volcano.

79

Gentle and explosive

157 When you think of an eruption, you probably imagine lava flowing out of a crater. Lava is produced in relatively gentle eruptions. An explosive eruption produces lots of ash and may even blast the mountain apart!

◀ The volcano of Kilauea on Hawaii's Big Island erupts quite gently. Lava fountains like this are common in Hawaiian eruptions.

158 Runny magma produces gentle eruptions. Bubbles of gas rise easily through runny magma and escape from the volcano with little build-up of pressure. So lava flows gently from the volcano's vent. Gentle eruptions occur over hot spots and constructive plate boundaries.

159 Gentle eruptions produce lots of lava. Rivers of lava often flow from side vents as well as the main vent, down the mountainside. If there is a lot of gas in the magma, lava is blasted upwards in towering lava fountains.

▲ In 1963, Mount Irazu in Costa Rica, South America, erupted explosively. It covered the town of San José — 54 kilometres away — in a thick layer of ash.

160 Thick magma produces explosive eruptions.
The bubbles of gas cannot escape easily from the thick, gooey magma. Often the vent is blocked by old, solidified lava, causing even more pressure to build up. Eventually the top of the volcano gives way and the magma explodes as the pressure and gases are suddenly released. Explosive eruptions occur at destructive boundaries.

161 Explosive eruptions produce clouds of ash. In
the early stages of an explosive eruption, a volcano can be erupting hundreds of thousands of tonnes of ash, gases and pyroclasts per second. Eruption columns grow extremely quickly — they can reach 20 kilometres into the sky in 30 minutes.

I DON'T BELIEVE IT!
When runny magma erupts from a volcano, it can form fountains of lava up to 300 metres high. That's as high as the Empire State Building in New York, USA!

81

Volcanic features

162 **Volcanic activity creates features on the landscape.** The heat in rocks in regions of volcanic activity cause features such as fumaroles, geysers, hot springs and boiling mud pools. These features can be seen in places where there are no actual volcanoes.

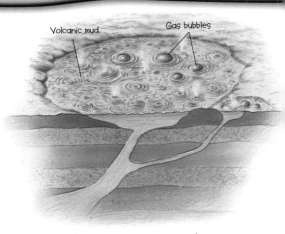

▲ A volcanic mud pool (or mudpot) forms where steam and hot gas bubble up through mud on the surface.

▼ Iceland's Blue Lagoon geothermal spa. Seawater is heated deep underground and it emerges as hot springs at the surface, rich in minerals. The nearby geothermal power station uses the heat to produce electricity.

163 Fumaroles are steaming holes in the ground. They form where groundwater (water under the ground) comes into contact with hot rock or magma and turns to steam. The steam rises through cracks, and vents at the surface as a fumarole. Gases, such as sulphur dioxide, are also emitted.

QUIZ

1. What makes the mud in a mud pool boil?
2. What does the word 'geyser' mean in Icelandic?
3. What is the most famous geyser?

Answers:
1. Steam and hot gas bubble up through surface mud 2. 'Geyser' is Icelandic for 'gush' 3. Old Faithful, Yellowstone National Park

▶ Strokkur geyser in Iceland erupts about every five minutes, shooting boiling water and steam about 20 metres into the air.

Steam and gases

▲ A fumarole is a hole that emits steam and sulphurous gases. Yellow sulphur crystals often form around the hole.

164 The word 'geyser' comes from Iceland. It is derived from the Icelandic word for 'gush'. The most famous geyser is Old Faithful in Yellowstone National Park, USA. It is called Old Faithful because every hour or so it produces a hot-water fountain 35 metres high.

165 A geyser is a fountain of boiling water and steam. Geysers form when groundwater is heated deep below the ground under pressure. The hot water moves up through rock layers to the surface to find a place to escape. When it starts to bubble up, releasing the pressure, a jet of super-heated water and steam blasts from a hole in the ground for a few seconds.

Hazards of a volcano

166 Volcanic eruptions can be extremely dangerous to anyone living in their vicinity. The main hazards are lava flows, pyroclastic flows, ash and side effects such as mudflows. In the past, volcanoes have killed thousands of people, destroying homes, and even whole villages and towns.

167 Lava flows are very destructive. They can knock down buildings, bury objects and they set light to anything that will burn. However, most lava flows creep along slower than walking pace, and people can normally run or drive away from the danger of an approaching lava flow.

▼ A lava flow creeps along, engulfing and incinerating palm trees on Hawaii.

▲ This aerial view shows the paths of the pyroclastic flows that swept down Mount Unzen, Japan.

168 The deadliest volcano hazards are pyroclastic flows. Temperatures inside these high-speed avalanches of searing hot ash, gas and rock reach hundreds of degrees Celsius. When a pyroclastic flow hits objects, such as trees or houses, the blast flattens them, and the heat burns them to a cinder.

169 Pyroclastic flows can travel as fast as a jet plane. Anyone caught in a pyroclastic flow cannot survive the heat. In 1991, hundreds of observers and journalists gathered at Mount Unzen, Japan, as it began to erupt. Forty-two of them were killed by a pyroclastic flow.

▲ These houses were buried by volcanic ash from an eruption on the island of Heimaey, Iceland, in 1973.

170 Volcanic ash is deadly. As ash falls down after an eruption, it is often still scorching hot. This can start fires and if breathed in, can cause suffocation. A layer of volcanic ash just a few centimetres thick can make the roof of a house collapse.

Side effects

171 **Volcanoes can set off floods, mudflows and tsunamis.** It is not just the material expelled by volcanoes, such as lava, bombs, ash and pyroclastic flows, which is dangerous. Eruptions can also cause hazardous side effects, which are just as deadly.

172 **A volcanic mudflow is a river of ash and water.** Mudflows are also called lahars. Some occur when hot ash falls on snow and ice on the upper slopes of volcanoes. Ash mixes with the meltwater and flows downhill. Others form from heavy rain falling on the ash deposits. When a mudflow stops flowing it sets solid like concrete.

QUIZ

1. What is a lahar?
2. What town was buried by a mudflow in 1985?
3. What happens to tsunami waves as they hit shallow water?

Answers:
1. Lahar is another name for a volcanic mudflow 2. Armero in Colombia, South America 3. They increase in size and become closer together

▲ Near the crater of Mount Ruapehu in New Zealand, a mudflow, or lahar, begins to flow down the slopes. The flow formed after an eruption in 2007.

173 **The town of Armero, Colombia, was devastated by a mudflow.** In 1985, the volcano Nevado del Ruiz erupted. It was not a large eruption, but ash melted snow on the summit, setting off a mudflow. It rushed down a river valley and swept through Armero. Practically the entire population of 22,000 died.

▶ The remains of the town of Armero, Colombia, after it was buried by a mudflow.

174 Volcanoes can cause floods. Landslides set off by eruptions can fall into lakes, causing floods in rivers below. In Iceland, volcanoes sometimes erupt under the ice cap. The eruptions melt huge volumes of ice, setting off vast floods that sweep out to sea.

175 Explosive eruptions can set off tsunamis. A tsunami is a huge wave that travels across the sea and causes floods on any coasts it hits. The eruption of the volcanic island of Krakatoa, Indonesia, in 1883, set off tsunamis that travelled thousands of kilometres around the world.

▼ When Krakatoa erupted, nearby islands were swamped by tsunamis set off by pyroclastic flows entering the sea.

Pyroclastic flow enters the sea

Far-apart, shallow ripples travel across the sea

As the waves approach shallower water, they increase in size and become closer together

Using volcanoes

▲ Wairakei power station in New Zealand is located on a field of geothermal activity. The pipes carry water heated by underground rocks.

176 Millions of people live near active volcanoes. About one in ten of all the people in the world could be in danger from eruptions. However, people living near volcanoes can benefit from them – heat from volcanoes can be turned into electricity and the soil is good for farming.

177 Volcanoes are sources of energy. The rocks around them are normally extremely hot. Heat energy from the Earth, called geothermal energy, can be collected and used for heating and to generate electricity. At geothermal power stations, water is pumped down into the ground where it is heated, creating hot water and steam. The hot water is used to heat homes and the steam to drive turbines and generators.

178 Sulphur is mined from around volcanoes. This yellow mineral is an important raw material for the chemical industries. Sulphur crystals are common around the vents of volcanoes and hot springs because magma gives off sulphurous gases. Sulphur is also extracted from volcanic rocks.

▶ In 2006, 20,000 people were evacuated due to the eruption of Mayon, the most active volcano in the Phillipines.

179 Volcanic soil is good for farming. Soil is normally made up of broken-down rock. Near volcanoes, soil is made up of eroded lava or ash and is rich in the minerals that plants need to grow. Mayon, a volcano in the Phillipines, regularly erupts explosively, but the land around Mayon is still farmed.

◀ A miner collects pieces of sulphur at a crater in Indonesia. Huge deposits of sulphur can build up around a volcano's crater.

180 Many people believe water filtered through volcanic rock is good for your health. Natural sources of water in volcanic regions are rich in minerals including calcium and magnesium, which are good for growth and general health. A lot of mineral water is bottled at its source and exported for sale.

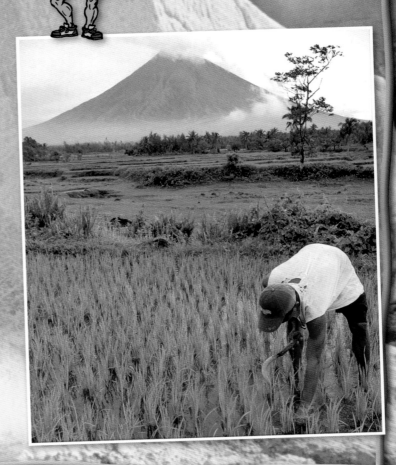

Volcano science

181 **The science of volcanoes is called volcanology.** Scientists called volcanologists study the structure of volcanoes, causes of eruptions, old lava flows and how ash travels in the air. They also monitor volcanoes to try to predict future eruptions.

▲ A volcanologist measures the levels of different gases coming from a fumarole.

▼ In 1994, the Dante II robot was lowered into the hot crater of Mount Spurr, Alaska. It collected gas and water samples and recorded video pictures.

182 Volcanologists analyze volcanic gases. The main gases emitted by volcanoes are steam, sulphur dioxide and carbon dioxide. The volume and proportion of gases coming from a volcano's vent indicates what magma is doing underground. An increase in sulphur dioxide shows that fresh magma may be near the surface and an eruption could happen soon.

TRUE OR FALSE?

1. More sulphur dioxide coming from a volcano means there could be an eruption.
2. Tiltmeters measure earthquakes.
3. Volcanologists wear silver suits to absorb the heat.

Answers:
1. True 2. False 3. False

183 Earthquakes show that magma is moving.

Volcanologists set up earthquake-detecting instruments called seismographs on volcanoes. If earthquakes become more frequent, an eruption may be about to happen. Tiltmeters are used to detect if the ground is bulging. This shows if magma is building up underneath.

184 Volcanologists study old lava flows.

Evidence of previous eruptions is a good guide to what might happen in the future. Old lava flows and ashfall on and around a volcano show the frequency and size of past eruptions. This gives a good indication of the areas that might be affected by future eruptions.

▼ Heat-reflecting silver suits protect volcanologists measuring the temperature of lava at Fournaise volcano, Reunion Island.

185 Volcanologists wear protective clothes.

Hot rocks, lava flows, bombs, falling ash and poisonous gases make active volcanoes dangerous places to be. When they visit volcanoes, volcanologists wear sturdy boots, hard hats and heat-resistant gloves. In very dangerous areas they also wear heat-reflecting overalls and gas masks.

Fighting volcanoes

186 People cannot stop volcanoes from erupting. However, we can reduce the damage that volcanoes cause by stopping or diverting lava and mudflows away from cities and towns. Injury and death can also be prevented by predicting eruptions accurately.

187 A lava flow was stopped with sea water. In 1973, an eruption on the island of Heimaey, Iceland, sent lava flows heading towards the island's harbour where its fishing fleet was moored. Islanders pumped sea water onto the lava for months. Eventually it was stopped and the harbour was saved.

▼ The towering lava flows destroyed many houses on the island of Heimaey, Iceland, during the eruption in 1973.

◄ During the eruption of Mount Etna, Italy, in 1983, bulldozers piled up rock in banks to channel a lava flow away from houses.

189 There are various ways to reduce the damage of lava flows. In the past people have built walls and dug channels to divert flows. Bombs have also been dropped on lava flows to make them spread out and slow down, as used on Mount Etna in 1992.

188 Mudflows can be reduced with dams. Deadly mudflows are fast-flowing and dense with ash and heavy debris. Special dams, called sabo dams, slow mudflows by trapping the ash and debris and letting the water flow harmlessly away.

▼ Sabo dams on the slopes of Sakurajima volcano in Japan are designed to slow mudflows.

190 Preparation saves lives. People living in danger zones near active volcanoes have a plan of action in case of eruption. Local authorities should also communicate with volcanologists and the emergency services when an eruption threatens so that people can be evacuated in good time.

191 Mount St Helens, USA, erupted in 1980. It is part of a range of volcanoes in western North America called the Cascades. The eruption of Mount St Helens was one of the most explosive and spectacular ever seen.

▲ Mount St Helens before the 1980 eruption. The bulge that grew on the north side is clearly visible.

192 Mount St Helens bulged outwards before the blast. The eruption began in March 1980 with a cloud of ash that grew to 6000 metres tall. In April, the north side of the volcano began bulging outwards. Gradually the bulge grew, showing that magma was building up underneath.

▶ Ash blasting from the vent of Mount St Helens during the eruption. The cloud grew more than 20 kilometres high.

► The scars of the devastating mudflows and pyroclastic flows can still be seen in this satellite image taken in 1997.

193 **The bulge collapsed on 18 May.** The pressure on the magma was released suddenly and the volcano exploded sideways. A pyroclastic flow hurtled across the landscape at more than 300 kilometres an hour. It flattened millions of trees, some 32 kilometres away. Landslides of rock, mixed with water, snow and ice, caused mudflows that travelled up to 30 kilometres away.

▼ The gaping hole blown in the north side of Mount St Helens.

194 Fifty-seven people were killed at Mount St Helens. They were forestry workers, volcanologists, campers and tourists. Most victims thought they were a safe distance away from the volcano. However, nobody expected the devastating sideways blast.

195 Mount St Helens is rebuilding itself. About 300 metres was blown off the top of the volcano in the 1980 eruption. Since then, a new lava dome (heap of solidified lava) has grown inside the crater — a sign that one day Mount St Helens will erupt again.

I DON'T BELIEVE IT!

Local man Harry Truman refused to leave his home near Mount St Helens despite warnings. The lodge he lived in was buried in the eruption.

Mount Pinatubo

196 Mount Pinatubo erupted violently in June 1991. It is a stratovolcano in the Philippines, close to the city of Manila. Its 1991 eruption was the most devastating of the 20th century.

197 Mount Pinatubo had been dormant for 600 years. The first signs of an eruption were explosions of steam from the summit. Volcanologists from the Philippines and USA quickly set up an observatory at the nearby Clark Air Base to monitor the activity. They set up instruments on the volcano that showed magma was on the move below.

198 An exclusion zone was set up around the volcano. At first, the zone extended 10 kilometres from the volcano. This was steadily increased to 30 kilometres. In total, 58,000 people were evacuated, which saved many lives.

▼ A truck races to escape a boiling pyroclastic flow rolling down from Mount Pinatubo.

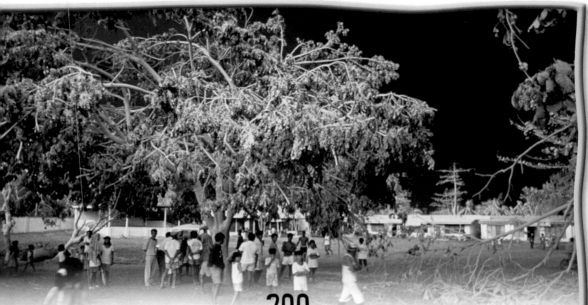

▲ Ash fell far from the eruption column of Mount Pinatubo, smothering local villages and countryside.

200 **Heavy rains caused devastating mudflows.** A typhoon hit the Philippines as Mount Pinatubo erupted, bringing days of torrential rain. The rain set off huge mudflows that swept away thousands of homes and 100 square kilometres of valuable farmland. More mudflows followed as the heavy rains returned in the following years.

199 **Mount Pinatubo erupted with giant explosions.** An ash cloud rose 40 kilometres into the sky and pyroclastic flows reached up to 20 kilometres from the volcano. They deposited ash and debris tens of metres deep along their route. Ash in the air made it dark in the middle of the day and gases from the eruption spread around the Earth. This caused temperatures to fall by 0.5°C for several months.

▶ A false-colour satellite image taken after Pinatubo's eruption shows mudflows in red and the large crater (centre) left after the eruption.

Mount Vesuvius

201 Mount Vesuvius, Italy, is the only active volcano on mainland Europe. In AD 79, when Italy was ruled by the ancient Romans, Mount Vesuvius erupted violently.

202 The eruption was seen by a Roman called Pliny the Younger. Pliny wrote letters describing the ash cloud – he said it looked like a giant pine tree. His uncle, Pliny the Elder, went to help people escape, but was killed by falling ash. Today, explosive eruptions are called Plinian eruptions after Pliny.

▶ Ash and pyroclasts raining down from Vesuvius would have caused complete panic in the streets of Pompeii.

203 The city of Pompeii was completely buried by ash. Pompeii lay 15 kilometres south of Mount Vesuvius. Ash and pumice rained down on the city, filling the streets and making buildings collapse.

I DON'T BELIEVE IT!

Before AD 79, Mount Vesuvius had not erupted for 800 years. The Romans did not realize it was a volcano or that there was any danger.

▲ The last major eruption of Mount Vesuvius happened in 1944. Two villages on the slopes were hit by lava flows.

204 People had little time to escape. Thousands died as they ran through the streets, suffocated by the hot, choking ash. Since excavations started in the 1750s, archaeologists digging through the layers of ash have uncovered the remains of people and animals.

205 Mount Vesuvius is still a dangerous volcano. It has erupted dozens of times since AD 79. Nearby towns and villages have been regularly destroyed by eruptions, yet millions of people still live close to the volcano.

Volcanoes at sea

206 **Many islands are the tops of volcanoes.** Volcanic islands grow over hotspots and other regions of volcanic activity under the sea. There are hundreds of hidden undersea volcanoes that have not broke the ocean's surface yet. These are called seamounts.

207 **Underwater eruptions produce pillow lava.** As lava is exposed to cold sea water, it cools quickly, forming round humps of lava that look like pillows piled on top of each other. Pillow lava also forms when lava flows reach the sea.

▲ Anak Krakatoa is a new island in Indonesia that first appeared out of the sea in 1927. It has grown in the place of the island of Krakatoa.

TRUE OR FALSE?

1. Mauna Kea is the world's tallest mountain.
2. More Hawaiian islands will form in the future.
3. Surtsey island is near Fiji.

Answers:
1. True – from the sea floor, Mauna Kea is slightly taller than Mount Everest. 2. True – as the tectonic plate moves over the hotspot more, more islands will form 3. False – Surtsey is near Iceland. The island that formed in 2006 is near Fiji

▶ This diagram shows how the Hawaiian islands have formed over a hot spot. The eight main Hawaiian islands are shown (as numbered).

8 Nihau   7 Kauai

6 Oahu

Extinct volcanoes

Active volcano

Mantle

Hot spot

Tectonic plate

208 Measuring from the sea floor, Mauna Kea is the world's tallest volcano and mountain. Mauna Kea is a dormant volcano on Hawaii in the Pacific Ocean, measuring 10,000 metres from the sea floor. The island of Hawaii is made up of five volcanoes – of these Kilauea and Mauna Loa are active.

5 Molokai

4 Lanai

3 Kahoolawe

Maui 2

◀ The eight main Hawaiian islands.

Hawaii 1

209 All of the Hawaiian islands are volcanic. They are the peaks of a chain of undersea volcanoes that have grown over a hot spot in the centre of the Pacific plate. New islands have formed over millions of years as the plate has moved and more will form in the future.

210 In 1963, a new island appeared near Iceland. At first, a cloud of steam and ash rose from the sea. Ten days later, an island one kilometre across and 90 metres high had built up. The new island was named Surtsey. More recently in 2006, sailor Fredrik Fransson came across a newly forming island off Fiji in the Pacific Ocean.

◀ A new volcanic island in the Pacific Ocean (left). Fredrik Fransson on board his yacht sails through a floating 'raft' of pumice (far left) erupted from the volcanic island.

The biggest volcanoes

211 Eruptions of the biggest volcanoes affect the whole planet. Ash and gases are blasted over 50 kilometres into the atmosphere. Winds that blow at high altitude spread the ash and gas for thousands of kilometres – sometimes right around the world.

VEI 8 – Mega-colossal
Ash column height 25 km +
Volume erupted 1000 km³

VEI 7 – Super-colossal
Ash column height 25 km +
Volume erupted 100 km³

VEI 6 – Colossal
Ash column height 25 km +
Volume erupted 10 km³

VEI 5 – Paroxysmal
Ash column height 25 km +
Volume erupted 1 km³

VEI 4 – Cataclysmic
Ash column height 10–25 km
Volume erupted 100,000,000 m³

VEI 3 – Severe
Ash column height 3–15 km
Volume erupted 10,000,000 m³

VEI 2 – Explosive
Ash column height 1–5 km
Volume erupted 1,000,000 m³

VEI 1 – Gentle
Ash column height 100–1000 m
Volume erupted 10,000 m³

▲ The Volcanic Explosivity Index. Each stage represents a ten-fold increase in explosivity.

212 The power of an eruption is measured on the VEI scale. VEI stands for Volcanic Explosivity Index and it is based on the amount of material erupted and the height of the ash column. Each stage on the scale has a name – 1 is a 'gentle' eruption and 8 is a 'mega-colossal' eruption. The eruption of Mount St. Helens had a VEI of 5 and that of Mount Vesuvius in AD 79 had a VEI of 4.

213 The biggest eruption in historical time had a VEI of 7. In 1815 the Indonesian volcano Tambora erupted. Ash spread around the world. It blocked sunlight and caused temperatures to fall and crops to fail. The following year, 1816, is known as 'the year without a summer' because of the cold weather. Over 90,000 people were killed by the eruption.

Before the 1883 eruption

Today

Anak Krakatoa

214 **The island of Krakatoa was destroyed in an eruption.** Krakatoa was a volcanic island in Indonesia. In 1883 it erupted in a series of huge explosions that blew the island apart. The eruption caused tsunamis that devastated nearby islands and coasts. Today, a new volcano – Anak Krakatoa (meaning 'child of Krakatoa') – is growing in the sea where Krakatoa once stood.

▲ An artist's impression of the eruption of Krakatoa in 1883 (main image). Most of the island was destroyed during the eruption (above right).

215 **The eruption of Toba had a VEI of 8.** Toba in Indonesia erupted about 74,000 years ago. Volcanologists think it was the biggest eruption in the last two million years. Its effects may have nearly wiped out the human population. Eruptions of this massive scale are called super eruptions.

◄ The 100-kilometre-long Lake Toba fills the caldera left by the super-eruption of Toba.

QUIZ

1. What does VEI stand for?
2. What does the name Anak Krakatoa mean?
3. Which volcanic eruption had a VEI of 8?

Answers:
1. Volcanic Explosivity Index 2. Child of Krakatoa 3. Toba, 74,000 years ago

103

Past and future

216 **The Earth was once covered by volcanoes.** When the Earth formed 4500 billion years ago, its surface was molten. It gradually cooled and a crust formed. At this time the Earth's surface was covered with millions of volcanoes.

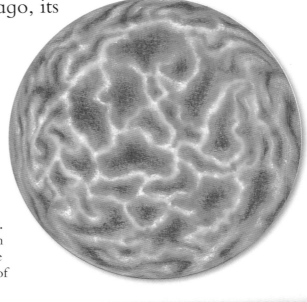

▼ The young planet Earth was a fiery ball of molten rock.

217 A VEI 8 eruption happens roughly once every 100,000 years. That is what volcanologists think as an average. A VEI 8 eruption would wipe out many countries and kill off much of the world's human population.

I DON'T BELIEVE IT!

There are volcanoes on Io, one of Jupiter's moons. They erupt giant fountains of sulphur that make the surface appear yellow.

218 We do not know when the next super-volcano will erupt. Super-eruptions are at the highest end (and beyond) of the VEI scale. The last super-eruption was Toba 74,000 years ago. The next one could happen in tens of thousands of years, more than a million years or even much sooner!

219 Yellowstone National Park, USA, could erupt soon! Yellowstone is over a hot spot in the crust. It is the site of a caldera that is 60 kilometres across. There were VEI 8 eruptions here two million, 1.3 million and 640,000 years ago. That means another one is due.

▶ Olympus Mons on Mars photographed from overhead by a space probe.

220 Other planets have volcanoes too. Astronomers have discovered more than 1000 volcanoes on Venus, but all are extinct. Mars has the largest volcano in the Solar System, called Olympus Mons, which is 24 kilometres high.

▼ Tourists flock to Yellowstone National Park to see the volcanic features, such as the Old Faithful geyser. The park lies on the site of a super-volcano.

Myths and legends

221 **People once thought eruptions were the work of gods.** Until scientists began to understand volcanoes, nobody knew how or why they erupted. People were scared by eruptions and thought that they meant the gods were angry.

▶ The word 'volcano' originates from Vulcan, the Roman god of fire.

222 **Vulcan was the Roman god of fire.** Roman legend says that Vulcan lived on the island of Vulcano, near Sicily. He was blacksmith to the gods, forging their weapons. Fire and smoke from Vulcano were thought to be caused by Vulcan hammering hot metal in his forge.

223 **Mount Fuji in Japan is a sacred mountain.** For hundreds of years, Japanese people have made pilgrimages to its summit. Mount Fuji is one of the world's most beautiful volcanoes, with a perfect snow-capped cone and lakes around its lower slopes. It appears many times in Japanese art and photography and is also shown on Japanese currency.

224 **Pele is the Hawaiian goddess of volcanoes.** Hawaiians believe that Pele lives on Kilauea on Hawaii. Drop-shaped pieces of volcanic glass erupted from Hawaiian voclanoes are known as Pele's tears and thin strands of the same material are called Pele's hair.

▼ The perfect cone of Mount Fuji. The mountain is sacred for many Japanese people.

▲ Pele, the Hawaiian goddess of volcanoes is also goddess of fire and lightning.

QUIZ

1. What was Vulcan the Roman god of?
2. Where was the goddess Pele thought to live?
3. What did the gods turn Popocatépetl and his princess into?

Answers:
1. Fire 2. Kilauea on Hawaii 3. Mountains

225 **A warrior was named after the Mexican volcano Popocatépetl.** In Aztec folklore, the warrior Popocatépetl fell in love with a princess. They wanted to marry but the princess's father would only agree if Popocatépetl went to battle for him. He was away for such a long time that the princess thought he was dead, so she drank poison and died. When Popocatépetl returned, he held the princess in his arms and it is said the gods turned them both into mountains. Popocatépetl made fire because of his anger.

WEATHER

226 Rain, sunshine, snow and storms are all types of weather. These help us decide what clothes we wear, what food we eat, and what kind of life we lead. Weather also affects how animals and plants survive. Different types of weather are caused by what is happening in the atmosphere, the air above our heads. In some parts of the world, the weather changes every day, in others, it is nearly always the same.

Equator

227 Tropical, temperate and polar are all types of climate. Climate is the name we give to patterns of weather over a period of time. Near the Equator, the weather is mostly hot and steamy. We call this a tropical climate. Near the North and South Poles, ice lies on the ground year-round and there are biting-cold blizzards. This is a polar climate. Most of the world has a temperate climate, with a mix of cold and warm seasons.

Tropical

Tropical forest

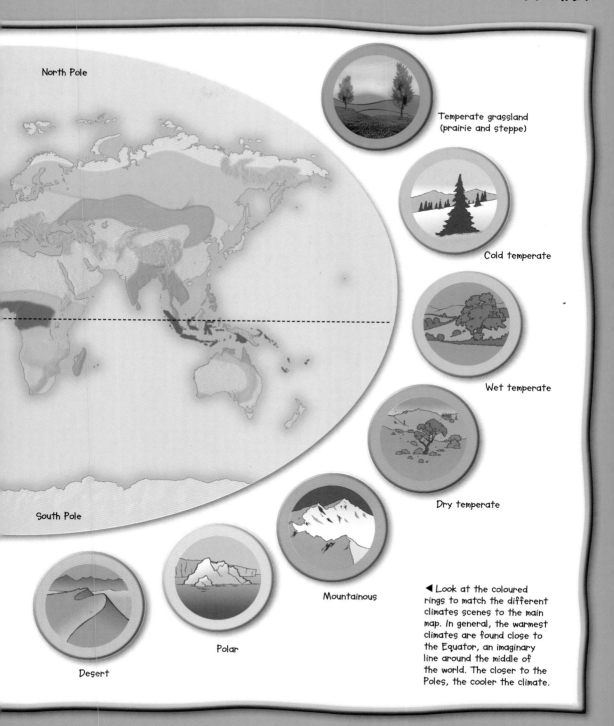

North Pole

Temperate grassland
(prairie and steppe)

Cold temperate

Wet temperate

Dry temperate

South Pole

Mountainous

Desert

Polar

◀ Look at the coloured rings to match the different climates scenes to the main map. In general, the warmest climates are found close to the Equator, an imaginary line around the middle of the world. The closer to the Poles, the cooler the climate.

The four seasons

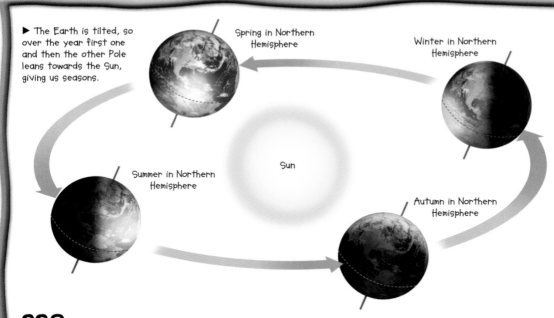

▶ The Earth is tilted, so over the year first one and then the other Pole leans towards the Sun, giving us seasons.

Spring in Northern Hemisphere

Winter in Northern Hemisphere

Sun

Summer in Northern Hemisphere

Autumn in Northern Hemisphere

228 **The reason for the seasons lies in space.** Our planet Earth plots a path through space that takes it around the Sun. This path, or orbit, takes one year. In June, for example, the North Pole leans towards the Sun. The Sun heats the northern half of Earth and there is summer.

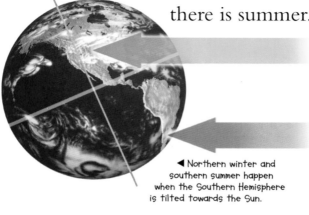

◀ Northern winter and southern summer happen when the Southern Hemisphere is tilted towards the Sun.

229 When it is summer in Argentina, it is winter in Canada. In December, the South Pole leans towards the Sun. Places in the southern half of the world, such as Argentina, have summer. At the same time, places in the northern half, such as Canada, have winter.

230 **A day can last 21 hours!**
Night and day happen because Earth
is spinning as it circles the Sun. At the
height of summer, places near the
North Pole are so tilted towards the
Sun that it is light almost all day long.
In Stockholm, Sweden, Midsummer's
Eve lasts 21 hours because the Sun
disappears below the horizon for only
three hours.

▲ At the North
Pole, the Sun never
disappears below
the horizon at
Midsummer's Day.

▼ Deciduous trees
like these lose their
leaves in autumn,
but evergreens
keep their leaves
all year round.

**I DON'T
BELIEVE IT !**
When the Sun shines all day
in the far north, there is 24-
hour night in the far south.

231 **Forests change
colour in the autumn.**
Autumn comes between
summer and winter. Trees
prepare for the cold winter
months ahead by losing their
leaves. First, though, they
suck back the precious green
chlorophyll, or dye, in their
leaves, making them turn
glorious shades of red,
orange and brown.

Fewer seasons

232 **Monsoons are winds that carry heavy rains.** The rains fall in the tropics in summer during the hot, rainy season. The Sun warms up the sea, which causes huge banks of cloud to form. Monsoons then blow these clouds towards land. Once the rains hit the continent, they can pour for weeks.

▶ When the rains are especially heavy, they cause chaos. Streets turn to rivers and sometimes people's homes are even washed away.

I DON'T BELIEVE IT !

In parts of monsoon India, over 26,000 millimetres of rain have fallen in a single year!

233 **Monsoons happen mainly in Asia.** However, there are some parts of the Americas that are close to the Equator that also have a season that is very rainy. Winds can carry such heavy rain clouds that there are flash floods in the deserts of the southwestern United States. The floods happen because the land has been baked hard during the dry season.

234 Many parts of the tropics have two seasons, not four.

They are the parts of the world closest to the Equator, an imaginary line around the middle of the Earth. Here it is always hot, as these places are constantly facing the Sun. However, the movement of the Earth affects the position of a great band of cloud. In June, the tropical areas north of the Equator have the strongest heat and the heaviest rain storms. In December, it is the turn of the areas south of the Equator.

Tropic of Cancer

Equator

Tropic of Capricorn

▲ The tropics lie either side of the Equator, between lines of latitude called the Tropic of Cancer and the Tropic of Capricorn.

235 In a tropical rainforest, you need your umbrella every day!

Rainforests have rainy weather all year round – but there is still a wet and a dry season. It is just that the wet season is even wetter!

▼ Daily rainfall feeds the lush rainforest vegetation.

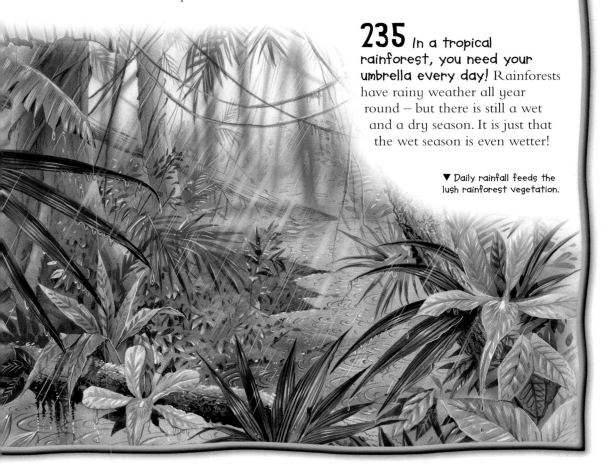

What a scorcher!

236 All our heat comes from the Sun. The Sun is a star, a super-hot ball of burning gases. It gives off heat rays that travel 150 million kilometres through space to our planet. Over the journey, the rays cool down, but they can still scorch the Earth.

237 The Sahara is the sunniest place. This North African desert once had 4300 hours of sunshine in a year! People who live there, such as the Tuareg Arabs, cover their skin to avoid being sunburnt.

238 The hottest place on Earth is Al Aziziyah in Libya. It is 58°C in the shade – hot enough to fry an egg!

▶ Desert peoples wear headdresses to protect their skin and eyes from the sun and sand.

▼ A mirage is just a trick of the light. It can make us see something that is not really there.

239 **The Sun can trick your eyes.** Sometimes, as sunlight passes through our atmosphere, it hits layers of air at different temperatures. When this happens, the air bends the light and can trick our eyes into seeing something that is not there. This is a mirage. For example, what looks like a pool of water might really be part of the sky reflected on to the land.

240 **Too much sun brings drought.** Clear skies and sunshine are not always good news. Without rain crops wither, and people and their animals go hungry.

241 **One terrible drought made a 'Dust Bowl'.** Settlers in the American Mid-West were ruined by a long drought during the 1930s. As crops died, there were no roots to hold the soil together. The dry earth turned to dust and some farms simply blew away!

▲ The 'Dust Bowl' was caused by strong winds and dust storms. These destroyed huge areas of land.

▲ El Niño has been known to cause violent weather conditions. It returns on average every four years.

242 **A sea current can set forests alight.** All sorts of things affect our weather and climate. The movements of a sea current called El Niño have been blamed for causing terrible droughts – which led to unstoppable forest fires.

Our atmosphere

243 **Our planet is wrapped in a blanket of air.** We call this blanket the atmosphere. It stretches hundreds of kilometres above our heads. The blanket keeps in heat, especially at night when part of the planet faces away from the Sun. During the day, the blanket becomes a sunscreen instead. Without an atmosphere, there would be no weather.

244 Most weather happens in the **troposphere.** This is the layer of atmosphere that stretches from the ground to around 10 kilometres above your head. The higher in the troposphere you go, the cooler the air. Because of this, clouds are most likely to form here. Clouds with flattened tops show just where the troposphere meets the next layer, the stratosphere.

KEY
① Exosphere 190 to 960 kilometres
② Thermosphere 80 to 190 kilometres
③ Mesosphere 50 to 80 kilometres
④ Stratosphere 10 to 50 kilometres
⑤ Troposphere 0 to 10 kilometres

◀ The atmosphere stretches right into space. Scientists have split it into five layers, or spheres, such as the troposphere.

245 Air just cannot keep

still. Tiny particles in air, called molecules, are always bumping into each other! The more they smash into each other, the greater the air pressure. Generally, there are more smashes lower in the troposphere, because the pull of gravity makes the molecules fall towards the Earth's surface. The higher you go, the lower the air pressure, and the less oxygen there is in the air.

▶ At high altitudes there is less oxygen. That is why mountaineers often wear breathing equipment.

High pressure

Cool air sinking

Air flow moves in clockwise direction

Centre of high pressure

Low pressure

Warm air rising

Air flow moves in anticlockwise direction

Centre of low pressure

246 Warmth makes air

move. When heat from the Sun warms the molecules in air, they move faster and spread out more. This makes the air lighter, so it rises in the sky, creating low pressure. As it gets higher, the air cools. The molecules slow down and become heavier again, so they start to sink back to Earth.

◀ A high pressure weather system gives us warmer weather, while low pressure gives us cooler more unsettled weather.

Clouds and rain

247 **Rain comes from the sea.** As the Sun heats the surface of the ocean, some seawater turns into water vapour and rises into the air. As it rises, it cools and turns back into water droplets. Lots of water droplets make clouds. The droplets join together to make bigger and bigger drops that eventually fall as rain. Some rain is soaked up by the land, but a lot finds its way back to the sea. This is called the water cycle.

RAIN GAUGE

You will need:

jam jar   waterproof marker pen
ruler   notebook   pen

Put the jar outside. At the same time each day, mark the rainwater level on the jar with your pen. At the end of a week, empty the jar. Measure and record how much rain fell each day and over the whole week.

248 Some mountains are so tall that their summits (peaks) are hidden by cloud. Really huge mountains even affect the weather. When moving air hits a mountain slope it is forced upwards. As it travels up, the temperature drops, and clouds form.

◀ Warm, rising air may be forced up the side of a mountain. At a certain level, lower temperatures make the water form clouds.

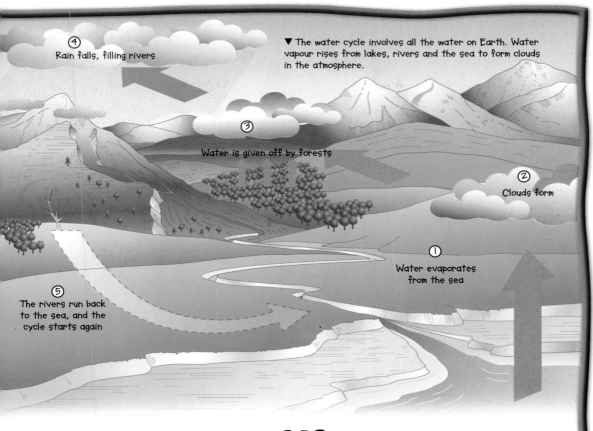

④ Rain falls, filling rivers

▼ The water cycle involves all the water on Earth. Water vapour rises from lakes, rivers and the sea to form clouds in the atmosphere.

③ Water is given off by forests

② Clouds form

① Water evaporates from the sea

⑤ The rivers run back to the sea, and the cycle starts again

▼ Virga happens when rain reaches a layer of dry air. The rain droplets turn back into water vapour in mid-air, and seem to disappear.

249 Some rain never reaches the ground. The raindrops turn back into water vapour because they hit a layer of super-dry air. You can actually see the drops falling like a curtain from the cloud, but the curtain stops in mid-air. This type of weather is called virga.

250 Clouds gobble up heat and keep the Earth's temperature regular. From each 2-metre-square patch of land, clouds can remove the equivalent energy created by a 60-Watt lightbulb.

Not just fluffy

251 **Clouds come in all shapes and sizes.** To help recognize them, scientists split them into ten basic types. The type depends on what the cloud looks like and where it forms in the sky. Cirrus clouds look like wisps of smoke. They form high in the troposphere and rarely mean rain. Stratus clouds form in flat layers and may produce drizzle or a sprinkling of snow. All types of cumulus clouds bring rain. Some are huge cauliflower shapes. They look soft and fluffy – but would feel soggy to touch.

Cumulonimbus clouds give heavy rain showers

▶ The main classes of cloud – cirrus, cumulus and stratus – were named in the 1800s. An amateur British weather scientist called Luke Howard identified the different types.

252 **Not all clouds produce rain.** Cumulus humilis clouds are the smallest heap-shaped clouds. In the sky, they look like lumpy, cotton wool sausages! They are too small to produce rain, but they can grow into much bigger, rain-carrying cumulus clouds. The biggest cumulus clouds, cumulus congestus, bring heavy showers.

Cumulus clouds bring rain

Cirrus clouds occur at great heights from the ground

Contrails are the white streaks
created by planes

Cirrostratus

254 Not all clouds are made by nature. Contrails are streaky clouds that a plane leaves behind it as it flies. They are made of water vapour that comes from the plane's engines. The second it hits the cold air, the vapour turns into ice crystals, leaving a trail of white snow cloud.

253 Sometimes the sky is filled with white patches of cloud that look like shimmering fish scales. These are called mackerel skies. It takes lots of gusty wind to break the cloud into these little patches, and so mackerel skies are usually a sign of changeable weather.

Stratus clouds can bring
drizzle or appear as fog

MIX AND MATCH

Can you match the names of these five types of clouds to their meanings?

1. Altostratus   a. heap

2. Cirrus   b. layer

3. Cumulonimbus   c. high + layer

4. Cumulus   d. wisp

5. Stratus   e. heap + rain

Answers:
1.C 2.D 3.E
4.A 5.B

121

Flood warning

255 **Too much rain brings floods.** There are two different types of floods. Flash floods happen after a short burst of heavy rainfall, usually caused by thunderstorms. Broadscale flooding happens when rain falls steadily over a wide area – for weeks or months – without stopping. When this happens, rivers slowly fill and eventually burst their banks. Tropical storms, such as hurricanes, can also lead to broadscale flooding.

▲ Flooding can cause great damage to buildings and the countryside.

256 **There can be floods in the desert.** When a lot of rain falls very quickly on to land that has been baked dry, it cannot soak in. Instead, it sits on the surface, causing flash floods.

◄ A desert flash flood can create streams of muddy brown water. After the water level falls, vegetation bursts into life.

268

You can tell how windy it is by looking at the leaves on a tree. Wind ranges from light breezes to hurricanes. Its strength is measured on the Beaufort Scale, named after the Irish admiral who devised it. The scale ranges from Force 0, meaning total calm, to Force 12, which is a hurricane.

▶ Turbines convert the wind's energy into electrical energy.

Force 0: Calm

Force 1: Light air

Force 2: Light breeze

Force 3: Gentle breeze

Force 4: Moderate breeze

Force 5: Fresh breeze

Force 6: Strong breeze

Force 7: Near gale

Force 8: Gale

Force 9: Strong gale

Force 10: Storm

Force 11: Violent storm

Force 12: Hurricane

▶ The Beaufort Scale.

269

Wind can turn on your TV. People can harness the energy of the wind to make electricity for our homes. Tall turbines are positioned in windy spots. As the wind turns the turbine, the movement powers a generator and produces electrical energy.

270

Wind can make you mad! The Föhn wind, which blows across Switzerland, Austria and Bavaria in southern Germany, brings with it changeable weather. This has been blamed for road accidents and even bouts of madness!

Thunderbolts and lightning

271 Thunderstorms are most likely in summer. Hot weather creates warm, moist air that rises and forms towering cumulonimbus clouds. Inside each cloud, water droplets and ice crystals bang about, building up positive and negative electrical charges. Electricity flows between the charges, creating a flash that heats the air around it. Lightning is so hot that it makes the air expand, making a loud noise or thunderclap.

▼ Cloud–to–cloud lightning is called sheet lightning, while lightning travelling from the cloud to the ground is called fork lightning.

272 Lightning comes in different colours. If there is rain in the thundercloud, the lightning looks red; if there's hail, it looks blue. Lightning can also be yellow or white.

▼ Lightning conductors absorb the shock and protect tall buildings.

▶ Dramatic lightning flashes light up the sky.

273 Tall buildings are protected from lightning. Church steeples and other tall structures are often struck by bolts of lightning. This could damage the building, or give electric shocks to people inside, so lightning conductors are placed on the roof. These channel the lightning safely away.

274 A person can survive a lightning strike. Lightning is very dangerous and can give a big enough shock to kill you. However, an American park ranger called Roy Sullivan survived being struck seven times.

HOW CLOSE?

Lightning and thunder happen at the same time, but light travels faster than sound. Count the seconds between the flash and the clap and divide them by three. This is how many kilometres away the storm is.

▼ A sudden hail storm can leave the ground littered with small chunks of ice.

275 Hailstones can be as big as melons! These chunks of ice can fall from thunderclouds. The biggest ever fell in Gopaljang, Bangladesh, in 1986 and weighed 1 kilogram each!

Eye of the hurricane

276 **Some winds travel at speeds of more than 120 kilometres an hour.** Violent tropical storms happen when strong winds blow into an area of low pressure and start spinning very fast. They develop over warm seas and pick up speed until they reach land, where there is no more moist sea air to feed them. Such storms bring torrential rain.

I DON'T BELIEVE IT !

Tropical storms are called different names. Hurricanes develop over the Atlantic, typhoons over the Pacific, and cyclones over the Indian Ocean.

▼ A Hurricane Hunter heads into the storm.

277 **The centre of a hurricane is calm and still.** This part is called the 'eye'. As the eye of the storm passes over, there is a pause in the terrifying rains and wind.

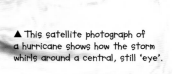

▲ This satellite photograph of a hurricane shows how the storm whirls around a central, still 'eye'.

278 **Hurricane Hunters fly close to the eye of a hurricane.** These are special weather planes that fly into the storm in order to take measurements. It is a dangerous job for the pilots, but the information they gather helps to predict the hurricane's path – and saves lives.

▲ A hurricane brings battering rain and massive waves.

279 Hurricanes have names. One of the worst hurricanes was Hurricane Andrew, which battered the coast of Florida in 1992. Perhaps there is a hurricane named after you!

280 Hurricanes whip up wild waves. As the storm races over the ocean, the winds create giant waves. These hit the shore as a huge sea surge. In 1961, the sea surge following Hurricane Hattie washed away Belize City in South America.

281 Typhoons saved the Japanese from Genghis Khan. The 13th-century Mongol leader made two attempts to invade Japan – and both times, a terrible typhoon battered his fleet and saved the Japanese!

▶ A typhoon prevented Genghis Khan's navy from invading Japan.

Wild whirling winds

282 **Tornadoes spin at speeds of 480 kilometres an hour!** These whirling columns of wind, also known as twisters, are some of the most destructive storms on Earth. They form in strong thunderstorms, when the back part of the thundercloud starts spinning. The spinning air forms a funnel that reaches down towards the Earth. When it touches the ground, it becomes a tornado.

▶ A tornado can cause great damage to anything in its path.

283 **A tornado can be strong enough to lift a train!** The spinning tornado whizzes along the ground like an enormous, high-speed vacuum cleaner, sucking up everything in its path. It rips the roofs off houses, and even tosses buildings into the air. In the 1930s, a twister in Minnesota, USA, threw a train carriage full of people more than eight metres through the air!

284 Tornados can happen anywhere in the world. They are especially active in the United States from Texas up through Oklahoma, Kansas, Nebraska and Dakota. Here, warm, moist air from the Gulf of Mexico meets cold air from the north, which causes storms to form.

Warm air

Cold air

▲ Tornadoes are powerful storms that can cause severe damage.

285 A pillar of whirling water can rise out of a lake or the sea. Waterspouts are spiralling columns of water that can be sucked up by a tornado as it forms over a lake or the sea. They tend to spin more slowly than tornadoes, because water is much heavier than air.

▲ Waterspouts can suck up fish living in a lake!

I DON'T BELIEVE IT !

Loch Ness in Scotland is famous for sightings of a monster nicknamed Nessie. Perhaps people who have seen Nessie were really seeing a waterspout.

▼ A whirling storm of sand in the desert.

286 Dust devils are desert tornadoes. They shift tonnes of sand and cause terrible damage – they can strip the paintwork from a car in seconds!

Pretty lights

287 **Rainbows are made up of seven colours.** They are caused by sunlight passing through falling raindrops. The water acts like a glass prism, splitting the light. White light is made up of seven colours – red, orange, yellow, green, blue, indigo and violet – so these are the colours, from top to bottom, that make up the rainbow.

REMEMBER IT!

Richard Of York Gave Battle In Vain

The first letter of every word of this rhyme gives the first letter of each colour of the rainbow – as it appears in the sky:

Red Orange Yellow Green Blue Indigo Violet

288 **Two rainbows can appear at once.** The top rainbow is a reflection of the bottom one, so its colours appear the opposite way round, with the violet band at the top and red at the bottom.

289 **Some rainbows appear at night.** They happen when falling raindrops split moonlight, rather than sunlight. This sort of rainbow is called a moonbow.

▲ Although a fogbow is colourless, its inner edge may appear slightly blue and its outer edge slightly red.

290 *It is not just angels that wear halos!* When you look at the Sun or Moon through a curtain of ice crystals, they seem to be surrounded by a glowing ring of light called a halo.

291 *Three suns can appear in our sky!* 'Mock suns' are two bright spots that appear on either side of the Sun. They often happen at the same time as a halo, and have the same cause – light passing through ice crystals in the air.

▼ An aurora – the most dazzling natural light show on Earth!

292 *Some rainbows are just white.* Fogbows happen when sunlight passes through a patch of fog. The water droplets in the fog are too small to work like prisms, so the arching bow is white or colourless.

▲ A halo looks like a circle of light surrounding the Sun or Moon.

▲ Mock suns are also known as parhelia or sundogs.

293 *Auroras are curtains of lights in the sky.* They happen in the far north or south of the world when particles from the Sun smash into molecules in the air – at speeds of 1600 kilometres an hour. The lights may be blue, red or yellow.

Made for weather

294 **Camels can go for two weeks without a drink.** They are adapted to life in a hot, dry climate. Camels do not sweat until their body temperature hits 40°C, which helps them to save water. Their humps are fat stores, which are used for energy when food and drink is scarce.

▼ These animals have adapted to life in very dry climates. However, they live in different deserts around the world.

295 **Lizards lose salt through their noses.** Most animals get rid of excess salt in their urine, but lizards, such as iguanas and geckos, live in dry parts of the world. They need to lose as little water from their bodies as possible.

Camels

296 **Even toads can survive in the desert.** The spadefoot toad copes with desert conditions by staying underground in a burrow for most of the year. It only comes to the surface after a shower of rain.

Iguana

Banded gecko

▶ Beneath its gleaming—white fur, the polar bear's skin is black to absorb heat from the Sun.

QUIZ

Rearrange the letters to find the names of four plants that can cope with a very dry climate.

1. ROAGAUS SACCUT
2. OBABBA ETRE
3. YLPCIRK REAP
4. SCUYTPALUE

Answers:
1. Saguaro cactus 2. Baobab tree 3. Prickly pear 4. Eucalyptus

297 Polar bears have black skin.
These bears have all sorts of special ways to survive the polar climate. Plenty of body fat and thick fur keeps them snug and warm, while their black skin soaks up as much warmth from the Sun as possible.

298 Acorn woodpeckers store nuts for winter.
Animals in temperate climates have to be prepared if they are to survive the cold winter months. Acorn woodpeckers turn tree trunks into larders. During autumn, when acorns are ripe, the birds collect as many as they can, storing them in holes that they bore into a tree.

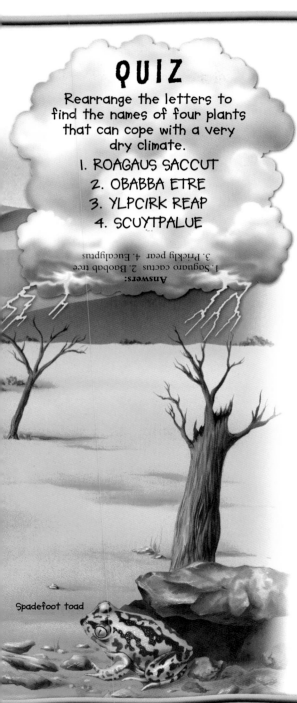

Spadefoot toad

▶ Storing acorns helps this woodpecker survive the cold winter months.

Weather myths

299 **People once thought the Sun was a god.** The sun god was often considered to be the most important god of all, because he brought light and warmth and ripened crops. The ancient Egyptians built pyramids that pointed up to their sun god, Re, while the Aztecs believed that their sun god, Huitzilpochtli, had even shown them where to build their capital city.

300 **The Vikings thought a god brought thunder.** Thor was the god of war and thunder, worshipped across what is now Scandinavia. The Vikings pictured Thor as a red-bearded giant. He carried a hammer that produced bolts of lightning. Our day, Thursday, is named in Thor's honour.

◀ In Scandinavian mythology, Thor was the god of thunder.

▲ The Egyptian sun god, Re, was often shown with the head of a falcon.

301 **Hurricanes are named after a god.** The Mayan people lived in Central America, the part of the world that is most affected by hurricanes. Their creator god was called Huracan.

302 **Totem poles honoured the Thunderbird.** Certain tribes of Native American Indians built tall, painted totem poles, carved in the image of the Thunderbird. They wanted to keep the spirit happy, because they thought it brought rain to feed the plants.

▶ A Native American Indian totem pole depicting the spirit of the Thunderbird.

303 **People once danced for rain.** In hot places such as Africa, people developed dances to bring rain. These were performed by the village shaman (religious woman or man), using wooden instruments such as bullroarers. Sometimes water was sprinkled on the ground. Rain dances are still performed in some countries today.

◀ Shamans wore a special costume for their rain dance.

MAKE A BULLROARER

You will need:
wooden ruler   string
Ask an adult to drill a hole in one end of the ruler. Thread through the string, and knot it, to stop it slipping through the hole. In an open space, whirl the instrument above your head to create a wind noise!

139

Rain or shine?

304 Seaweed can tell us if rain is on the way. Long ago, people looked to nature for clues about the weather. One traditional way of forecasting was to hang up strands of seaweed. If the seaweed stayed slimy, the air was damp and rain was likely. If the seaweed shrivelled up, the weather would be dry.

◄ Kelp picks up any moisture in the air, so it is a good way of telling how damp the atmosphere is.

I DON'T BELIEVE IT!

People used to say that cows lay down when rain was coming — but there is no truth in it! They lie down whether rain is on the way or not!

305 'Red sky at night is the sailor's delight'. This is one of the most famous pieces of weather lore and means that a glorious sunset is followed by a fine morning. The saying is also known as 'shepherd's delight'. There is no evidence that the saying is true, though.

Groundhog

306 Groundhogs tell the weather when they wake. Of course, they don't really, but in parts of the USA, Groundhog Day is a huge celebration. On 2 February, people gather to see the groundhog come out. If you see the creature's shadow, it means there are six more weeks of cold to come.

▼ A blood-red sunset is delightful to look at, but it can't help a sailor to predict the next day's weather.

▲ Records of ancient weather were scratched on to this piece of shell.

▲ The Moon is clearly visible in a cloudless night sky. Its light casts a silvery glow over the Earth.

307 '**Clear moon, frost soon**'. This old saying does have some truth in it. If there are few clouds in the sky, the view of the Moon will be clear – and there will also be no blanket of cloud to keep in the Earth's heat. That makes a frost more likely – during the colder months, at least.

308 The earliest weather records are over 3000 years old. They were found on a piece of tortoiseshell and had been written down by Chinese weather watchers. The inscriptions describe when it rained or snowed and how windy it was.

Instruments and inventors

309 The Tower of Winds was built 2000 years ago. It was an eight-sided building and is the first known weather station. It had a wind vane on the roof and a water clock inside.

310 The first barometer was made by one of Galileo's students. Barometers measure air pressure. The first person to describe air pressure – and to make an instrument for measuring it – was an Italian, Evangelista Torricelli. He had studied under the great scientist Galileo. Torricelli made his barometer in 1643.

▲ This is how the Tower of Winds looks today. It was built by Andronicus of Cyrrhus in Athens around 75 BC. Its eight sides face the points of the compass: north, northeast, east, southeast, south, southwest, west and northwest.

◄ Torricelli took a bowl of mercury and placed it under the open end of a glass tube, also filled with mercury. It was the weight, or pressure, of air on the mercury in the bowl that stopped the mercury in the tube from falling.

311 Weather cocks have a special meaning. They have four pointers that show the directions of north, south, east and west. The cockerel at the top swivels so that its head always shows the direction of the wind.

► Weather cocks are often placed on top of church steeples.

312 A weather house really can predict the weather. It is a type of hygrometer – an instrument that detects how much moisture is in the air. If there is lots, the rainy-day character comes out of the door!

▶ Weather houses have two figures. One comes out when the air is damp and the other when the air is dry.

◀ This early thermometer shows both the Fahrenheit and the Celsius temperature scales.

313 Fahrenheit made the first thermometer in 1714. Thermometers are instruments that measure temperature. Gabriel Daniel Fahrenheit invented the thermometer using a blob of mercury sealed in an airtight tube. The Fahrenheit scale for measuring heat was named after him. The Centigrade scale was introduced in 1742 by the Swedish scientist Anders Celsius.

QUIZ

1. What is another name for the liquid metal, mercury?

2. What does an anemometer measure?

3. What does a wind vane measure?

4. On the Fahrenheit scale, at what temperature does water freeze?

Answers:
1. Quicksilver 2. Wind speed
3. Wind direction 4. 32°F

World of weather

314 Working out what the weather will be like is called forecasting. By looking at changes in the atmosphere, and comparing them to weather patterns of the past, forecasters can make an accurate guess at what the weather will be tomorrow, the next day, or even further ahead than that. But even forecasters get it wrong sometimes!

315 The first national weather offices appeared in the 1800s. This was when people realized that science could explain how weather worked – and save people from disasters. The first network of weather stations was set up in France, in 1855. This was after the scientist Le Verrier showed how a French warship, sunk in a storm, could have been saved. Le Verrier explained how the path of the storm could have been tracked, and the ship sailed to safety.

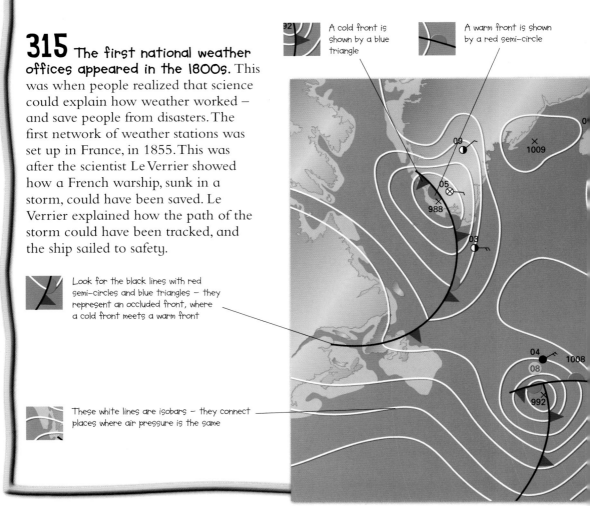

A cold front is shown by a blue triangle

A warm front is shown by a red semi-circle

Look for the black lines with red semi-circles and blue triangles – they represent an occluded front, where a cold front meets a warm front

These white lines are isobars – they connect places where air pressure is the same

WEATHER SYMBOLS

Learn how to represent the weather on your own synoptic charts. Here are some of the basic symbols to get you started. You may come across them in newspapers or while watching television. Can you guess what they mean?

316 Nations need to share weather data. By 1865, nearly 60 weather stations across Europe were swapping information. These early weather scientists, or meteorologists, realized that they needed to present their information using symbols that they could all understand. To this day, meteorologists plot their findings on maps called synoptic charts. They use lines called isobars to show which areas have the same air pressure. The Internet makes it easier for meteorologists to access information.

This symbol shows the strength of the wind – the circle shows how much cloud cover there is

This symbol shows that the wind is very strong – look at the three lines on the tail

This shows an area of calm, with lots of cloud cover

◀ Meteorologists call their weather maps synoptic charts. They use the same symbols, which make up a common language for weather scientists all around the world.

Weather watch

317 Balloons can tell us about the weather. Weather balloons are hot-air balloons that are sent high into the atmosphere. As they rise, onboard equipment takes readings. These find out air pressure, and how moist, or humid, the air is, as well as how warm. The findings are radioed back to meteorologists on the ground, using a system called radiosonde. Hundreds of balloons are launched around the world every day.

▶ A weather balloon carries its scientific instruments high into the atmosphere.

318 Some planes hound the weather. Weather planes provide more atmospheric measurements than balloons can. *Snoopy* is the name of one of the British weather planes. The instruments are carried on its long, pointy nose, so they can test the air ahead of the plane.

▼ Snoopy's long nose carries all the equipment needed to monitor the weather.

319 Satellites help save lives.

Their birds'-eye view of the Earth allows them to take amazing pictures of our weather systems. They can track hurricanes as they form over the oceans. Satellite-imaging has helped people to leave their homes and get out of a hurricane's path just in time.

I DON'T BELIEVE IT!

Some of the best weather photos have been taken by astronauts in space.

▲ A weather satellite takes photographs of Earth's weather systems from space.

▶ Currents carry the floating weather buoys around the oceans.

320 Some weather stations are all at sea.

Weather buoys float on the surface of the oceans, measuring air pressure, temperature and wind direction. They are fitted with transmitters that beam information to satellites in space – which bounce the readings on to meteorologists. Tracking the buoys is just as important. They are carried along by ocean currents, which have a huge effect on our weather systems.

Changing climate

321 Climate change destroyed the dinosaurs – but no one can agree on what caused it. The best explanation is that a huge piece of space rock, called a meteorite, smashed into Earth. It threw up a giant cloud of dust that blocked out the Sun, plunging the world into cold and dark.

▼ Could a meteorite have crashed to Earth and changed the climate? A meteorite crater found in the Gulf of Mexico dates to 65 million years ago – exactly the time that the dinosaurs died out. Perhaps the impact changed the warm climate the dinosaurs were so used to.

322 Greenland used to be green! This island lies in the Arctic Ocean and is mostly covered by a huge ice sheet. Even in Viking times, Greenland was cold, but Viking settlers built at least two farming colonies there. These died out around the 1400s, after the climate cooled.

◄ Vikings settled on Greenland's coastline. Inland areas were covered in ice.

323 A volcano can change the climate!

Big volcanic explosions can create dust that blots out the Sun, just as a meteorite impact can. Dust from the 1815 eruption of a volcano called Tambora did this. This made many crops fail around the world and many people starved.

324 Tree-felling is affecting our weather.

In areas of Southeast Asia and South America, rainforests are being cleared for farming. When the trees are burned, the fires release carbon dioxide – a greenhouse gas which helps to blanket the Earth and keep in the heat. Unfortunately, high levels of carbon dioxide raise the temperature too much.

◀ Like all plants, rainforest trees take in carbon dioxide and give out oxygen. As rainforests are destroyed, the amount of carbon dioxide in the atmosphere increases.

325 Air temperatures are rising.

Scientists think the average world temperature may increase by around 1.5°C this century. This may not sound like much, but the extra warmth will mean more storms, including hurricanes and tornadoes, and more droughts, too.

QUIZ

1. What may have caused the death of the dinosaurs?

2. Which settlers once lived along the coast of Greenland?

3. Which gas do plants take in?

Answers:
1. Meteorite impact 2. Vikings 3. Carbon dioxide

Carbon dioxide layer traps heat

Heat from the Sun

Trapped heat bounces back to Earth

▶ Too much carbon dioxide in the atmosphere creates a 'greenhouse effect'. Just as glass traps heat, so does carbon dioxide. This means more storms and droughts.

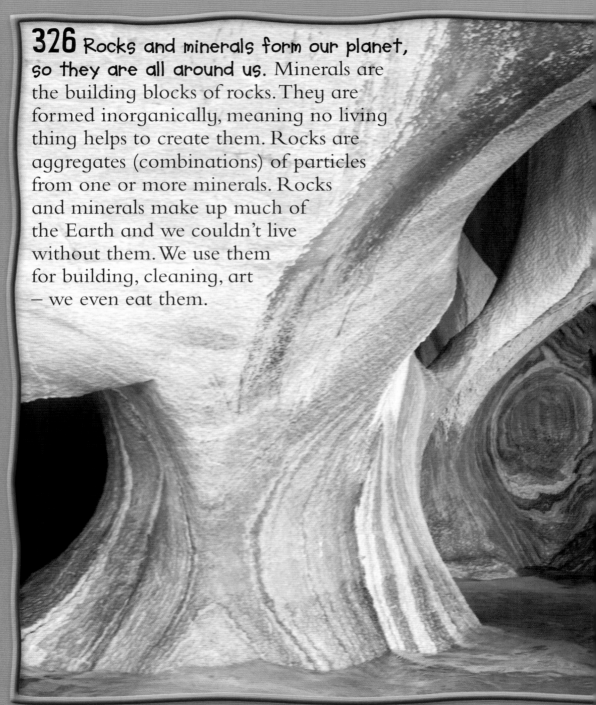

ROCKS AND MINERALS

326 Rocks and minerals form our planet, so they are all around us. Minerals are the building blocks of rocks. They are formed inorganically, meaning no living thing helps to create them. Rocks are aggregates (combinations) of particles from one or more minerals. Rocks and minerals make up much of the Earth and we couldn't live without them. We use them for building, cleaning, art — we even eat them.

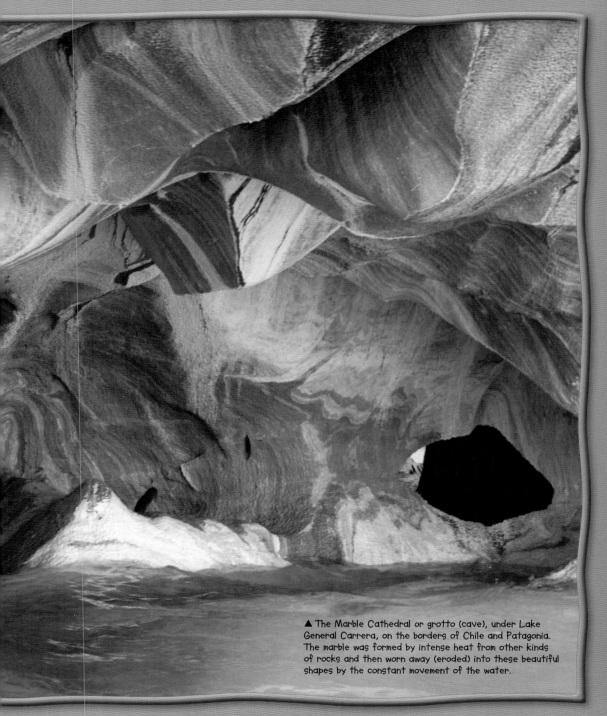

▲ The Marble Cathedral or grotto (cave), under Lake
General Carrera, on the borders of Chile and Patagonia.
The marble was formed by intense heat from other kinds
of rocks and then worn away (eroded) into these beautiful
shapes by the constant movement of the water.

The rock cycle

327 **There are layers inside the Earth.** The first is the crust (the solid outer shell), which is between 6 and 70 kilometres thick. Under this is the mantle – a layer of hot rock that is around 2500 kilometres thick. The uppermost layers of the mantle are fused to the crust. Beneath these layers is an outer core of liquid metal and an inner core – a solid ball of hot iron.

Inner core

Outer core

Mantle

Crust

▲ Under the crust and mantle are layers of liquid metal and, in the centre, a solid ball of sizzling iron.

▶ The rock cycle is the long, slow journey of rocks down from the surface and then up again. Rocks are often changed during this process.

Weathering of rocks at surface

Erosion and transport

Laying down of sediment

328 **All rock goes through a cycle over millions of years.** During the rock cycle rocks form deep in the Earth, move and sometimes change, go up to the surface and eventually return below the ground. There are three kinds of rock – igneous, sedimentary and metamorphic. They form in different ways and have different features.

Burial and becoming more compact under pressure

SEDIMENTARY ROCK

Deep burial and metamorphism (changing structur

329 Rocks can go around the cycle in lots of ways. Igneous rocks were once molten (liquid), and have hardened beneath or above the surface. Metamorphic rock forms when rock is changed by heat, pressure or a combination of the two. Sedimentary rocks are formed when sediment – small particles of rock – becomes buried.

I DON'T BELIEVE IT!

The outer rock layer of the Earth is made of seven main segments (plates). Over time, these plates have moved across the surface of the Earth at a rate of between 5 and 15 centimetres a year, creating volcanoes, mountains and oceans.

330 Exposed rock is eroded (worn away) over time. This is a process in which tiny pieces (particles) of rock are loosened and transported as a result of gravity, wind, water or ice. Gradually these particles may become buried under more rock particles, forming sediment. If the sediment is buried deep enough to reach the mantle it will be heated by magma (hot molten rock), which may melt or bake it. Uplift and erosion can then expose them again.

IGNEOUS ROCK

Magma forms crystals as it cools

METAMORPHIC ROCK

Melting to form magma

153

Formed in fire

331 Rock that forms when hot molten rock (magma or lava) cools and hardens is called igneous rock. Igneous rock is divided into two types, extrusive and intrusive, depending on where it forms.

◄ When the pressure in the magma chamber is high enough, the volcano erupts and spews out its lava with incredible force.

332 Igneous rock is known as 'extrusive' if it forms above Earth's surface. This can happen if it erupts or flows from a volcano as lava. Sometimes lava settles, sealing the volcano until pressure builds for another eruption. Extrusive rock can form over thousands or even millions of years. As extrusive rock cools, its fine grains grow into larger crystals.

333 Intrusive rock cools and solidifies inside the Earth's crust below the surface. It only becomes visible when the rocks above it wear away. Granite and dolerite are two examples of intrusive rock.

QUIZ

1. What is igneous rock before it hardens?
2. Where does 'extrusive' rock form?
3. How were the columns at the Giant's Causeway formed?

Answers:
1. Molten rock, or magma 2. Above ground 3. They formed as lava cooled and shrank

▶ An ancient volcanic eruption formed the Giant's Causeway, which consists of around 40,000 columns of basalt that interlock like a giant jigsaw.

334 The most common type of igneous rock is basalt, which often cools in hexagonal columns. At the Giant's Causeway in Northern Ireland, thousands of these columns were created as lava cooled and shrank over millions of years. Legend says that the columns, some as much as 2 metres in height, are stepping stones for giants to walk across the sea.

335 Sometimes gas creates holes in rock. Crystals form inside the holes, creating geodes – dull-looking stones from the outside, lined with brilliant crystals on the inside. Geodes are often sold cut in half and polished to reveal their glittering insides.

▶ Geodes are rock cavities with crystal formations or circular bands inside them.

Incredible igneous

▼ Volcanic ash settled over the dead of Pompeii. Over time the bodies rotted away leaving cavities in the ash. The scientists who uncovered these filled them with plaster to create casts of the victims' bodies.

336 The igneous rock, basalt, is so durable that it was used to pave the ancient Roman city of Pompeii. However, in AD 79 the nearby volcano Vesuvius erupted, covering the town with fresh ash. Buildings, streets and many people were buried and lay untouched for centuries.

▼ Pumice is frothy lava turned solid. It is widely used to make lightweight concrete.

337 Pumice is solidified lava. It is so light it will float until water soaks into it. It has tiny holes with sharp edges all over it, making it ideal for rubbing down rough surfaces and cleaning skin. Stonewashed jeans are treated with ground-up pumice.

338 Granite has a high content of the mineral quartz. This makes it very tough so it is often used for construction. It can be seen in many famous buildings, such as parts of London's Tower Bridge and some of the ancient Egyptian pyramids and obelisks.

▲ Curling is an event at the Winter Olympics. Teams slide granite stones towards a target.

339 **The sport of curling uses granite stones.** Teams slide large, heavy, polished granite discs along ice towards a target. Two sweepers with brooms brush the ice to make the stone go in the direction that they want.

◀ Ancient Egyptian obelisks such as this have survived for thousands of years because granite is so tough it takes ages to erode.

TRUE OR FALSE?

1. Pumice is one of the heaviest types of rock.

2. Granite is often used in building because it is so strong.

3. In tennis, players pass granite stones to one another.

Answers:
1. False, it is very light 2. True 3. False, granite stones are used in curling

340 **Igneous rock is crushed to make aggregate.** This is the material used for the foundations of roads and railways. It forms a strong, stable base on top of which the road surface can be laid. You can sometimes see it as the layer underneath the tarmac when roads are being repaired.

Lots of layers

341 When rocks are weathered or eroded they break into tiny pieces called sediment. This sediment is eventually buried and compacted (packed tightly together) under pressure until it becomes solid, forming sedimentary rock. It is found in layers known as strata.

342 The walls of the Grand Canyon in Arizona, USA, are sedimentary rock. The canyon is 350 kilometres long and has a depth of 1.6 kilometres in places. It was created by the flowing force of the Colorado River, which wore away the rock. Rock layers are clearly visible along the sides of the canyon.

343 Limestone is a sedimentary rock mostly formed from crushed shells. It contains the remains of millions of sea creatures that have piled up over millions of years, and so it often contains fossils.

I DON'T BELIEVE IT!

Uluru in Australia is the most famous block of freestanding rock. It is a 348-metre-high lump of sandstone and is 300 million years old.

344 Some sedimentary rocks are formed when saline (salt) water evaporates. This can happen when a bay or gulf is cut off from the sea and starts to dry up. These mineral-rich rocks are known as evaporites and include gypsum, rock salt (halite) and potash.

345 Coal is a sedimentary rock formed over millions of years. Vegetation from swampy forests died and rotted away. As the water dried out, the vegetation became first peat and eventually coal. Both peat and coal can be mined and burned as fuel.

◄ The Grand Canyon was formed by two billion years of erosion from the Colorado River exposing countless layers of sedimentary rock.

Super sedimentary

▲ Flint was tied to wood to make tools that were used for fighting and farming.

346 **Some of the first tools were made of flint.** Flint, also called chert, is a mineral found in sedimentary rock. Its glassy texture, along with its hardness, made it a good material for tools such as axes. Stone Age people found it so useful that they dug mines to extract it.

▲ Coloured chalks are made from gypsum mixed with powdered paint.

347 Sedimentary rock such as limestone and sandstone is fairly soft and easy to cut. This makes it particularly useful when the stone for a building is to be carved and shaped. Examples include St Peter's Basilica in Rome and Durham Cathedral in England.

348 Chalk is a fine limestone made from the crushed remains of tiny sea plants. The white sticks we use to write with aren't actually the rock chalk, but a mineral called gypsum. Real chalk is too soft to use.

◄ El-deir monastery near Petra in Jordan. The 42-metre-high façade of sedimentary rock that now forms one of the new wonders of the world.

GROW YOUR OWN STALACTITE

Make sure you ask an adult to help you. Dissolve some Epsom salts (magnesium sulphate) in two jars of hot water. Drape string between the two jars with each end in the liquid, holding it in place with a paper clip. Leave for a few days and a stalactite should start to form on the string.

349 Stalactites are an amazing feature of some limestone caves. A stalactite develops when a drop of water evaporates, leaving behind a mineral deposit of calcite. If this keeps happening, a spike of mineral starts to 'grow' as more water drips down. Stalactites only grow a few millimetres a year.

▼ Stalactites are formed by slow dripping water, just like icicles, except the water has evaporated leaving its minerals behind. The shapes made when stalactites and stalagmites join into pillars have been called 'organ pipes' and 'hanging curtains'.

350 Sometimes the minerals falling from a stalactite collect on the cave floor and start to 'grow' up, making a stalagmite. Eventually the two might meet and join, forming a column. A good way to remember the difference between stalactites and stalagmites is: Watch out! If stalactites grow down, stalag*mites might* grow up.

The rock that changes

351 Metamorphic rock is rock that has been changed by heat or pressure (or both) into a new form deep underground. Pressure from movement of the Earth's crust, the weight of the rocks above and heat from magma cause metamorphic changes. Most of these happen at temperatures of 200–500°C. The rock does not melt – that would make igneous rock – but it is altered.

352 The appearance and texture of rock changes as a result of heat and pressure. Crystals break down and form, and a rock's chemical structure can change as its minerals react together. If the change is made under pressure, the rock crystals grow flat and form layers. If shale is compressed it forms slate.

▼ Slate forms when fine clay settles in layers and is then compressed and heated.

1. Bands of shale form solid layers

Shale

2. Movement creates curves

Slate

▼ Part of a slate landscape on Valencia Island off the coast of Ireland. This useful rock has been quarried and mined for thousands of years.

353 Sometimes rocks don't stop changing. For example, over centuries shale becomes slate, which looks the same as shale but is far harder and is more likely to split into sheets. However, if slate is then heated and squeezed it will be transformed again into phyllite, then schist and finally gneiss. This is the incredibly hard rock that forms the Alps.

▼ The Alps is a long mountain range stretching from east to west across Europe, formed about 40–20 million years ago.

354 Eclogite is one of the rarest, but most interesting, metamorphic rocks. It is full of crystals and minerals so it is very coarse-grained. Eclogite is green and often studded with red garnets, and sometimes even diamonds. It forms deep in the Earth's mantle, reaching the surface through volcanoes.

▼ No other rock contains as many interesting crystals and minerals as eclogite, which is formed by extremely high pressures and temperatures.

163

Marvellous metamorphic

355 **The metamorphic rock marble is used in building.** It is especially good for curved buildings, such as the Taj Mahal in India. The dome is made of white marble and seems to change colour through the day. It took 20,000 workers 22 years to finish the temple and the surrounding buildings in 1648.

▼ The Taj Mahal is an intricately carved, symmetrical tomb made of white marble. It is now a World Heritage Site.

▶ Marble can be cut in any direction and has been used by artists for thousands of years.

356 **Marble was a favourite material of Greek and Roman sculptors.** Pure marble only contains one mineral – calcite – so it is not formed in bands. This means it is smooth and can be easily carved, so it is perfect for creating complex shapes. The best-known marble comes from Italy.

366 Fossils can tell us the age of rocks.
If scientists can identify a fossilized animal or plant, they will be able to identify the time period in which it lived, so the rock that the fossil has been found in must also date from that period.

367 Sometimes footprints, burrows and animal droppings are fossilized. These 'trace fossils' are created when mud or sand fills cavities before they are washed away. Scientists can work out the size and speed of dinosaurs from trace fossils of their footprints.

Neanderthal

NEOGENE
23 million years ago
(MYA) onwards

Diatryma

PALAEOGENE
65.5–23 MYA

Deinotherium

Lambeosaur

CRETACEOUS
145.5–65.5 MYA

Hoplopteryx

Archaeopteryx

Allosaurus

JURASSIC
200–145.5 MYA

Acanthodes

Thrinaxodon

Dimetrodon

PERMIAN–
TRIASSIC
299–200 MYA

Ammonite

Dragonfly

DEVONIAN–
CARBONIFEROUS
410–299 MYA

Trilobite

Amphibian

Shark tooth

CAMBRIAN–
ORDOVICIAN
540–410 MYA

▲ Geologists can work out how old rock is by studying the fossils within it.

The changing landscape

368 Rocks form our landscape but they are slowly changing all the time. They are always being pulled down by gravity, but rocks can also be pushed up from below or worn down in different ways. Many things affect how fast rock is broken down, but it happens to all exposed rock eventually.

369 When movement wears down rocks it is known as erosion. This might be a pebble being ground down as it rolls down a river or glacier, or the top of a hill on a beauty spot being pounded by the feet of countless visitors.

370 When rocks break down without moving it is known as weathering. This can be because of rain, frost, sun or wind. Flowing water wears rock away, which is often how valleys form. If the water falls inside a crack and then freezes and expands, it can shatter the rock. This is called frost damage.

371 Even wind can break down rock, as the movement of small particles in the air slowly wears it away. This happens faster in deserts where the sand and dust carried by the wind rub at the rock.

▶ Sometimes the lower rock of a cliff face is eroded, leaving an overhang.

372 On the coast, breakwaters (strong walls) are sometimes put up to protect against sea erosion. The current, along with powerful waves, breaks up rock and moves vast amounts of sand. Some beaches would disappear without the protection of breakwaters.

373 Pollution can damage buildings made from rock. During the Industrial Revolution in the 18th century, people noticed that buildings crumbled more in towns where lots of coal was being burnt. Minerals in the rock were being eaten away by acid in the atmosphere created by the burning coal. Acid rain is still a big problem today, damaging many buildings worldwide.

▲ The strange landscape of Monument Valley in Arizona, USA, was formed as tiny particles of sand and dust carried by the wind wore away the softer rock, leaving landforms known as 'buttes'.

What are minerals?

374 Minerals are natural substances that form crystals. There are over 4000 different minerals but only about 30 are found all over the world. Quartz and feldspar are two of the most common types of mineral.

Cubic

▼ Crystal shapes are set by the arrangement of atoms and molecules inside the mineral.

Tetragonal

Orthorhombic

Monoclinic

375 A mineral is a chemical compound (a combination of two or more substances) or element (a single fundamental substance). Rocks are made from minerals. Limestone is made mainly of the mineral calcite (calcium carbonate), and granite contains quartz, mica and feldspar.

Triclinic

Hexagonal

Trigonal

376 Minerals form crystals. They can do this in several ways. Some are formed as hot molten magma cools. Others come from water (the white powder left when water evaporates is a mineral deposit). Crystals can also be formed when minerals are altered by heat or pressure.

377 Crystals have seven basic shapes. Some just look like a jumble of different surfaces and angles. They have flat, often shiny faces and sharp edges.

378 The tiny grains you can see in most rocks are actually minerals, often forced together. Large crystals form in cracks and holes in rocks, where they have space to grow. The deeper the rock, the longer it generally takes to reach the surface, and the more time the crystal has to grow.

379 Some minerals are so valuable that they are mined. This might mean scraping them from the ground, or blowing up the rocks that hold them. Minerals buried deep underground are reached by drilling down and digging tunnels. People have mined minerals for thousands of years.

▶ Miners have to follow the direction of the mineral-rich band in the seam of rock.

Mineral detectives

380 **Minerals can be tricky to identify.** Mineralogists (scientists who study minerals) use a number of tests to identify minerals. These are crystal shape, colour, streak, magnetism, density, how it splits, and how it reacts to acid.

381 The same mineral can be different colours, so it can be more helpful for mineralogists to assess how well a mineral reflects light. This is known as lustre. It might shine like metal (metallic), or glisten like glass (vitreous) or be transparent, or block light (opaque).

▲ These giant selenite crystals are believed to be the biggest crystals in the world.

▼ These long, thin crystals belong to a mineral called stibnite.

382 Another way to identify a mineral is to test how easy it is to scratch. Minerals are given a 'hardness' rating from 1 to 10. If a mineral can be scratched with a fingernail, its hardness is less than 2.5. If it can be scratched with a bronze coin it has a hardness of 4. If it can be scratched with a penknife it has a hardness 6. The softest mineral, with a score of 1, is talc. Diamonds score 10, because only other diamonds can cut them.

▼ The hardness scale was devised in 1812 by Friedrich Mohs and is still used today.

① Talc   ② Gypsum   ③ Calcite   ④ Fluorite

383 The way crystals split is known as cleavage. They break along lines of weakness, known as cleavage planes. Some, such as mica, break into flat sheets or flakes. Others split in two planes like a square rod – orthoclase feldspar does this. Galena breaks in three planes so that the face looks like steps.

▶ Some mica crystals can be split into wafer–like sheets that are so thin they can become almost transparent.

384 The real mineral colour test is the streak test. When the mineral is rubbed against the back of a white porcelain tile it will always mark the tile with the same colour. For example quartz can be purple, green, red, yellow or black, but it leaves a white streak on tiles.

▶ The most common mineral on Earth's land surface, quartz, is usually colourless or white, but it can be many colours.

GET A REACTION

A group of minerals called carbonates all react to acid. You can test this by dropping a rock into vinegar. If the rock has carbonates in it, it will fizz and bubble. Try this with a lump of chalk or limestone, as their main ingredient is calcite. The fizzing is carbon dioxide gas being released as the mineral dissolves.

⑤ Apatite	⑥ Orthoclase	⑦ Quartz	⑧ Topaz	⑨ Corundum	⑩ Diamond

Brilliant colours

385 The caves of Lascaux in France are decorated with nearly 2000 figures painted onto the walls by cave dwellers nearly 17,000 years ago. They painted horses, stags, bison and huge bulls using ground-down minerals.

◄ Charcoal is just burnt wood, so there was a plenty of it around for Stone Age artists.

386 Minerals were used for thousands of years to make pigments. At first, earth colours were used, but they were not very bright. Gradually people discovered how to make brilliant blues and greens and the new pigments were traded over long distances. Today most pigments are synthetic (man-made).

◄ The Lascaux cave paintings are one of only a few surviving examples of prehistoric art.

► One word for a deep but bright blue is azure, taken from the pigment azurite.

387 Pigments need to have a binding agent to hold them in place.

Otherwise they just turn back to powder after any water has evaporated. One natural binding agent is egg yolk (the yellow part of the egg).

► Artists have long prized the intense blue made from the semi-precious stone lapis lazuli.

388 Chalk was the first substance to be used as white pigment, while earth colours were made with iron minerals.

A copper compound called azurite made a beautiful blue, bettered only by the rarer and more expensive lapis lazuli. The mineral pigment terra verte was used to make green paint, and was so common around Verona, Italy, that it was also known as Verona Green.

▲ Made from a copper compound, green malachite has been in use as a pigment since the Bronze Age in Egypt.

389 Ancient Egyptian beauties used mineral make-up!

Women of the time used green malachite, along with the black minerals galena or lead sulphide, for eye make-up. Other minerals were used for beauty treatments, and the mineral jasper was used to cure eye infections.

► The abundant minerals found or traded by the ancient Egyptians were used for make-up and body decoration.

Metal minerals

390 **Most minerals are mixtures known as compounds.** However, there are about 20 'native elements' that rarely mix and are mostly pure. Most of these are metals and without them our world would be very different.

391 **Metals are mined, quarried or dredged up.** At this point they are known as ore, the word for rock containing metals. The ore is heated beyond its melting point (this is called smelting), and the precious metal is poured out as a liquid and put in a mould to set.

392 **Silver has long featured in jewellery but it is also used in the electronics industry.** It is found as small specks or thin wiry shapes in igneous rock. Today, silver is less valuable than gold, but in the past it has been rarer than gold, and so more valuable. It goes dull and black very quickly so it has to be polished to make it shiny.

▲ At a smelting works metal ore is heated past its melting point and the liquid is poured to set in a mould.

▶ With its red-gold colour, copper makes one of the most distinctive metals, and is found in many minerals.

393 Aluminium is quite a common metal — it makes up 8 percent of the weight of the Earth's crust. It is found in about 270 minerals but is mainly extracted from the ore bauxite. It is light but strong, and is used to make vehicles such as cars and planes as well as many other things. Aluminium isn't magnetic, unlike iron.

▲ ▶ Bauxite ore produces aluminium, a strong but light metal that is ideal for forming the body of vehicles such as planes.

▶ Bronze is the most popular material for metal sculptures. This bronze and marble sculpture is *The Thinker* by Rodin.

394 Metals can be mixed together to make alloys. One of the most important alloys in our history is bronze, a blend of copper and tin. Copper is soft, so wasn't useful for tools or containers as it didn't stay sharp or in shape. Adding tin made it harder and allowed people to make swords, armour, ploughs and cooking pots.

395 Platinum is one of the rarest metals. It is 30 times more scarce than gold and is usually found as fine grains. Most platinum is found in two parts of the world — Russia and South Africa. It is used in jewellery, laboratories and in catalytic converters (devices used to reduce damaging substances in car emissions). Some coins were made from it in the past.

Panning for gold

◀ Gold panners scoop up the riverbed and shake their pans to see if any pieces of gold are hidden in the rocks and mud.

396 **Gold is one of the most valuable materials.** It has been used as money and as jewellery and decoration for centuries. One of the reasons that it is so precious is that it is very hard to find. Gold is a pure element – it rarely mixes with other minerals.

◀ Gold sometimes forms in veins of quartz that are then extracted and smelted.

397 **Gold forms in igneous and sedimentary rocks.** It is sometimes found in lumps known as nuggets, but more commonly as tiny specks. People still pan for gold today, filtering gravel and sand in the hope that they will find some heavier gold grains in their sieve.

TRUE OR FALSE?

1. The mineral pyrite is worth the same as gold.
2. Gold is often used in jewellery.
3. Gold was only recently discovered.

Answers:
1. False 2. True
3. False, it has been used since ancient times

398 The ancient Egyptians decorated their temples with gold. The Turin Papyrus, drawn in 1160 BC, shows a gold mine in the Egyptian desert. Gold is good to work with as it can be softened and shaped relatively easily. It is also very strong and polishes well.

◄ 'Bling' is the slang term for flashy jewellery with lots of gold in it, as worn here by the rapper Slick Rick.

▲ Tutankhamun's death mask was made of solid gold decorated with semi-precious stones and glass. It weighs 10 kilograms.

399 When lots of people travel to an area where gold has been found it is called a gold rush. Gold rushes occurred in Roman times and during the Spanish conquest of the Americas. In the 19th century whole towns were founded in America, Brazil and Australia when gold-panners moved in and started their search.

400 Some minerals look like gold. Known as 'fool's gold', pyrite and chalcopyrite have often been mistaken for the real thing because they resemble it so closely. Both are harder than real gold.

► Fool's gold can still be useful – it makes sparks when struck and was used in early firearms.

Special effects

401 A firework display is a big mineral burn-up. The colours depend on which mineral is used. For example, celestite burns red, while greens are from barite, tourmaline burns yellow and copper burns blue. Firework makers mix minerals into compounds to create new colours. Flashes and shower effects are made with aluminium. The smell from fireworks is actually the mineral sulphur burning.

◄ The blues in a firework display are produced by copper minerals being burnt.

402 Ultraviolet (UV) light makes some minerals glow fantastic colours that are completely different to their dull appearance in daylight. This is called fluorescence after the best example, fluorite. This mineral shines blue or green in UV light, probably because it has traces of radioactive uranium.

403 Gypsum can be dried into a powder. This powder forms the base for many plasters (such as plaster of Paris) and cements. It is also used in fertilizers and paper.

▲ Fluorite shines in UV light and it also glows when gently heated.

▶ Coal mining is dangerous because the seams of coal are deep under the ground.

▲ Coal can be treated so that it burns without producing smoke.

404 Fossil fuels such as coal, oil and gas are made from minerals found in the remains of plants that lived millions of years ago. They are used to get energy because they burn well. Coal is solid, and mostly made up of the element carbon.

405 Kaolin is named after Kao-ling hill in China, where it has been quarried for 1400 years. Made from the mineral kaolinite, it is a soft, white and fine-grained clay used to make porcelain. It has many uses – it is also found in some light bulbs, medicines and glossy paper.

▶ This kaolin (china clay) mine is in St Austell, Cornwall, UK.

A mineral meal

Cheese is an excellent source of the mineral apatite

406 Our bodies need minerals to stay healthy. The mineral apatite helps to form teeth and bones (its chemical name is calcium phosphate). We get it from dairy foods such as cheese.

407 We need iron in our blood. It is found in red meat and eggs. Potassium keeps our muscles working (bananas are full of it). Zinc helps us fight diseases and heal cuts – it is found in meat and beans.

▶ People have mined salt for thousands of years. Salt was once so valuable that Roman soldiers were paid with it.

408 The most commonly used mineral is salt. Also known as table salt and rock salt, its chemical name is halite, or sodium chloride. Salt forms where salty water evaporates. Thick layers of it can be found in some sedimentary rock. Some salt is mined underground. Shafts are dug and the salt is loosened with an explosion and then removed.

Eggs are a source of iron

Pulses such as beans provide zinc

Bananas are an excellent source of potassium

▲ The minerals we need to keep our bodies healthy come from the foods we eat. This is one reason why it is so important to eat a varied diet.

409 Your body is like a machine, and it needs minerals to function. In total, about four percent of your body is made up of minerals. This includes small amounts of manganese, copper, iodine, cobalt, fluoride, selenium and many others.

▶ Calcite defines point 3 on the hardness scale. It forms as sharply pointed or flattened six-sided crystals.

410 Plants take minerals from the soil as part of the mix of nutrients they need to live. Minerals used by plants include sulphides, sulphates, calcium and magnesium. They are taken up through the roots.

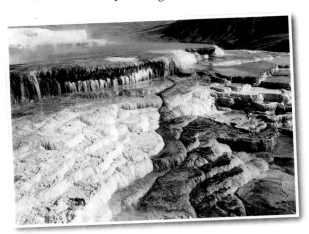

QUIZ

1. Which fruit is packed with potassium?
2. What is the most commonly used mineral?
3. Red meat and eggs provide us with which mineral?

Answers:
1. Bananas 2. Salt 3. Iron

411 Have you ever noticed the cream-coloured 'fur' that collects in kettles? It is actually a form of calcite, one of the most common minerals in the world. It dissolves in water and then gets left behind. Calcite is the main ingredient in limestone, marble and chalk.

Gems and jewels

412 Gemstones are crystals of natural minerals that shine or sparkle in beautiful colours. They are very popular set in jewellery such as rings, earrings, necklaces and bracelets. They look dull when they are dug up in rocks, but then they are cut to shape and polished to sparkle.

413 The mineral corundum forms blue sapphires and red rubies. These are two of the most precious gemstones. Corundum is very hard (second only to diamonds) and is used to make emery boards that people use to file their nails. It is colourless when pure and is made red by tiny amounts of chromium, or blue by the presence of iron and titanium.

◀ One of the British Crown Jewels, the Imperial State Crown contains diamonds, pearls, sapphires, emeralds and rubies.

I DON'T BELIEVE IT!

Gems are given a carat rating, which refers to their weight (a carat is about one-fifth of a gram). The word carat comes from the ancient Greek practise of weighing gems using carab tree seeds.

▼ Ruby is regarded as the king of gemstones because of its rich red colouring and its strength.

▶ Everybody has a birthstone and some people like to wear their own special gem.

414 One of the earliest highly prized gems was emerald. The Egyptians sent slaves to work in the desert mining these green gems. The Inca of South America regarded them as sacred and decorated their golden statues and jewellery with them.

415 Some gemstones are identified with certain months. For example, May is emerald and October is opal. There are even meanings given to gemstones, such as peace for amethyst and energy for topaz.

416 There are 130 different gemstones, of which the rarest are diamonds, emeralds, rubies and sapphires. Dealers describe gemstones using the four Cs: clarity, colour, cut and carat (weight). The largest stones are usually the most valuable.

January
Garnet

February
Amethyst

March
Aquamarine

April
Diamond

May
Emerald

June
Pearl

July
Ruby

August
Peridot

September
Sapphire

October
Opal

November
Topaz

December
Turquoise

Diamonds are forever

◄ Large machinery is used to uncover diamond-rich gravel at this coastal diamond mine in Namibia, Africa.

417 Diamonds are the hardest known mineral. They are named after the Greek word for indestructible, *adamas*. They are the toughest known material, scoring 10 on the mineral hardness scale. They are used in jewellery, and also in industry for cutting and drilling through dense materials such as rock.

418 Most diamonds are mined from a rock called kimberlite. They form deep in the Earth, up to 200 kilometres below the surface, under high pressure and at temperatures between 900 and 1300°C. Some diamond mine tunnels have to be cooled for people to work in because they are heated by the Earth's magma.

◄ The Millennium Star diamond is one of the most famous in the world. It took three years to cut it into this perfect pear shape using lasers.

◄ This diamond-bearing rock formed deep in the Earth and was brought up by an erupting volcano.

▶ This 18th-century skull is studded with 8601 diamonds to create a piece of art that has been valued at £50 million.

419 When they are cut and polished, diamonds sparkle beautifully. This makes them very popular for jewellery, but it wasn't until the Middle Ages that jewellers cut and polished diamonds and discovered their amazing brilliance.

420 If diamonds are heated above 900°C they become graphite, the mineral that is mixed with clay to form the 'lead' in pencils. It gets its name from the Greek word for writing, *graphein*. Graphite is a soft and very stable mineral and it is also used for lots of things from tennis rackets to steel making and nuclear power stations.

▶ Diamonds mean glamour, so movie stars such as Elizabeth Taylor (1932–2011) (shown here at the 42nd Annual Academy Awards in 1970) spend huge amounts of money on them.

189

How to be a geologist

421 Geology is the study of the Earth including its rocks and minerals. Some people do it as a hobby, others as a job. Geologists might be called in to help plan where to build roads and houses or to look for precious gems or minerals. Many are employed helping to search for valuable resources such as metals, gas and oil.

▼ Geologists study how rocks form and measure how much they move as the Earth changes.

STUDYING ROCKS

Study a piece of rock through a magnifier. How many colours can you find? You might find it's made of tiny grains with shiny surfaces – crystals. Try to find any tiny dark flecks of mica, or glassy grains of quartz. Look for evidence of sea creatures – you might be looking at the fossil of something that swam in the oceans millions of years ago.

422 If you want to collect rocks, fossils and minerals you must have permission from the landowner and go with an adult. You need a notepad, map, guidebook, magnifier, gloves, boots and maybe a helmet. Carry a digital camera so you can take pictures of what you find.

423 Don't collect from cliffs and quarry walls as they can be dangerous. Only use a hammer if you've been shown how. You can just collect information, noted down or photographed. Wrap any specimens in newspaper or other material to stop them getting damaged.

424 Beaches are great places to hunt for rocks and fossils. Fossils can be exposed as the wind and waves wash away soil and loose rock. You could start by studying pebbles. Different colours probably indicate different minerals. Some rocks may have been in the same place for centuries, others could have come in on the tide that day. You can also look at the rock strata of cliffs.

▲ A geologist picks up a piece of molten rock from a lava flow. The study of volcanoes is called volcanology.

24

425 Geology really started about 250 years ago with James Hutton (1726–97). Hutton showed that rivers wash away rocks and even eventually whole hills and mountains. He also noticed that rocks were formed from crystals and could be changed by the Earth's heat. He was one of the first people to show that our planet was far older than had been thought. We now know it is about 4.6 billion years old and has been through many stages and changes.

◄ In Hutton's time many people believed that all rocks formed in the sea. His idea that they came from deep in the Earth was thought very strange at first.

FOSSILS

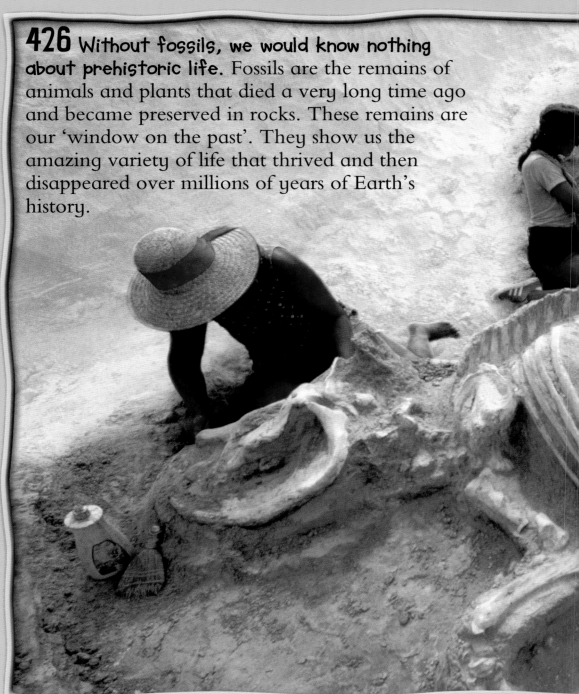

426 **Without fossils, we would know nothing about prehistoric life.** Fossils are the remains of animals and plants that died a very long time ago and became preserved in rocks. These remains are our 'window on the past'. They show us the amazing variety of life that thrived and then disappeared over millions of years of Earth's history.

▲ A preserved rhinoceros skeleton gradually emerges from ten-million-year-old rocks at a fossil excavation or 'dig' in Nebraska, USA. Removing the remains is just the first part of recreating how this great beast looked, lived and died.

What are fossils?

427 Fossils are the preserved remains of once-living things, such as bones, teeth and claws. Usually the remains were buried in sediments – layers of tiny particles such as sand, silt or mud. Very slowly, the layers and the remains inside them turned into solid rock.

428 In general it takes at least 10,000 years, but usually millions, for fossils to form. So the remains of living things that are a few hundred or thousand years old, such as the bandage-wrapped mummies of pharaohs in ancient Egypt, are not true fossils.

▲ A seed cone fossil of the extinct plant *Williamsonia*.

429 Many kinds of once-living things have formed fossils. They include all kinds of animals from enormous whales and dinosaurs to tiny flies and beetles. There are fossils of plants too, from small mosses and flowers to immense trees. Even microscopic bacteria have been preserved.

◄ Teeth are very hard and so make excellent fossils – especially those from *Tyrannosaurus rex*!

194

450 Moulds and casts form with a whole fossil, and also with holes and spaces within a fossil. For example, the fossil skull of an animal may have a space inside where the brain once was. If this fills with minerals it can form a lump of rock that is the same size and shape as the original brain. These types of cast fossils are known as endocasts.

451 Usually, the slower fossilization happens, the more details it preserves of the original living parts. Incredible tiny features are shown even under the microscope.

▲ Sometimes many animals are fossilized together. Perhaps these fish were trapped when the water they were in dried up. Their remains show amazing detail.

I DON'T BELIEVE IT!

Fossil skulls of the ancient humans called Neanderthals show that many of them had bigger brains than people of today!

203

Special preservation

▲ This frog dried out before its flesh could rot away, leaving its mummified remains.

452 **Once–living things can be preserved in many different ways.** Mummification is when a dead plant or animal is left to dry out slowly. Some dinosaurs and animals have been preserved in this way in the windblown sands of deserts.

453 **Amber is the sap (sticky resin) from prehistoric trees, especially conifers, that has been fossilized.** If small creatures became trapped by the resin, they are preserved within it. Insects, spiders, frogs, and even leaves and seeds have all been preserved in this way.

◀ Amber preserves amazingly small details, even the delicate wings of this fly.

494 At first there may be lots of loose rocks, boulders or soil to remove, called overburden. Big, powerful tools might be used such as mechanical diggers, road drills (jackhammers) or even dynamite!

▲ It can take weeks to clean a large fossil such as this elephant skull and tusk.

495 Small bits of loose rock might be sieved to find tiny fossils. Soft, fragile fossils can be covered with material such as plaster or fibre-glass, which hardens into a protective jacket. This allows the fossil to be lifted out.

496 As fossils are exposed, experts decide whether they are worth digging out. Gradually the excavation methods become more careful, using hammers, chisels, small picks and brushes to avoid damaging the find. It can be a lengthy, difficult task. The dig site might be a baking desert, tropical swamp or freezing mountainside.

Cleaning up fossils

497 When fossils reach the workroom, which might be in a museum or university, experts decide which ones to prepare. This means cleaning away unwanted bits of rock and stone around the fossil (the matrix) without damaging the fossil itself.

498 Many kinds of tools and equipment are needed to clean or expose a fossil. They range from small hammers, chisels and drills, to engraving tools, pins and picks, sanders, files and different brushes. The preparator (person working on the fossil) stops regularly to examine the specimen and decide which part to clean next.

◄ Museum preparators work carefully to remove unwanted bits of rock and leave only the fossil.

WHAT ORDER?

List these tools and equipment in the order you would use them to find, dig up and clean a rare fossil.

A. Wooden toothpick
B. Hammer and chisel
C. Stick of dynamite
D. Soft-bristled paintbrush
E. Dentist's drill

Answer:
C B E A D

▲ The enlarged view through a stereo microscope shows lots of detail, to avoid scratching or chipping the specimen.

499 Microscopes are often used to show tiny details of a fossil during preparation. Usually this is a stereoscopic microscope with two eyepieces, like binoculars, mounted on a stand with the specimen beneath.

▶ It may take a year to dissolve rock with acid and expose the fossils — these are unhatched dinosaur eggs.

Dinosaur embryo

500 When the fossil is one type of rock and the matrix is another, preparators may use chemicals to expose the fossil. Different acids are tested on small parts of the matrix and fossil, to see if they dissolve the former but not the latter.

501 Very few animals or plants die neatly in one piece and are preserved whole. So it's incredibly rare to find a whole fossilized plant or animal with all the parts positioned as they were in life. Most fossils are bits and pieces that are crushed and distorted. Putting them back together is very difficult!

On display

502 In a well-organized fossil collection, specimens are given catalogue numbers showing where and when they were found. They are studied, described and identified, and logged into a computer database or card index. Then the specimen can be easily recognized.

▼ London's Natural History Museum has some of the world's best fossil displays, such as these dinosaurs.

503 Usually only exceptional fossils are chosen to display in museums, galleries and exhibitions. They might be very large for their kind, preserved in great detail, be extremely rare, found by a famous fossil-hunter, or simply very beautiful.

504 Fossil displays vary hugely. Some are shelves or cabinets with simple labels. Others have fossils and reconstructions of the original animals or plants, set into a realistic scene. They may have special lighting, descriptions and diagrams, and even press-button video shows.

I DON'T BELIEVE IT!

In 2002, experts re-examined the fossil jaws of a tiny creature called *Rhyniognatha* found in 1919. They realized it was probably the earliest known insect, and that it was almost 400 million years old.

505 Some fossils are so rare, delicate or valuable that they are not displayed — copies are. Copies or replicas of very rare fossils might be sent to other museums so more people can study them.

506 Copies are used for big creatures such as dinosaurs, whales and mammoths. The original fossils are solid rock and can weigh many tonnes. Lightweight copies are easier and safer to put on a frame or hang by wires, to build up the animal in a lifelike position.

Fossils come alive!

507 One of the most exciting parts of fossil study is to reconstruct (rebuild) the original plant or animal. This needs a detailed knowledge of anatomy, or body structure. For example, fossils of prehistoric birds are compared to the same body parts of similar birds alive today. This is called comparative anatomy.

508 Tiny marks or 'scars' on fossil bones show where the animal's muscles attached in real life. These help to reveal muscle shapes and arrangements so experts can gradually put the flesh on the (fossil) bones.

Fossil bones
Faint scars on fossil bones can help scientists work out how and where muscles were attached

▲ This reconstruction of an ankylosaur, an armoured dinosaur, is being done head-first. The tail is still bare fossils of the bones.

509 We can see how a living creature walks, runs and jumps using the joints between its bones. If fossil bones have their joints preserved, their detailed shapes and designs show the range of motion and how the animal moved.

MULTI-COLOURED BIRD

You will need:
pictures of *Archaeopteryx*   colour pens
tracing paper   white paper

No one knows what colour the first bird *Archaeopteryx* was. Look at pictures of it in books and on web sites. See how its feather colours and patterns differ. Trace an outline of *Archaeopteryx* from a book and colour it to your own amazing design.

226

Soft tissues
Flesh, guts and muscles can be added to the skeleton as scientists compare the fossil to similar living animals

Skin
The external covering of skin, scales, horns and claws are added by studying fossil examples and using intelligent guess work

510 Gradually, soft parts such as the guts of an animal or the petals of a flower, can be guessed and added to the reconstruction. Again, experts use information from fossil relatives and living cousins.

511 The outward appearance of an animal might be known from fossils such as an outer shell, scaly skin, feathers or fur. However, fossils are not original living parts – they have changed to rock. So the colour of fossil skin is the colour of the type of rock, not the animal. Experts guess at colours and patterns for their reconstructions.

227

Trading, stealing, faking

512 Fossils are big business. Thousands of people work at digs, in workrooms and in museums, exhibitions and galleries. A find such as a new dinosaur can hit the news headlines and make the discoverer famous – and rich!

513 The biggest, most complete fossil *Tyrannosaurus rex* was found in 1990 near Faith, Dakota, by Sue Hendrickson. The dinosaur was nicknamed 'Sue' and there was a long legal dispute about who owned it. Finally it was sold to the Field Museum of Chicago for more than seven million dollars!

◀ Street traders offer fossils for sale in North Africa. There is no guarantee the fossils came from the local area.

In 2008, a 7-metre-long fossil *Triceratops* dinosaur went on sale for £400,000 along with a fossil skull of a sabre-tooth cat for £35,000.

▶ Chinese palaeontologist Dong Zhiming with some smuggled dinosaur eggs. Every year police, customs and security staff uncover illegal collections such as this.

514 Real fossils, replicas and models are sold around the world by museums, shops, mail-order catalogues and on the Internet. Buyers range from leading museums to individuals who like the idea of a home fossil collection without the trouble of digging them up.

▼ Rare or unusual fossils, such as this ammonite shell showing detailed internal structure, can fetch huge sums of money at auction.

515 Stealing and faking fossils has been going on for centuries. In 1999 scientists announced a fossil creature called *Archaeoraptor* that seemed to be part-bird and part-dinosaur. *Archaeoraptor* showed how small meat-eating dinosaurs evolved into birds. However, further study revealed that the specimen was indeed part-dinosaur and part-bird, because it was a fake with separate fossils cleverly glued together.

Famous fossils

516 Many fossils and prehistoric sites around the world are massive attractions, visited by millions of people. The Petrified Forest National Park in Arizona, USA has hundreds of huge fossilized trees and smaller specimens of animals such as dinosaurs, dating from about 225 million years ago. It receives more than half a million visitors yearly.

▲ The coelacanth is known as a 'living fossil', meaning it is very similar to its long-extinct relatives.

517 The coelacanth fish was known only from fossils and thought to have been extinct for more than 60 million years. In 1938 a living coelacanth was caught off southeast Africa and more have been discovered since. Living things that are very similar to their prehistoric relatives are known as 'living fossils'.

▶ Thousands of fossil tree trunks and branches litter the ground at Arizona's Petrified Forest National Park.

518 There are only about ten fossils of *Archaeopteryx*, the first known bird. They all come from the Solnhofen area of southern Germany. They are amazingly detailed and almost priceless.

▶ Each specimen of *Archaeopteryx* is closely guarded.

519 'Lucy' is a fossilized part-skeleton from a very early human-type creature. It was discovered in 1974 in Ethiopia, Africa and dates back about 3.2 million years. Thousands of people flock to see 'her' every year.

◀ Piltdown Man was really the skull of a human from about 500 years ago combined with the jawbone of an orang-utan.

I DON'T BELIEVE IT!
Animal droppings can become fossils known as coprolites. Leftovers in them can show what an animal ate. Luckily they are no longer squishy and smelly, but have become solid rock.

520 Piltdown Man is perhaps the most famous fossil fake. It was found in southeast England in 1912 and thought to be an early kind of human. In 1953 it was exposed as a hoax by new scientific methods.

Looking to the future

521 As fossil-hunting goes on around the world, scientific methods and equipment become more powerful every year. Ground-penetrating radar, X-rays and CT (computerized tomography) scanners can 'see' fossils inside solid rock.

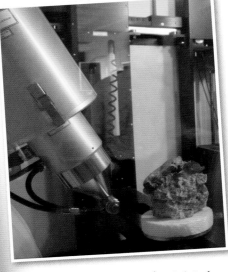

▲ A CT scanner examines the fossil skull of an ancient type of otter.

522 As we improve ways to study fossils, old specimens are looked at again to see new details. The dinosaur *Oviraptor* or 'egg thief' was named because one of its fossils suggested it was stealing the eggs of another dinosaur. Then X-rays of similar eggs showed baby *Oviraptor*s inside. The 'egg thief' fossil was probably looking after its own eggs.

◄ This *Oviraptor* may have died shielding its eggs from a predator, 75 million years ago.

523 Some amazing fossils of the 1990s–2000s are from Liaoning Province in northeast China. Dated to 130 million years ago, they show details of creatures and plants, including dinosaurs with feathers and a cat-sized mammal that preyed on baby dinosaurs.

▲ Fossils of the tiny feathered dinosaur *Microraptor* have been found in China.

524 New fossils provide more evidence for evolution, such as how fish changed gradually into land animals. *Panderichthys* was a fish-like creature from 380 million years ago. It had features such as finger-like bones developing in its fins.

525 Important fossil discoveries cause news and excitement around the world. They affect our ideas about prehistoric life, how Earth has changed through time, evolution and extinction. They can also help to fill in the details of where we came from.

NAME GAME

Match these nicknames of fossils with their scientific names.
A. 'Lucy' B. 'Stan' C. 'Jaws'
D. 'Spike'

1. Triceratops (dinosaur)
2. Megalodon (giant shark)
3. Australopithecus afarensis (early human)
4. Tyrannosaurus (dinosaur)

Answers:
A3 B4 C2 D1

▲ *Panderichthys* was about one metre long. Its fossils come from Latvia in northeastern Europe.

233

POLAR LANDS

526 **The polar regions are found at the top and bottom of the Earth and they are the coldest, windiest places in the world.** Here, the land and sea stay frozen for most of the year, and snow and ice stretch as far as the eye can see. Only a few creatures are tough enough to survive these frozen conditions.

▼ Ice-breakers like the *Apu* have enough power to smash through metre-thick ice in polar seas. They clear the way for following ships, which must keep up because the ice re-freezes in a few hours.

The ends of the Earth

North Pole

ARCTIC REGION

ANTARCTIC REGION

Axis

South Pole

528 **The Earth really has four poles!** There are the Geographic North and South Poles, which are defined by the position of the Earth's axis, but there are also the Magnetic North and South Poles. The Magnetic Poles are some distance from the Geographic Poles.

◀ The Earth spins around an imaginary line called the axis, which passes through the Geographic North and South Poles.

529 **The Earth is like a giant magnet.** Deep inside the Earth are layers of hot, liquid metals, especially iron. As the Earth turns, the iron moves, creating a magnetic force. The Magnetic Poles are the two places where this force is strongest.

Antarctic Peninsula

527 **The North and South Poles are at the top and bottom of the Earth.** Every 24 hours, Earth turns once around its axis. The axis is an invisible line that runs through the middle (core) of the Earth, from Pole to Pole.

530 Because of the moving liquid metals inside the Earth, the magnetic poles wander, and may move a few metres every year. Throughout history, the poles have flipped. This is known as magnetic reversal – the Magnetic North Pole becomes the Magnetic South Pole, and the Magnetic South Pole becomes the Magnetic North Pole. The last flip was about 780,000 years ago.

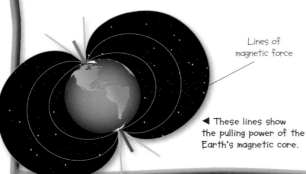

Lines of magnetic force

◀ These lines show the pulling power of the Earth's magnetic core.

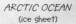

ARCTIC OCEAN
(ice sheet)

Geographic North Pole
*

▶ The North Pole is in the middle of the Arctic Ocean, which is covered by a floating ice sheet.

GREENLAND

531 **The northern polar region is called the Arctic.** The word Arctic comes from the ancient Greek word *arktos*, meaning 'bear'. This refers to the star pattern (constellation) called the Little Bear, or *Ursa Minor*. It contains a star near the North Pole, known as the Pole Star.

Geographic South Pole
*

ANTARCTICA

◀ ▼ The South Pole is towards one side of the vast, ice-covered land mass of Antarctica. In early April penguins gather at traditonal breeding sites on the sea ice.

SOUTHERN OCEAN

I DON'T BELIEVE IT!

Antarctica is the coldest place on Earth. At Vostok Base, the coldest-ever temperature was −89°C in 1983. That's more than four times colder than inside a freezer!

532 The southern polar region is called the Antarctic. Ant or anti means 'against' or 'opposite to'. So the Antarctic is simply the region opposite the Arctic, on the other side of the Earth.

Extreme seasons

533 The Earth's axis is not completely vertical. It is tilted at an angle of around 23°. The movement of the Earth around the Sun, combined with this angle, gives our world its seasons.

▲ At the North Pole, the Sun never disappears below the horizon at Midsummer's Day.

534 The Earth moves around (orbits) the Sun. Over the course of a year, first one and then the other Pole leans towards the Sun, giving us seasons.

535 In most polar lands, summer is long and light, and on some days the Sun never sets. Winter is long and dark, and on some days the Sun never rises. The further north or south you are in the world, the more extreme the seasons will be.

▲ Midnight Sun (the presence of the Sun throughout the night), means that people can travel at any time, day or night.

NO SUNSET

You will need:
an apple   a desk lamp

Imagine your apple is the Earth, and the lamp is the Sun. The stem of the apple represents the North Pole. Hold the apple in front of the lamp and angle the stem towards the light. Spin the apple around its core. Despite the spinning, the area around the North Pole has light all the time, while the other side stays in darkness. This illustrates midsummer at the Arctic Circle.

536 When the North Pole is facing away from the Sun, the area around it is in perpetual darkness. The Sun does not rise for at least one night in midwinter. This area is known as the Arctic Circle. The Antarctic Circle is a similar area around the South Pole. When it is midwinter in the Arctic it is midsummer in Antarctica, so at the Antarctic Circle, the Sun does not set for at least one day.

537 Sometimes at night, the polar skies are lit by shimmering, waving curtains of multi-coloured lights. These are called the *Aurora Borealis* or Northern Lights in the Arctic. Around Antarctica they are called the *Aurora Australis* or Southern Lights.

▼ Campers in the forests of the far north see the Northern Lights as a wavy glow. Tonight it is yellow-green. Tomorrow it may be blue or red!

538 The lights are made by tiny particles given off by the Sun, known as the solar wind. These get trapped by the Earth's magnetism and start to glow. This happens very high in the sky, above 100 kilometres, which is three times higher than a passenger jet plane can travel.

Land around a frozen sea

539 The Arctic is a mostly frozen area of the Arctic Ocean that is surrounded by land. The Arctic Ocean is the smallest, shallowest ocean, with an area of about 14 million square kilometres, and an average depth of 1000 metres. During winter, the ice over the ocean becomes up to 3 metres thick. In summer it shrinks, but it never disappears.

▼ In spring, enormous herds of caribou (reindeer) migrate north to feed on the plants of the tundra.

540 The floating ice layer over the Arctic Ocean cracks and melts around the edges to form dangerous pack ice (icebergs) and icefields. Around the shores of the Arctic Ocean, massive lumps of ice break from ice sheets and form glaciers (frozen rivers), which float out into the ocean as icebergs.

541 Around the Arctic Ocean it is too cold and windy for any trees to grow. The main plants are tussock grass, small bushes, low-growing mosses and lichens. These treeless zones are known as tundra. The Arctic hares that live here have very short ears, to stop them losing body heat.

542 Around the tundra, millions of conifers form huge areas known as boreal forests, or taiga. These are some of Earth's last unexplored wildernesses. Conifer trees' needle-like leaves and downward-sloping branches mean that snow slides off easily. If too much snow gathered, the branches would become heavy and break.

543 The deer known as caribou in North America are called reindeer in northern Europe and Asia. They wander through the forests in winter, then trek out to tundra areas for the summer, in long journeys known as migrations. Packs of wolves follow them and pick off the old, young, sick and dying.

544 In some Arctic regions, the soil just below the surface never thaws, even in summer. These areas are called permafrost. The layer of ice does not let surface water drain through down into the soil below. So permafrost areas are usually boggy and swampy.

FLOATING ICEBERG

Icebergs are much bigger than they look. Make a big lump of ice by putting a plastic bowl of water into a freezer. Float this lump in a sink filled with water. How much is above the surface? In an iceberg it is usually about one-eighth of the total volume above, leaving seven-eighths below.

▶ When there is less ice in summer, brown bears wander from the forests towards the Arctic Ocean shores.

241

Sea around a frozen land

545 Antarctica is different to the Arctic in many ways. The Arctic is a sea surrounded by land, while the Antarctic is land surrounded by sea. Antarctica is a huge landmass about 14 million square kilometres in area, mostly covered by ice. It has mountains, valleys, and old volcanoes, but nearly all of these are hidden under the ice.

Corrie (bowl)

Glacier

Crevasses (cracks)

Melting nose or snout

Squeezed snow and ice

► Snow and ice slide slowly from the polar ice caps as long glaciers, down to the sea.

546 Around Antarctica is the Southern Ocean, also called the Antarctic or Southern Polar Ocean. It is larger and deeper than the Arctic Ocean, with an area of around 20 million square kilometres and an average depth of 4500 metres. It merges into southern parts of the Atlantic, Indian and Pacific Oceans.

◄ Massive chunks split off the ice cap into the sea, and float away as they melt.

547 During the long, dark winter, the Antarctic ice sheet spreads into the surrounding ocean. It forms layers known as ice shelves, which float on the surface. As summer arrives, the shelves shrink back again.

548 Huge ice blocks break off the ice shelves to form massive icebergs. This ice was originally snow, so it is made of fresh water. It differs from the sea ice that forms in the middle of the Arctic Ocean.

549 Each summer, a small area of Antarctica becomes ice-free. This is mainly along the Antarctic Peninsula towards South America. The land is mostly rock and thin soil, where only a few small plants and animals can survive.

I DON'T BELIEVE IT!

Antarctica's ice cap is an average of 1600 metres deep. In places the ice goes down 3350 metres before reaching the rocky surface of the continent. Here there are streams, rivers and lakes, all far below the ice surface.

▶ Most of an iceberg is hidden below the sea's surface, and sometimes scrapes along the sea bed.

Animals of Arctic lands

550 Many kinds of animals live on the lands of the far north. Most of them have thick fur or feathers to keep out the cold and wind in winter. In spring, they shed (moult) their winter fur or feathers, and grow a thinner summer coat.

◄ Ptarmigan change their feathers for camouflage, from white in winter to brownish in summer.

551 Snowy owls make nests on the tundra. They lay their eggs in shallow hollows in the ground. The female looks after her chicks while the male finds food.

▶ Snowy owl chicks feed on small animals such as mice, voles, lemmings and young birds.

552 The ptarmigan gets new feathers for winter. In preparation for the colder months, the ptarmigan grows thick, white feathers. These help it to merge into the natural background, which is known as camouflage. Its winter feathers are also warmer than its brown summer feathers.

WHITE ON WHITE

How do snowy owls 'hide' out in the open? Make a snowy owl by cutting out an owl face shape and feathers from white paper. Draw the eyes and beak. Hold the owl in front of surfaces of different colours. See how it stands out more against dark colours and less against pale colours.

◀ The Arctic ground squirrel hibernates for up to seven months every year. When it emerges from its burrow it feeds mostly on a variety of plants, seeds and berries.

555 In North America, musk oxen live out on the tundra. They have very long, thick fur, with some hairs reaching almost one metre in length. Herds of musk oxen are hunted by arctic wolves. If the adult musk oxen sense danger, they form a defensive circle around their young to protect them.

553 Smaller animals of the far north include the Arctic hare, snowshoe hare, various kinds of voles, Siberian and Norway lemmings, and Arctic ground squirrels. Some of them live under the snow in winter, which is warmer than out in the freezing winds above.

554 The moose of North America is known as the elk in Europe. It eats all kinds of plant foods, from soft waterweeds in summer to twigs and bark in winter. Some move south in autumn to the shelter of the forests for the cold winter. Only the males have antlers.

▶ The moose, or elk, is the biggest deer. A large male can be 2 metres in height.

Realm of bears and wolves

▲ Arctic foxes often follow polar bears, to feed on the leftover bits of their kill.

556 The biggest land hunter in the Arctic, and in the world, is the polar bear. However, it often hunts in water and on ice, too! A big male polar bear can measure 3 metres in length and weigh over half a tonne.

557 The polar bear's favourite food is seals. Camouflaged against the snow, polar bears hunt by creeping up on their prey, then pouncing. They also wait by seals' breathing holes for one to appear above the water. Then the bear bites the seal or hooks it out of the water with its huge claws.

▶ In midwinter, the mother polar bear gives birth to two or three tiny babies, called cubs, in a snow cave she digs.

559 Wolves of the far north tend to follow their prey, such as caribou and musk oxen, until it tires. Wolves work in packs to kill a large victim, or they can hunt alone for smaller prey such as Arctic hares, voles and lemmings.

558 Polar bears can swim for hours in icy water, and walk across land, ice or frozen snow. Their fur is very thick, and their paws are wide so they sink less in soft snow. They also have a layer of fat under their skin, called blubber, which keeps in body heat.

▼ Wolves try to break up and scatter a herd of musk oxen so they can attack the young.

560 Only the chief male and female of the wolf pack (the alpha pair), mate and have cubs. Other pack members help look after the cubs, and bring them food. They also help to defend the pack from polar bears and brown bears.

Arctic seals

561 **Many kinds of seals live in the Arctic region.** These include ringed seals, bearded seals, harp seals, spotted seals, ribbon seals and hooded seals. Most feed on fish, squid and small shrimp-like creatures called krill, which are also eaten by whales.

◀ Seals make breathing holes by bashing their noses, teeth and flippers against the thin ice.

562 **Seals have very thick fur to keep out the cold water.** Like their main enemy, the polar bear, they also have a layer of fatty blubber under the skin to keep them warm. They swim well but have to come up to breathe every few minutes. Sometimes they use breathing holes they make in the ice.

563 **In spring, mother seals come onto the ice to give birth.** Their babies, or pups, have very thick, fluffy fur to keep them warm. Each mother seal usually has only one pup. She feeds it on very rich milk, and it grows very quickly.

▼ Walruses often use their flippers and tusks to haul themselves out of the water onto rocky shores, to sunbathe during the brief summer.

564 Mother seals have to return to the water to feed, leaving their pups alone on the ice. At this time pups are in danger from polar bears, wolves and other predators. Within a couple of weeks the young seal is big enough to look after itself.

565 The walrus is a huge seal with two long upper teeth, called tusks. It shows these off at breeding time to impress its partner. Tusks are also used in feeding, to lever shellfish off the seabed. A big walrus can grow to 3 metres in length and weigh 1.5 tonnes!

Whales of the far north

567 The beluga is also called the white whale. It makes a variety of sounds such as whistles, squeals, twitters and chirps. These can be heard even above the surface. Old-time sailors nicknamed it the 'sea canary'. Both the beluga and narwhal are 4 to 6 metres in length and weigh about one tonne. They eat prey such as fish, squid and shellfish.

▲ The beluga whale has very bendy lips, and purses them as though kissing, to suck in its food.

568 The beluga and narwhal migrate within the Arctic, from the southern areas of the Arctic Ocean to the even icier waters further north. They follow the edge of the ice sheet as it shrinks each spring, then grows back again each autumn.

566 The cold seas of the Arctic are visited in summer by many kinds of whales, including the biggest of all, the blue whale. However, there are some whales that stay in the Arctic all year round, such as the beluga and narwhal.

I DON'T BELIEVE IT!

The massive bowhead whale has the largest head and mouth of any animal. Its head is almost one-third of its 18 metre-long-body. The brush-like baleen strips in its huge curved mouth can be more than 4 metres in length!

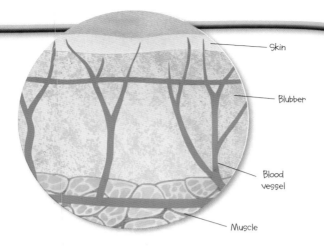

Skin

Blubber

Blood vessel

Muscle

▲ Whales, seals and other polar mammals have a thick layer of blubber under their skin. In whales it is about five times thicker than the fat beneath human skin.

569 The male narwhal has a tooth in its upper jaw that grows very long and pointed, to form a spear-like tusk. This can reach 3 metres in length. It is sometimes used to pierce a hole in the ice so the whale can come up to breathe.

570 The northern right and the bowhead whale are baleen whales. They have long brush-like fringes of baleen in their mouths to filter tiny animals, called plankton, from the sea. These whales can weigh up to 80 tonnes! They are among the world's rarest whales, with just a few hundred right whales left.

571 One of the most powerful Arctic hunters is the killer whale, or orca. It is not a true whale, but the largest kind of dolphin. It lives in large family groups called pods and hunts fish, seals and even great whales.

► At breeding time, male narwhals use their tusks to battle with each other.

Summer visitors

572 Some animals migrate north to the Arctic for its short summer. At this time, Arctic days are long and food is plentiful. In autumn, as the long winter approaches, animals return south to warmer regions.

573 The Arctic tern has the longest migration of all animals. It breeds in summer at the Arctic, then follows the warm weather south to the Antarctic, to have another summer. It covers an amazing 35,000 kilometres every year.

▼ The Arctic tern swoops down to the sea's surface to eat small creatures such as baby fish and krill.

▼ Snow geese flock to the tundra of North America in huge family groups, where each pair raises three to five chicks.

574 The mighty sperm whale is also a summer visitor to the Arctic. The huge males swim from the tropics to the edge of the pack ice. They dive to great depths to catch fish and giant squid.

▲ Grey whale babies (calves) join their mothers on the long journey north each spring, but many are attacked by sharks and killer whales.

575 Many kinds of geese and other birds migrate to the Arctic in summer, such as snow geese, Brent geese and barnacle geese. These birds make nests and rear their chicks quickly. They feed on grasses, rushes, sedges and other plants of the boggy tundra, as well as eating flies, grubs and other small creatures from pools along the seashore.

576 Grey whales swim along the coasts of the North Atlantic in spring, to feed in the waters off Alaska and in the Bering Sea throughout the summer. Then they return to subtropical waters off Baja California, Mexico, and spend the winter resting and giving birth. Their yearly journeys total 20,000 kilometres, and are the longest migration of any mammal.

QUIZ

Do some research and see if you can put these animals in order of the distance they cover on their yearly migration:

A Bowhead whale
B Barnacle goose
C Sperm whale
D Arctic tern
E Caribou

Answers:
D C B E A

In the Southern Ocean

577 During summer, the Southern Ocean around Antarctica is rich with life. The water is not very warm, but it contains many nutrients and there is lots of daylight. This means billions of tiny plants and animals, called plankton, grow. They become food for bigger creatures such as fish and squid.

578 The great supply of krill and plankton attracts some huge visitors to the Antarctic region. These include the world's largest animals, such as the blue whale, fin whale and humpback whale, which migrate here for summer.

579 Southern Ocean seals include the leopard, crabeater and Southern elephant seal. Despite its name, the crabeater seal does not actually eat crabs – it is mainly a krill-feeder. The leopard seal is about 3 metres in length and very fierce. It catches fish, seabirds, penguins, and even other seals.

580 A Southern elephant seal is almost as big as a real elephant! These seals spend weeks at sea feeding, then come to remote beaches to breed. The huge males, called beachmasters, rear up, roaring and biting each other, before mating with the females.

▼ Male elephant seals battle each other to win an area of the beach, otherwise they do not breed. Sometimes they become badly injured in the fight, and die.

581 Elephant seals are the deepest-diving of all seals. They can dive down more than 1000 metres and stay under the water for over an hour before they need to surface for breath. They eat mainly fish and squid, as well as crabs and shrimps from the ocean floor.

I DON'T BELIEVE IT!

A male southern elephant seal can be more than 5 metres in length. When it is well fed, it weighs almost two tonnes! It gets its name from its huge size, and from its long, floppy nose.

Antarctic waters

582 Apart from seals, whales, fish and squid, many other creatures thrive in Antarctic waters. They include jellyfish that drift with the currents, trailing their long tentacles. The tentacles sting passing creatures, which are then pulled up to the mouth on the underside of the jellyfish's umbrella-like body (bell).

583 The temperature of polar seas often falls below 0°C. However, the waters do not always freeze, so animals are safe from being frozen solid. This is because sea water contains salts, so its freezing point is lower than fresh water. Ice crystals also break up as they form, due to the movement of the seas' currents and waves.

▼ The *Isotealia* anemone lives in waters from about 50 to 500 metres deep. It grabs any kind of food, including jellyfish and sea urchins.

▶ The huge desmonema jellyfish grows to more than one metre across. It catches fish, krill, sea worms and starfish.

584 Cousins of jellyfish, known as sea anemones, also live along the coasts of Antarctic islands. They too have stinging tentacles that pull in prey such as shrimps and prawns. However the mainland shores of Antarctica itself are too cold for most kinds of seaside animals.

QUIZ

Do some research to find out which fish is most closely related to the Antarctic ice-fish.

A Flatfish
B Sharks
C Trout
D Perch

Answer: D

585 Several polar fish have special substances in their blood and body fluids that work like natural **anti-freeze.** Even if trapped in solid ice, these animals can survive for a while by going into suspended animation – staying still and using almost no energy.

▶ There are several kinds of Antarctic ice-fish, which have blood that is thickened by certain natural chemicals to stop it freezing.

Antarctic birds

586 Antarctica is visited by hundreds of kinds of birds each year. Most of them fly over the open ocean, since there is very little unfrozen land on which to nest. In contrast, the islands close to Antarctica are home to some breeding birds, such as albatrosses and petrels.

587 The wandering albatross has longer wings than any other bird, at more than 3 metres from tip to tip. Albatrosses form long-lasting breeding pairs that come together on remote islands to raise their single chick. The young albatross may not fly until it is almost one year old.

▼ Research scientists measure the wingspan of an albatross.

▶ Tussock birds are always on the lookout for any morsels of food. This bird is pecking bits of flaking skin from an elephant seal.

588
The blackish cinclodes, also called the tussock bird, eats almost anything it can find. It snaps up shellfish and shrimps along the coast and eats dead crabs and starfish washed up on the shore. Tussock birds also wander around seabird colonies to feed on the rotting fish that the parent birds cough up, or regurgitate, for their chicks.

589
Skuas are powerful seabirds with large, sharp beaks. They chase terns, gulls and similar birds and attack them in mid air, forcing them to drop their food, which the skua then gulps down.

▶ The skua's strong beak can easily stab into a penguin's egg. Then the bird laps up the soft inner parts or hacks apart the chick inside.

Sliding and diving

590 Penguins live only in the south, around Antarctica — there are none in the Arctic. They cannot fly, but they use their flipper-like wings to swim with great speed and skill. Most of the 17 kinds of penguins live on the islands and shores of the Southern Ocean, on the icebergs and ice floes there, and on the continent of Antarctica itself.

▼ Penguins' outer feathers overlap in water or when the weather is cold, and stand upright when it is warmer.

Long feathers

Down feathers

Skin

1. Long feathers overlap, trapping warm air next to the skin

Warm air escaping

Long feathers

Down feathers

Skin

2. Long feathers separate, letting warm air escape

591 The biggest penguins are emperors. They can be up to 120 centimetres in height and weigh more than 30 kilograms. They breed on Antarctic ice, and the female lays just one egg, passes it over to the male, and leaves. She sets off on the long journey back to the sea to feed.

▶ Adelie penguins slide down an icy cliff and take to the water, in search of their main food — krill.

STAND UP!

You will need:
card   felt-tip pens   tape

Make a penguin about 30 centimetres tall from card. Carefully cut out the head and body, two flippers, and two feet, and colour them with felt-tip pens. Tape the parts together and try to make the penguin stand upright. It's quite tricky! Luckily a penguin has a short, stiff tail. Cut this out and tape it on to make standing easier.

592 The male emperor penguin spends almost two months of the worst midwinter weather with the egg on his feet, keeping it warm until it hatches. Then the female returns, walking and sliding across the ice, to take over caring for the chick. At last the hungry male can head to the sea to feed.

593 The king penguin is the second–largest penguin. It stands about 90 centimetres in height and weighs up to 15 kilograms. Its main foods are fish, squid and plankton. King penguins can dive down to 200 metres.

▲ Emperor penguins travel to traditional breeding sites to find a partner and mate. When an egg hatches, the parent bird brings up (regurgitates) food from its stomach to feed its chick.

Polar peoples

594 People have lived in Arctic regions for over 10,000 years. Today, groups exist around northern North America, Scandinavia (northern Europe) and Siberia (north Asia). They include Inuit, Aleuts, Koryak, and Chukchi people. They live in some of the world's most difficult conditions.

I DON'T BELIEVE IT!

Wind chill makes cold temperatures much worse! Cold wind blowing past a warmer object, such as a human body, draws away heat in seconds. If the temperature is −20°C, strong winds can double this to −40°C. It freezes body parts in seconds.

595 In recent times, the traditional way of life in polar regions has changed greatly. New ways of travel are available, from skidoos and other snowmobiles to helicopters, snowplanes and icebreaker ships. Many polar people are no longer cut off from the lands farther south. They can trade more easily for consumer goods such as clothes, tools, TVs and prepared foods.

▼ Snowmobiles have skis at the front for steering, and tracks at the rear to push the vehicle along. Here, a Saami person crosses a snow-covered lake in Finland.

596 Commercial fishing is big business in some Arctic areas. Ships catch large numbers of fish or krill, especially in summer. Whaling and sealing are banned, but ships continue to catch food that these animals eat, so the populations can still be harmed.

ski-doo

48 G

► Traditional fishing skills are still vital. This man is fishing for halibut through a hole in the ice in Greenland.

597 One of the most helpful modern items for northern people has been the gun. In the past, spears or hooks and lines were used to catch seals and other food. Even when using guns, hunters still need patience. Arctic animals are very wary and it is difficult to creep up on them unseen in the white, icy wilderness.

▼ Tourism is a growing business in Ilulissat, Greenland, a World Heritage Site. Visitors come to see icebergs breaking off the Sermeq Kujalleq glacier.

598 The discovery of oil, coal, minerals and other resources have brought many newcomers to the Arctic. Settlements have grown up along the coasts. The houses are heated by oil, from wells in the area, or coal mined locally, since there are no trees to burn as fuel.

Living in the cold

599 Over time, Arctic people have developed skills and knowledge to survive in this harsh environment. Plants are scarce, so food is mainly animals such as seals, shellfish, fish and whales. A stranded whale can provide enough food for a week.

600 Arctic animals provide not just food, but many other resources for polar people. The fatty blubber is burned in lamps for heat and warmth. Weatherproof clothes and boots are made from the furry skins of seals, caribou and other creatures.

1. Large blocks of squashed snow or loose ice are cut with a large-bladed snow-knife.

601 Tools and utensils such as knives, bowls and spoons are also made from local animals. They are carved from the bones and teeth of smaller toothed whales, from the horns of caribou and musk oxen, from the tusks of walrus and narwhals, and from the bendy, springy baleen or whalebone of great whales.

2. The blocks are stacked in a circular pattern, sloping inwards in a gradually rising spiral.

◀ Snow houses called igloos are usually a temporary shelter, made for just a night or two while out on a winter hunting expedition.

3. The blocks slope together to make a dome shape that keeps out wind and snow.

▶ Kayaks are usually paddled by hand with paddles made from driftwood. Some modern ones have outboard motors. Here, a kayak is launched by hunters in Alaska.

602 Since so much food is obtained from the sea, boats are very useful. The canoe-like kayak is made by stretching waterproof animal skin such as whale hide over a frame of carved driftwood, or perhaps bone. The parts are tied together with animal sinews.

603 Kayaks are light and easily carried, and slide well across snow and ice. Larger kayaks are used for carrying a family's possessions to a new hunting area.

◀ The joints between the blocks in an igloo are sealed with snow to keep out the wind. The entrance is low down to prevent the warm air inside from escaping.

QUIZ

Try and find out which materials Antarctic people use to make the following items:

A. Boots
B. An overcoat
C. A head-dress

Answers:
A. Waterproof sealskin
B. Reindeer hide
C. Seabird feathers

Life of a herder

604 Some people of the far north live inland. People in northern Europe such as the Saami (Lapps), and the Nenet of Siberia, depend on reindeer herds that provide them with almost everything they need.

▼ Nenet people gather reindeer in a herd to be checked and counted.

605 The reindeer herds follow their natural migrations. They move north to tundra areas for summer and head south to the forests for winter. Herders travel with them, to keep the herds together and protect them from wolves and bears.

606 As the people and deer move, the reindeer pull sleds loaded with the herder's tents, utensils and other belongings. The animals are counted regularly and spare reindeer are herded to the local towns, where they are traded for items such as sharp metal knives.

I DON'T BELIEVE IT!

In the last 50 years the Nenet people have lost more than 7 million hectares of reindeer grazing lands due to pollution, the creation of coal mines, new vehicle tracks, oil pipelines, and introduced animals eating the plant food.

607 Reindeer can provide a huge variety of resources. Their fur and skins make clothes, boots, floor rugs, sleeping blankets and tents. They provide fresh milk and blood to drink, and their meat is very nutritious. The antlers and bones are carved into utensils and tools. They are also used, along with teeth, to make beautiful works of art, showing scenes of fishing, hunting, herding and the natural world.

▲ Saami hunters live in tents of reindeer hide stretched over log poles, which can be easily packed and transported by sled.

On top of the world!

608 Many adventurers have tried to reach the North Pole, which is located near the middle of a floating layer of ice in the Arctic Ocean. Before today's satellite navigation, it was hard to know if you were in the right place. Then, explorers had to prove that they really did reach their destination. They couldn't leave a flag in the floating, breaking ice.

▶ Nansen's ship *Fram* was stuck in ice for almost three years, but its design meant that it survived.

609 English admiral William Parry tried to reach the North Pole in 1825. So did Norwegian explorer Fridtjof Nansen in 1893–96 in his ship *Fram*. Yet neither of them made it. In 1909, American Robert Peary and his team claimed to have reached the North Pole, but experts do not agree if they really did.

610 The first people to fly over the North Pole in a plane may have been Richard Byrd and Floyd Bennet in 1926. However, as with Peary, it's not certain if they really did. A few days later, Roald Amundsen – the first person to reach the South Pole – flew over the North Pole in an airship, the *Norge*.

◀ Some experts disagree with Robert Peary's claim that he marched across the floating ice to the North Pole.

611 Claims to be first to stand at the North Pole continued, such as Russian explorer Pavel Gordiyenko and his team in 1952. In 1968, American explorer Ralph Plaisted and two colleagues made the first surface trip there.

QUIZ

You're off to the North Pole. What do you pack?

A. Swimming costume
B. GPS satellite–navigation recorder
C. Skis or snow boots

Answers:
A. No – too cold!
B. Yes – shows where you are.
C. Yes – allows you to move over the ice, to and from your waiting ship.

612 In modern times, more and more expeditions have reached the North Pole across the ice. In 2007, Dutch performer Guido van der Werve spent a day there, turning in the opposite direction to the Earth's spinning, so in fact he stayed completely still. It is even possible for rich tourists to fly to the exact North Pole for a few hours' visit.

▶ In 2007, Lewis Gordon Pugh swam one kilometre through water in cracks between the North Pole ice, to highlight the problem of global warming.

Race to the South Pole

614 Once ships arrived at Antarctica, there was still a dangerous journey across the ice to the South Pole. Irish explorer Ernest Shackleton made several trips there. In 1901–02 in the ship *Discovery*, and in 1914–16 in *Endurance*. These trips did not reach the South Pole, but helped to establish bases for further exploring across the ice cap.

▶ In Ernest Shackelton's 1914–15 expedition, his ship *Endurance* was frozen into the ice for ten months and finally crushed. Yet all the crew were eventually rescued.

613 It was difficult to even get close to the South Pole. In 1820, Russian naval officer Fabian Gottlieb von Bellingshausen was perhaps the first person to see the Antarctic mainland. American seal-hunter John Davis may have been first to set foot on the continent, in 1821. In 1839, English naval commander James Clark Ross set sail on a voyage to map Antarctica's outline. Many of these people have areas of Antarctica named after them.

SLIPPERY SLOPE

You will need:
length of wood   ice cubes   stones   wood   plastic

Hold up one end of the wood, like a ramp. Put an ice cube at the top and let it slide down. The ice melts into water, which works like slippery oil. Try sliding the other substances such as plastic, wood and stone. The ramp has to be much steeper!

▲ Amundsen's expedition saved the weight of carrying food by killing and eating the sled dogs one by one.

615 In 1911 two expeditions set off to reach the South Pole, led by Norwegian Roald Amundsen, and English naval officer Robert Scott. The world was gripped by news of their 'race to the Pole'. Amundsen, his team and his dog sleds got there first on 14 December 1911, and returned safely. Scott and his team, pulling their own sledges, arrived a month later. Tragically, on the way back they ran out of supplies and were stranded by blizzards. They did not survive.

616 The South Pole can now be visited by rich tourists. Several overland expeditions make the trek each year. There is a permanent scientific base called the Amundsen–Scott South Pole Station, where people live and work, usually for a period of six months.

▶ In 1997, mother-of-two Laurence de la Ferriere walked across Antarctica to the South Pole unaided.

Polar lands in peril

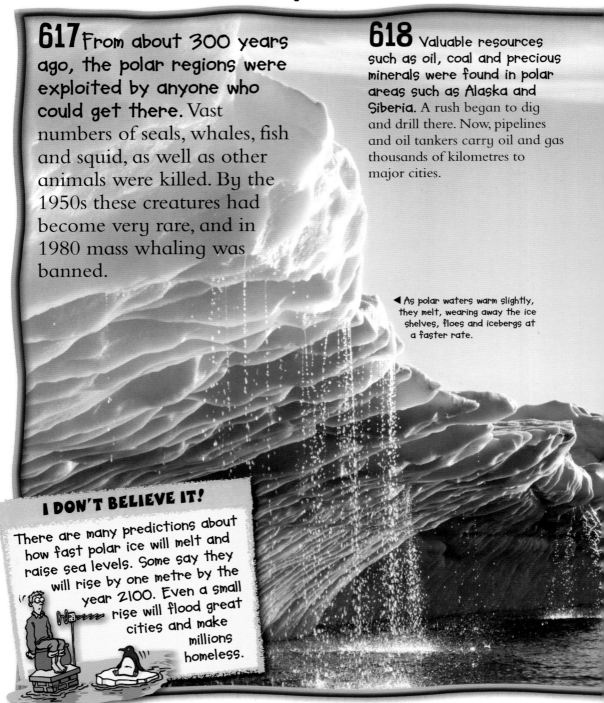

617 From about 300 years ago, the polar regions were exploited by anyone who could get there. Vast numbers of seals, whales, fish and squid, as well as other animals were killed. By the 1950s these creatures had become very rare, and in 1980 mass whaling was banned.

618 Valuable resources such as oil, coal and precious minerals were found in polar areas such as Alaska and Siberia. A rush began to dig and drill there. Now, pipelines and oil tankers carry oil and gas thousands of kilometres to major cities.

◄ As polar waters warm slightly, they melt, wearing away the ice shelves, floes and icebergs at a faster rate.

I DON'T BELIEVE IT!

There are many predictions about how fast polar ice will melt and raise sea levels. Some say they will rise by one metre by the year 2100. Even a small rise will flood great cities and make millions homeless.

619 **Pollution has begun to affect the polar lands.** Dangerous chemicals such as pesticides from farming, and toxins from industry, flow into Arctic waters. The protective ozone layer above Antarctica has been made thinner by chemicals from aerosol spray cans. Oil spills from tankers have devastated parts of the Arctic.

620 **Climate change will have terrifying results around the world.** The habitats of polar bears, seals, penguins and many other animals are disappearing. Floods will affect low-lying areas far from polar lands, where billions of people live in cities. Polar scientific bases have been set up to study these problems.

▶ Cleaning penguins' coats of pollution strips their feathers of natural oils, without which the birds could freeze to death. Rescued birds are fitted with woolly jumpers to keep them warm.

621 **The greatest threat to polar regions may still be to come.** Global warming due to the greenhouse effect is causing climate change, as world temperatures rise. This is making the ice caps melt, causing sea levels to rise.

▼ The striped pole marks the exact spot of the South Pole. It is repositioned every New Year's Day, as the ice moves around 10 metres yearly.

Protecting the Poles

622 Countries have signed agreements to protect polar lands and oceans from damage. Even tourism can be a problem. Cruise ships bring visitors that disturb whales and other wildlife, and leave waste.

▼ Scientists monitor emperor penguin breeding colonies near the Weddell Sea, Antarctica, to see the effect of climate change on their breeding.

623 In 1994 the Southern Ocean was declared a vast sanctuary, or safe area, for whales. This meant it was also safe for many other kinds of wildlife. However some countries still hunt whales, and ships also go there to catch krill, fish and squid. As we catch more, whales and other large animals have less to eat.

624 Some parts of the Arctic are also being protected. Some countries want to drill for oil and gas, and mine for coal, precious minerals and metals. Big companies sometimes try to change the minds of governments or break the rules. These activities create jobs for people, but create risks of pollution.

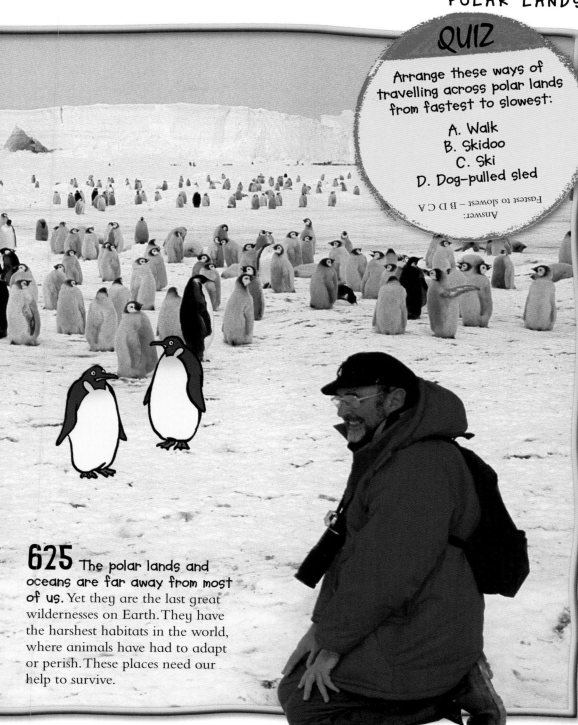

QUIZ

Arrange these ways of travelling across polar lands from fastest to slowest:

A. Walk
B. Skidoo
C. Ski
D. Dog-pulled sled

Answer:
Fastest to slowest – B D C A

625 The polar lands and oceans are far away from most of us. Yet they are the last great wildernesses on Earth. They have the harshest habitats in the world, where animals have had to adapt or perish. These places need our help to survive.

RAINFORESTS

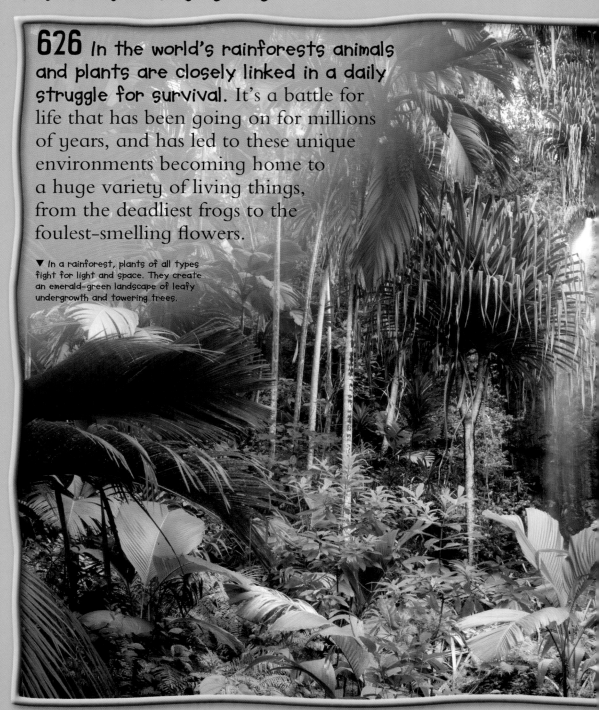

626 In the world's rainforests animals and plants are closely linked in a daily struggle for survival. It's a battle for life that has been going on for millions of years, and has led to these unique environments becoming home to a huge variety of living things, from the deadliest frogs to the foulest-smelling flowers.

▼ In a rainforest, plants of all types fight for light and space. They create an emerald-green landscape of leafy undergrowth and towering trees.

What is a rainforest?

627 Rainforests are places where lots of rain falls every year – usually more than 2000 millimetres. They are filled with enormous, broad-leaved trees and a bewildering collection of living things. Rainforests usually grow in warm, steamy parts of the world.

628 Trees provide habitats (homes) for millions of rainforest animals and plants. Much of the wildlife in these forests cannot survive anywhere else – just one of the reasons why people want to make sure rainforests are kept safe.

Toco toucan

629 Of all the different habitats found on Earth, rainforests have the biggest range of living things. They are home to more than 80 percent of all insects and a single rainforest in South America has 18,000 different types of plants. The word 'biodiversity' is used to describe the range of living things that live in one habitat.

Tapir

EMERGENT LAYER

CANOPY

UNDERSTOREY

FOREST FLOOR

Queen Alexandra's
birdwing butterfly

630 Rainforests
have four main layers.
The bottom layers are the
dark, dank forest floor and
understorey, where the
shortest plants live. Here,
bugs, frogs, fungi and many
other living things thrive.
The middle layer is the
forest canopy and the top layer is the emergent layer.
This is where the tallest trees poke up above a blanket
of green leaves. The trees are home to vines, mosses,
monkeys, lizards, snakes, insects and thousands of
species (types) of bird.

◄ Most animals and
plants live in the
rainforest canopy
layer. The understorey
is very gloomy because
not much sunlight
reaches it.

I DON'T BELIEVE IT!

People who live in rainforests
can build their entire homes
from plant materials. Walls are
made from palm stems or bamboo
and leaves can
be woven to
make roofs
and floors.

Red-eyed
tree frog

631 Rainforests are home to people as well as
animals and plants. Many tribes (groups of people)
live in these dense, green forests around the world,
finding food, medicines and shelter amongst the trees.
Some of them still follow a traditional lifestyle,
hunting animals and gathering plants for food.

Not just jungles

632 Hot, steamy rainforests are sometimes called jungles. They are found in Earth's tropical regions. These are areas near the Equator, an imaginary line that encircles the Earth, where daily temperatures are around 25°C and it rains most days.

▼ A boy rows a canoe made from a hollow tree trunk on the Amazon River in Brazil.

633 Around 60–100 million years ago, most of the world's land was covered with tropical rainforest. Now only a tiny area – six percent – is covered. This is partly due to deforestation (people cutting down trees) and partly because the Earth's climate has changed, becoming cooler and drier.

634 Temperate rainforests grow in cool, wet places. 'Temperate' means having a moderate climate. Trees here are usually conifers such as pine trees. Temperate rainforests are home to the world's largest trees – Californian redwoods. These can live for 2000 years, and the tallest reach 115 metres in height.

► Redwoods, or sequoias, are giant trees that sprout from tiny seeds. The trees produce cones that each contain up to 300 seeds.

▶ Mangrove trees grow long and tangled roots, which slow down the movement of water and create a habitat for animals.

635 **Mangrove swamps are another type of warm, wet rainforest.** The trees that grow here live with their roots steeped in layers of mud, silt and salty water. Around half of the world's mangrove forests have been cut down in the last 50 years and it is expected that almost all mangrove forests will have disappeared by 2050.

636 **Rainforests on mountains higher than 2500 metres are often shrouded in mist.** They are given the name 'cloud forests', and here the temperatures are lower than in a tropical rainforest. Mosses, ferns and liverworts are plants that thrive in these permanently damp conditions. The trunk and branches of a tree in a cloud forest can be completely covered in a bright-green coating of moss.

▶ Cloud forests can be eerie places where trees and plants are permanently shrouded in a fine mist.

HUG A TREE!

Visit a local woodland or forest and find out the names of some of its trees. Use a sketchbook or camera to record images of wildlife you see there. Find out which are the widest tree trunks by hugging them. Can you find one that is so broad your fingers don't touch?

Where in the world?

637 Tropical forests grow in the region close to the Equator. The area just south of the Equator is called the Tropic of Capricorn, and the area just north of the Equator is called the Tropic of Cancer.

NORTH AMERICA

▼ Grizzly bears live in forests near the Pacific coast and hunt salmon in the cold, fresh rivers.

Equator

SOUTH AMERICA

639 Amazonia is the huge tropical rainforest of Brazil and neighbouring South American countries. Further south, temperate rainforests grow, cloaked in cold mist. In the Chilean temperate rainforests, ancient trees called alerces grow. The oldest alerce is thought to have lived for over 4000 years.

638 Wet winds and cool fogs from the Pacific Ocean sweep onto the coast of North America, creating the perfect climate for temperate rainforests. This is ideal for giant conifers – evergreen trees that live there. The forests are home to black bears, mountain lions and blacktail deer.

◀ Piranhas are sharp-toothed Amazon fish. They feed on a variety of animals including other fish and snails.

◀ Atlas moths are the world's largest moths. They flutter through the canopies of Asian cloud forests.

EUROPE

ASIA

▼ Cassowaries are large birds that cannot fly. They live in the forests of Australia and New Guinea.

AFRICA

◀ African bush vipers live in the forest canopy, slithering down to hunt frogs and lizards.

OCEANIA

Quiz
1. What is the Equator?
2. Where does the cassowary live?
3. How old is the oldest-known alerce?

Answers:
1. An imaginary line that encircles the Earth. 2. New Guinea and Australia 3. More than 4000 years old

640 Cloud forests usually grow on, or near, mountain ranges, where there is plenty of rain and mist. In China, the Yunnan cloud forest grows over tall mountains and deep gorges. The name *Yunnan* means 'south of the clouds' – it's a mysterious place that few people have visited.

KEY 🌳 Tropical forest   🌴 Cloud forest   🌲 Temperate forest

Tree of life

641 **The brazil-nut tree produces balls of seeds.** Each ball is the size of a melon and as hard as stone. This amazing tree grows in tropical rainforests and provides a home and food for many living things.

642 When the seed balls are ripe they crash to the ground. Only the agouti, a dog-sized rodent, has teeth tough enough to break through the case to reach the tasty brazil nuts inside. Agoutis bury some of the nuts, which may then grow into trees. Without agoutis new brazil-nut trees could not grow.

▲ Between 12 and 24 nuts grow inside each brazil-nut tree seed case. Inside each nut is a seed.

Strangler fig

643 Strangler figs grow up and around the trunks of rainforest trees. Over years, the fig continues to grow until it eventually strangles its host tree to death. Once the tree has rotted, only the tangled web of fig roots and stems remain, like a spooky tree skeleton.

◀ Agoutis' teeth continue to grow throughout their lives, allowing them to bite through nutshells.

▼ Brazil-nut tree flowers open before sunrise. By the end of the day, all the petals will have fallen off.

644 Brazil-nut trees also depend on a single type of insect to survive – orchid bees. These are the only insects strong enough to get inside the tree's heavy, hooded flowers to pollinate them, so the nuts – which contain seeds – can grow into new plants.

▶ Female orchid bees visit brazil-nut flowers to feed on nectar, while male orchid bees visit orchids to collect perfume.

645 Fallen leaves at the base of tropical trees quickly disappear. Dead matter, called leaf litter, is broken down by fungi, or eaten by bugs. This process is known as decomposition, and it helps the goodness from the leaves return to the forest soil in a natural method of recycling.

Male orchid bee

◀ A brazil-nut tree can grow to 60 metres in height and produce more than 100 kilograms of nuts every year.

646 When a number of different living things all depend on one another for survival they are described as an ecosystem. Rainforest habitats are large ecosystems, and a brazil-nut tree is a small ecosystem. When brazil-nut trees are cut down, many other living things that depend on them die, too.

Amazing Amazon

647 The Amazon rainforest is the largest tropical rainforest in the world. It covers 6 million square kilometres, which means it is nearly the same size as Australia. Around half of all animal and plant species live in Amazonia, as this forest is known.

◄ An Amazonian Hercules beetle can grow to 18 centimetres in length. It is one of the world's largest insects.

648 The giant Amazon River wends its way through the forest, bringing life and death to many of its inhabitants. This is the world's biggest river, stretching for about 6400 kilometres and pouring 770 billion litres of water into the Atlantic Ocean every day. People and animals of the forest use the river for transport, food and water.

649 Insect experts who travelled to Amazonia in the 1840s discovered more than 8000 new species (types) of beetle. Alfred Wallace and Henry Bates were amongst the first of many scientists who realized that this rainforest has a fantastic range of animal and plant life, many of which do not exist anywhere else. Charles Darwin, a 19th century scientist, described it as 'a great wild, untidy, luxuriant hothouse'.

▼ The Amazon River basin holds 20 percent of the world's fresh water.

650 The waters of the Amazon are home to many types of animal and plant. Giant waterlilies with 2-metre-wide leaves grow in slow-moving stretches of the river, but just beneath them lurk hungry alligators, sharp-toothed piranha fish and blood-sucking leeches.

651 There are more than 400 species of reptile, such as snakes and lizards, in the Amazon rainforest. More freshwater fish live in the Amazon River than anywhere else on Earth, and more than 225 types of amphibian, such as frogs and toads, live in and around the water.

▶ Large green iguanas like to lie on branches that hang over the Amazon River and soak up the sun's warming rays.

I DON'T BELIEVE IT!

Giant Amazonian leeches are blood-sucking worms that can grow up to 30 centimetres in length! They have sharp teeth and pain-numbing spit that stops blood from clotting so they can enjoy a long feast.

People of the Amazon

652 The Amazon was given its name by a Spanish explorer who ventured down the river in the 1540s. Francisco de Orellana was attacked by the local long-haired people who reminded him of the mythical female warriors described by the ancient Greeks, so he named the Amazon after them.

▶ Inside the *shabono*, Yanomani people build circular huts called *malocas*. At night, the young people sleep in hammocks, outside the *malacos*.

653 When Europeans first went to the Amazon rainforest in search of treasure, there were around seven million people living there. Today, 500 years later, there are fewer than a million. The Amazonian people live as groups, or tribes, and have different cultures and languages from one another.

654 The Yanomani people still follow many of their ancient traditions today. Villagers share one large home, known as the *shabono*, and women grow crops such as sweet potatoes. Men hunt using blowpipes and bows and arrows. The rainforest is the children's school, where they learn how to survive in, and protect, their jungle home.

◀ Several families make up one Yanomani village. They live, work and play together, passing on traditions and skills.

655 The Embera people use the poison produced by rainforest frogs to hunt animals to eat. Men wipe the tips of their blowpipe darts on the frogs' backs before firing them. One golden poison dart frog has enough poison to kill ten men. In recent years several rainforest frogs have become extinct (died out), but no one knows why this is.

▲ The golden poison frog produces poison on its skin, which the people of the Embera tribe carefully wipe on their darts.

656 Although many Amazonian people live in protected areas of rainforest, many more face an uncertain future. Large parts of Amazonia are being taken over by mining and logging companies. They cut down large parts of the forest, forcing local people to move elsewhere.

▶ Embera women clean and prepare food in rivers and lakes, but many have become polluted.

Forests of Oceania

657 **Hundreds of millions of years ago there was a giant continent called Gondwana.** Around 140 million years ago, Gondwana began to split, and eventually Australia, New Zealand and New Guinea broke away from the rest of the landmass. Wildlife that evolved in these places is very different from that found elsewhere.

658 **Walking through the cloud forests of New Guinea is an incredible experience.** The air is damp, and every surface is covered with plants, especially mosses and ferns. When the clouds open, torrential rain drenches each living thing.

659 **Dragons live in Australia's rainforest, waiting to pounce on passers-by.** These are not real dragons, but lizards called Boyd's forest dragons – and they attack bugs, not people! They live on trees, where their patterned scales help them to stay hidden from view.

▶ Australian tree kangaroos scamper through branches. When they are scared, they can jump down from trees in one giant leap.

I DON'T BELIEVE IT!

In the last 200 years most of Australia's rainforests have been replaced by farms and towns. If the southern cassowary, an endangered bird of this region, becomes extinct, so will around 150 rainforest plants that rely on it to spread their seeds.

▼ Korowai families live in tall tree houses. They eat sago (from plants) beetle grubs, and hunt wild pigs.

◄ Boyd's dragon lizards sit motionless, waiting for prey to pass by, then pounce at speed.

660 During the last Ice Age, rivers of ice (glaciers) covered parts of New Zealand. Today the climate is warmer so wet and cool rainforests have replaced the glaciers. New Zealand's Fiordland forest is home to the Takahe parrot, which has lost the ability to fly because it had no natural predators in its forest home.

661 Tribal people on the island of New Guinea live in homes up to 50 metres off the ground. The tree houses built by tribes such as the Korowai and Kombai provide safety against warring tribes or dangerous creatures, especially disease-carrying mosquitoes.

Magical Madagascar

662 Madagascar is the world's fourth largest island. It lies to the east of Africa, in the warm waters of the Indian Ocean. The rainforests here cover 10,000 square kilometres, and are mostly found on the island's eastern coast.

663 When Madagascar split away from the rest of Africa about 165 million years ago, its animals and plants began moving on a unique path of change. Now this tropical place is a haven for some amazing animals such as lemurs and coloured lizards called chameleons. Between 80 and 90 percent of the 250,000 species found here live nowhere else, and new species are discovered all the time.

▼ Ring-tailed lemurs live together in groups that are ruled by females. They feed on plants and, unlike most lemurs, spend much of their time on the ground.

664 Lemurs are animals with long legs and bushy tails that leap through trees. They are related to monkeys and apes and, like their cousins, are intelligent and inquisitive creatures. The ring-tailed lemur lives in groups of up to 25 family members. They like to sit in the sun, but scatter if a member of the group sounds an alarm call to warn of danger nearby.

◄ The wings of the African sunset moth are ablaze with beautiful colours. Like most colourful moths, it is active during the day.

665 People have been living on Madagascar for around 2000 years. Travellers from Arabia, Asia, Africa and Indonesia have all settled here, along with Europeans. Four out of every five adults earns a living from agriculture. More than 90 percent of Madagascar's rainforests have been destroyed to provide farmland for the growing population.

◄ The rosy periwinkle is used to make drugs that fight deadly diseases.

666 The pretty rosy periwinkle plant is found in Madagascar's rainforests and is used to fight cancer. It contains chemicals that are used to make drugs that combat this deadly disease. The rosy periwinkle is endangered in the wild because its forest home has been largely destroyed.

I DON'T BELIEVE IT!

Lemurs in Madagascar have been seen rolling giant millipedes over their fur. No one knew why, until scientists discovered that the many-legged bugs release chemicals that keep flies and fleas off the lemurs — like a natural fly spray!

▶ A Madagascan aye-aye taps a tree with its long middle finger. It listens for sounds of moving grubs beneath, and hooks them out.

293

African adventures

667 The Congo rainforest (or Central African rainforest) lies in the centre of Africa, in the basin of the Congo River. It is the second largest rainforest, with an area around twice the size of France. More than 50 million people depend on it for survival.

▲ The Central African rainforest is home to more than 11,000 types of plant and 400 types of mammal, such as African forest elephants.

669 Walking through the African rainforest is a challenging, frightening, noisy activity! Plants block every step and strange noises come from all corners, including squeaks, trilling, singing, cheeps, growls and roars. Deadly snakes and spiders lurk in dark corners, and biting or stinging insects will sniff out human flesh in seconds.

668 Before European explorers ventured into Africa's jungles the native people lived in harmony with their environment. They survived as hunter-gatherers – they only killed what they needed to eat, and collected fruits by hand. Europeans wanted to use the rainforests to make money – a practice that continues today.

◀ Grey parrots are common in Arican rainforests, where they feed on fruits and seeds.

670 The Batwa people of Central Africa are pygmies, which means they are unusually short.
They have lived in African rainforests for thousands of years, collecting honey and hunting. When farmers destroyed the Batwas' forests, they were left without homes and with no way to get food. Most now live in great poverty.

► Some Batwa men still climb trees to collect honey, but most members of the tribe have been forced to leave their forest homes.

671 African hardwoods are prized for their great beauty and durability.
These woods come from tropical trees and have been used for centuries to make fine furniture and decorative objects. Mahogany, ebony and teak are all exotic woods from African rainforests.

▼ Around 90 percent of the rainforests in West Africa have been wiped out by farming.

QUIZ
Three of these countries are in Africa, and three are in South America. Can you put them in the right continents?

Colombia Gabon Congo
Guyana Brazil Ghana

Answers:
Africa: Congo Gabon Ghana
South America: Brazil Colombia
Guyana

Forests of the Far East

672 The word 'jungle' comes from a Hindi word meaning 'thick forest'. Most Asian rainforests lie on the mainland, from India to Bhutan and Malaysia, or on tropical islands such as Sumatra.

▼Orang-utans live in trees, but they do spend some time on land. They can walk through water, but do not swim.

673 Borneo cloud forests provide shelter and food for one of the world's most endangered apes. Orang-utans live in trees and feed on the fruit of more than 400 different types of tree, especially durians and figs. If they can't find fruit, they eat leaves and bark.

674 Palm trees provide an important source of food — sago. Women make it from palm pith (the spongy substance inside a trunk or branch). They chop and soak it, before treading on it to turn it into a pulp. The pulp dries to a flour that can be cooked. Tribal people also enjoy delicious sago grubs — the large maggots that live inside rotting palm trees.

RAIN RECORD

It rains almost every day in a rainforest. To measure your rainfall you need a clear plastic container, a ruler and a notebook.
1. Place the empty container outside, away from trees.
2. At the same time every day measure the water in the container.
3. Empty your container after each measurement.
4. Record your results in a notebook.

Powerful, curved beak

◀ The Philippine eagle has a wingspan of more than 2 metres and is a formidable predator, catching prey such as flying lemurs in mid-flight. It is in danger of extinction because more than 90 percent of its Philippine forest home has been cut down.

Sharp talons

675 The people of the Indonesian rainforests are called Orang Asli and they have had a hard battle for survival in recent times. In Malaysia, they were often captured and sold as slaves to local chiefs. Many Orang Asli still live in the rainforests, hunting monkeys with blowpipes made from bamboo.

Flying lemur

676 Known as the lord of the jungle, the Philippine eagle soars over Asian rainforests, hunting monkeys and squirrels. It is one of the world's biggest raptors (birds of prey), but also one of the most endangered. There are now probably no more than 500 alive.

Cloud forests

677 **Trekking through the Monteverde cloud forest of Costa Rica can be done on foot — or by air!** Visitors can fly between the trees on zip wires, passing through low-lying clouds to get a bird's-eye view of the treetops. On the ground, every surface is wet, as it is either drizzling or pouring with rain for much of the day.

▲ Three-toed sloths are slow-moving mammals. Their camouflage is their only defence against jaguars — the big cats of South America that hunt them.

▼ Mountain gorillas live in the cloud forests of Africa's Virunga National Park. They are highly endangered animals, despite being our close cousins.

678 At night, cloud forests buzz with life, but the sleepy sloth rarely stirs. These animals from Central and South America are such slow movers that plants grow in their fur, giving perfect camouflage! Three-toed sloths hang from branches and sleep upside-down for up to 18 hours every day, only coming down to the ground once a week. It takes them one minute to travel just 3 metres.

679 Epiphytes are rainforest plants that grow very well in cloud forests. They emerge from the nooks and crannies of tree trunks and branches, to reach more sunlight than they would on the forest floor. Dirt collects in these places and turns to soil. The epiphytes' roots grow into this soil, where they collect nutrients and water.

▲ Trees in cloud forests are covered in epiphytes and they grow roots from their trunks and branches. These hanging roots can be tens of metres in length and absorb water from the damp atmosphere.

◀ In the mating season a male quetzal grows two tail feathers that may reach one metre in length.

GO SLOW

Measure out 3 metres on the floor. How quickly can you cover this distance when you run? Probably very quickly! Now try to cover the same distance as slowly as you can, so it takes a whole minute – just like a three-toed sloth. Now do it again, upside down (only joking!)

680 As a resplendent quetzal flies through Mexico's cloud forest its tail feathers shimmer in the sunlight. Male quetzals, known as birds of the gods, have the longest tail feathers of any bird in the region, and they are often regarded as one of the world's most beautiful birds. Quetzals eat wild avocados, swallowing the fruit whole. The seeds pass through their bodies, helping new avocado trees to grow.

Peculiar plants

681 It is thought that more than 60 percent of plant species live in rainforests. Plants do an important job in making the soil stable so rain doesn't wash it away. They also take carbon dioxide out of the air, and put oxygen – the gas we breathe – back into it.

682 One of the stinkiest plants is the giant titan arum. This freaky flower can grow to 3 metres in height and produces a pongy perfume to attract insects. The insects pollinate the plants so that it can produce seeds. The titan arum only flowers once every seven years.

◀ Titan arums only grow wild in the Indonesian island of Sumatra. They smell of rotting meat.

▶ Durians are called 'kings of fruits' and are eaten in Indonesia and Malaysia.

683 The smell of a ripe durian fruit can be detected nearly one kilometre away. Visitors to the rainforests of Southeast Asia say durians stink like rotting fish, but the local people and the animals don't mind – they know the soft flesh tastes sweet. Tigers, sun bears and mouse deer all eat durians that have fallen to the forest floor.

▶ Look inside a pitcher plant and you can see how it traps bugs.

Slippery surface

Insects caught in thick liquid

684 **Pitcher plants are killers.** These pretty green plants lure bugs using a tempting scent. As insects land on the rim of the pitcher, their feet lose their grip on the waxy surface, sending them tumbling into the trap. The plant produces acid, which digests the insect's body, dissolving it within hours. The enormous rajah pitcher plant can even digest mice and birds!

685 **The biggest flower on Earth — the rafflesia — grows in the rainforests of Borneo.** This monster bloom can reach one metre across and smells of rotting flesh. The rafflesia lives on other plants and steals its food and water from its 'host'.

▶ Rafflesia plants are parasites so they do not need roots, stems or leaves. Their foul smell attracts flies that pollinate the flowers.

On the move

◄ Green vine snakes live in Southeast Asia and mostly prey upon frogs and lizards.

686 Moving through a rainforest is difficult. Trees, roots and shrubs fill every space, and there are few natural paths, so animals have to fly, swing, crawl or leap to find food, shelter and mates.

687 Walking in a jungle at night is especially challenging, as an inky darkness descends when the sun sets. Animals that hunt at night are called nocturnal. Some bats use echolocation – a type of sixth sense – to hunt and find their way through the web of branches, while others, such as flying foxes, use their exceptional eyesight.

688 Green vine snakes have pencil-thin bodies and can move between branches soundlessly, reaching up to one metre between trees. With their tails firmly wrapped around a branch these snakes dangle down, looking for prey they can catch with a single venomous bite.

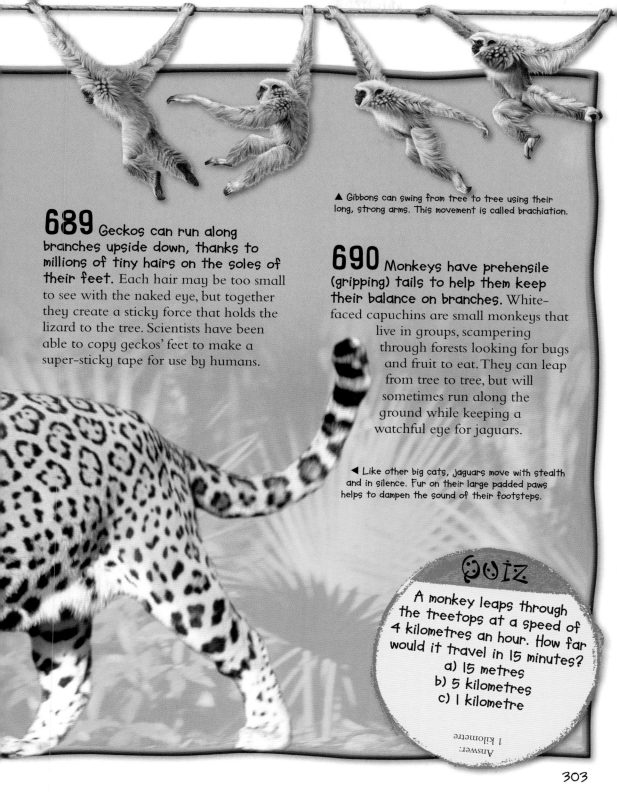

▲ Gibbons can swing from tree to tree using their long, strong arms. This movement is called brachiation.

689 Geckos can run along branches upside down, thanks to millions of tiny hairs on the soles of their feet. Each hair may be too small to see with the naked eye, but together they create a sticky force that holds the lizard to the tree. Scientists have been able to copy geckos' feet to make a super-sticky tape for use by humans.

690 Monkeys have prehensile (gripping) tails to help them keep their balance on branches. White-faced capuchins are small monkeys that live in groups, scampering through forests looking for bugs and fruit to eat. They can leap from tree to tree, but will sometimes run along the ground while keeping a watchful eye for jaguars.

◀ Like other big cats, jaguars move with stealth and in silence. Fur on their large padded paws helps to dampen the sound of their footsteps.

QUIZ

A monkey leaps through the treetops at a speed of 4 kilometres an hour. How far would it travel in 15 minutes?
a) 15 metres
b) 5 kilometres
c) 1 kilometre

Answer:
1 kilometre

Fantastic feathers

691 **Birds of paradise are the jewels in a rainforest crown.** These animals are dressed in feathers of fine colours and are adorned with crests, ruffs and streamers. Males use their bright, bold plumage to catch the attention of females, but they also do splendid dances and displays to make sure they can't be ignored!

692 **The mating dance of the male cock-of-the-rock is one of nature's most extraordinary sights.** Groups of males, with their bright-orange heads, collect on a branch near the forest floor, and put on a performance for a watching female. They flutter their wings, bob their heads and scuttle along the branch. The female mates with the male whose show has most impressed her.

▼ Male cocks-of-the-rock never hide themselves behind dull colours. Their startling plumage catches the attention of females — and predators.

693 **Wilson's bird of paradise has bare blue skin on its head, which is so bright it can be seen at night.** Males prepare a patch of ground to use as a stage, clearing it of all leaves and twigs. Their tails contain two skinny, curly silver feathers and their backs are metallic green. Like all birds of paradise, the females are not as brightly coloured as their mates.

I DON'T BELIEVE IT!

Hummingbirds are tiny, colourful birds of the rainforest that feed on sugary nectar from flowers. The bee hummingbird is the world's smallest bird, with a body length of just 57 millimetres and a wingspan of only 65 millimetres.

▼ When a male Raggiana bird of paradise is resting, its fan of orange-red feathers is hidden from view, but if a female nears, it will show itself in all its glory.

694 Birds of paradise live in Australia, New Guinea and some Asian islands. When dead samples of these birds were sent to Europe hundreds of years ago, their legs had been removed. This led scientists to believe that these creatures had come straight from paradise, and could not touch the ground until death, which is how they got their name.

Kaleidoscope of colour

695 Rainforests are full of shades of green, but the animals that live in them are often bold and bright in colour. Strong colours help animals send signals to one another in a habitat where it is easy to be hidden from view.

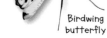

Postman butterfly

Birdwing butterfly

Blue morpho butterfly

▲ The wings of many butterflies are covered in tiny scales that reflect light rays to create a range of shimmering colours.

▶ A strawberry poison-dart frog from Costa Rica has bright colours to warn of the poison it has on its skin.

696 While some animals use colour to draw attention to themselves, others use it to hide. Giant stick insects, like many other bugs in the forest, are patterned in mottled shades of green, grey or brown so they blend in with their surroundings. Camouflage is one way to avoid being eaten in the jungle, but there are many other ways to stay alive.

Parasol fungi

697 The forest floor is littered with brightly coloured 'umbrellas'. These little growths, called toadstools or mushrooms, are fungi – living things that are similar to plants but do not need sunlight. Orange, gold, red, blue and yellow are common fungi colours, which may alert grazing animals to the poisons they contain.

Cup fungi

◀ The giant stick insect can reach 45 centimetres in length.

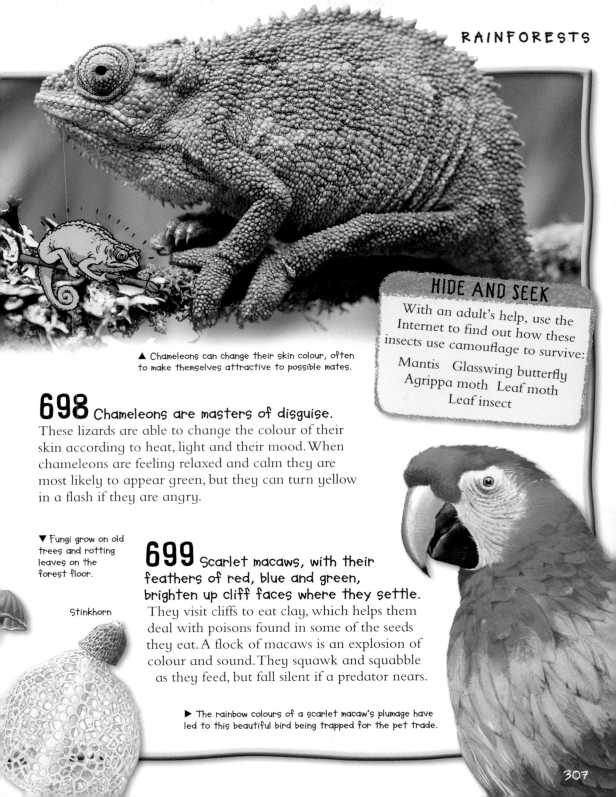

▲ Chameleons can change their skin colour, often to make themselves attractive to possible mates.

HIDE AND SEEK

With an adult's help, use the Internet to find out how these insects use camouflage to survive:

Mantis   Glasswing butterfly
Agrippa moth   Leaf moth
Leaf insect

698 Chameleons are masters of disguise.
These lizards are able to change the colour of their skin according to heat, light and their mood. When chameleons are feeling relaxed and calm they are most likely to appear green, but they can turn yellow in a flash if they are angry.

▼ Fungi grow on old trees and rotting leaves on the forest floor.

Stinkhorn

699 Scarlet macaws, with their feathers of red, blue and green, brighten up cliff faces where they settle.
They visit cliffs to eat clay, which helps them deal with poisons found in some of the seeds they eat. A flock of macaws is an explosion of colour and sound. They squawk and squabble as they feed, but fall silent if a predator nears.

▶ The rainbow colours of a scarlet macaw's plumage have led to this beautiful bird being trapped for the pet trade.

The key to survival

700 Surviving in a rainforest is a battle for most animals. Food and shelter are plentiful, but habitats are so crowded it is easy for predators to hide. As a result, many creatures have developed amazing ways to stay alive.

701 Some rainforest animals pretend to be poisonous. When explorer Henry Bates (1825–1892) examined butterflies in the Amazon he found one type of patterned butterfly that tasted foul to birds, and another type that looked very similar, which didn't. He concluded that some animals copy (mimic), the appearance of others that are poisonous to avoid being eaten.

▲ Leaflitter toads are named for their clever camouflage. They resemble the decaying leaves of their forest floor habitat.

▼ Goliath tarantulas don't build webs to catch their prey – they hunt just like bigger predators, stalking animals such as frogs.

702 Poisons are common in many rainforest creatures. However, the Goliath tarantula spider uses flying hairs, as well as poisons, to keep safe! Probably the world's largest spider, it reaches 30 centimetres across, with 2.5-centimetre-long fangs. If threatened, Goliath tarantula spiders shoot hairs at attackers, which cause irritation and pain.

703 Rainforest ants morph (change) from black insects into red berries. Parasite worms living inside the ants cause their rear ends to swell and turn red. Birds mistake the ants for juicy berries and eat them. The worms' eggs are then spread through the bird's droppings. Without this clever bit of mimicry, birds would not eat the ants, which taste bitter, so the worms would not be able to reproduce.

▶ Tiny termites are responsible for building large, round nests that hang on branches throughout the rainforest.

I DON'T BELIEVE IT!

Animals that hunt other animals are called predators, and jaguars are amongst the largest Amazonian predators. Sadly these big cats used to be killed for their fine, spotted fur, which was used to make coats, hats and handbags.

Termite nest

704 Working together means ants and termites, which live in colonies of many millions, are giants of the jungle. Termites build huge nests in trees, while leafcutter ants join forces to collect fallen leaves and carry them to their nests. The leaves become food for fungi growing in the nest, which the ants then collect and eat.

▼ Forest floors teem with columns of leafcutter ants, carrying leaf pieces more than 20 times their own body weight.

Inside the nest is a complex tunnel network

309

The jungle's bounty

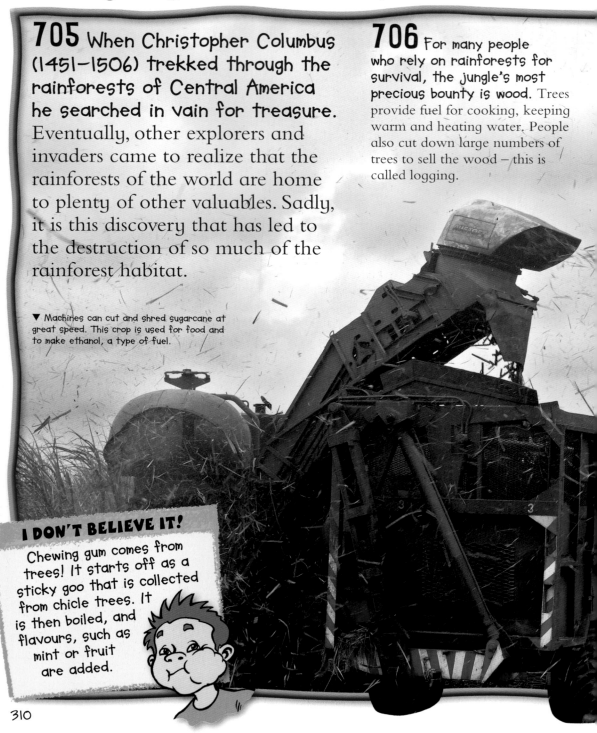

705 When Christopher Columbus (1451–1506) trekked through the rainforests of Central America he searched in vain for treasure. Eventually, other explorers and invaders came to realize that the rainforests of the world are home to plenty of other valuables. Sadly, it is this discovery that has led to the destruction of so much of the rainforest habitat.

▼ Machines can cut and shred sugarcane at great speed. This crop is used for food and to make ethanol, a type of fuel.

706 For many people who rely on rainforests for survival, the jungle's most precious bounty is wood. Trees provide fuel for cooking, keeping warm and heating water. People also cut down large numbers of trees to sell the wood – this is called logging.

I DON'T BELIEVE IT!

Chewing gum comes from trees! It starts off as a sticky goo that is collected from chicle trees. It is then boiled, and flavours, such as mint or fruit are added.

▲ Cocoa beans grow inside pods.

▲ Latex drips into a collecting cup.

▲ Star fruits, or carambolas, can be sweet or sour.

707 Chocolate, sugar and rubber come from rainforest plants. Cocoa pods are cut open to reveal seeds (cocoa beans) which are dried, cleaned and made into chocolate. Sugar comes from a grass called sugarcane that grows in tropical areas. Rubber is harvested from trees as a white sticky gum called latex, which is made into many useful products such as tyres and hoses.

709 Many delicious fruits, vegetables, nuts, spices and herbs come from rainforests, although they may be cultivated (grown) in other places. Shops around the world sell ginger, cloves, pepper, nutmeg, pineapples, bananas, starfruits and sweet potatoes, all of which originally came from rainforests.

708 Scientists are discovering that rainforest plants can be used to treat diseases. The people of the rainforests have known this for thousands of years. Quinine is a chemical that comes from the bark of the cinchona tree. It has been used by Amazonian Indians to prevent malaria – a deadly disease spread by mosquitoes. It is thought many rainforest plants could be used to treat cancer in the future.

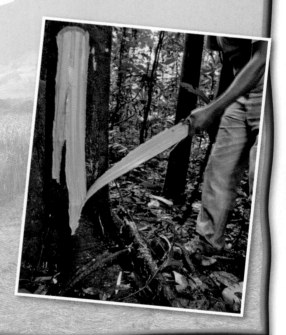

▶ The outer bark of a cinchona tree is peeled back to reveal yellow inner bark, which contains quinine.

Paradise lost

710 Mangrove forests are one of the world's fastest disappearing habitats. Half of them have been destroyed in just 50 years. The trees are cut down so the swampy ground can be used to cultivate shrimps to be sold as food. Coastal areas that have lost their mangrove forests are more likely to suffer from tsunamis, storms and flooding.

711 The red-vented cockatoo is one of the world's rarest birds. Chicks are taken from nests and sold as pets – there may now be as few as 1000 left. The giant elephant birds of Madagascar died out centuries ago when their eggs were taken for food.

712 Gold mines, which use the poisonous metal mercury, have been established in some rainforests. Water that contains mercury can kill anything that comes into contact with it, and may have caused the disappearance of many types of frog and toad.

▲ This mangrove swamp in Indonesia has been devastated by shrimp farming. Mangroves protect land from water damage and are home to many animals, which, once destroyed, may take centuries to recover.

713 Humans' closest relatives are being eaten to extinction. Primates such as gorillas, chimps and bonobos are sold as meat in Africa, while monkeys and langurs are served as luxury dishes in Asia. Primates also suffer when their habitats are affected by human conflicts.

▲ WWF international staff patrols search for evidence of poaching activities in central Africa.

714 When the forest dies, so does a way of life. Now the future looks uncertain for millions of tribal people whose families have depended on rainforests for centuries. When they lose their forest homes, it is hard for people to retain the knowledge and skills that help them to survive.

▶ Wild populations of great apes such as chimpanzees are disappearing fast.

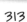

313

Burning issues

715 Cutting down forests is called deforestation. Many forests are lost when they are turned into plantations – large fields that are used to grow single crops, such as bananas or rubber. Scientists believe that at least 19 million precious rainforest trees are cut down every day for wood or to make way for crops.

716 Around one-sixth of the Amazon rainforest has been destroyed, yet deforestation continues around the world. New roads are being built in the South American and African rainforests, which make it easier to fell trees. As many countries with rainforests are poor, selling wood can seem a good way for people to pay for food.

▼ It only takes a few hours for modern machines to fell trees and remove vegetation so the land can be used for farming.

I DON'T BELIEVE IT!
Orang-utans are close to extinction because their forests are becoming palm plantations. Palm oil is used in food and as a fuel. It is expected that orang-utans will be gone from the wild in less than ten years.

▲ Aerial photos show how huge areas of rainforest are being destroyed so the land can be used for cattle and crops.

▼ Slash and burn is used to clear the ground. When it is done too often, or over a large area, entire habitats may be changed or destroyed forever.

717 The Amazon rainforest is being cut down to provide land for cattle. These animals are used for beef, which is sent to developed nations for use in hamburgers and similar foods. There are more than 200 million herds of cattle in the region, and that number is likely to grow.

718 Large areas of rainforest are destroyed using 'slash and burn'. Trees and plants are cut down, and the remains are burned. The cleared ground is used for growing crops, or as land for cattle. This method of deforestation ruins the soil, so the farmers then have to move on to a new patch of forest.

719 Deforestation has been found to affect our atmosphere and climate. Removing these massive ecosystems could cause droughts and flooding. Once forests are gone, the soil is not held together so well, causing soil erosion, so landslides become more common and plants can no longer grow.

Forests for the future

720 We must preserve the world's rainforests if we value the people and wildlife that live in them. Less than eight percent of these ecosystems are currently strictly protected from deforestation, but governments could turn rainforests into national parks so they cannot be used for farming or logging.

▲ Tourists pay to go on canopy walks and admire the rainforests from above. Money from tourism can be used to protect these habitats and give local people jobs.

▼ Solar panels collect the Sun's energy, which can be turned into electrical energy to provide light and heat.

721 Rainforest people can be shown how to use solar power to produce energy for light and cooking. Solar power is sustainable, which means it will never run out – unlike rainforest trees. Wood fires produce dirty smoke, but solar energy, which comes from the sun, is pollution-free.

722 Technology may help save the Congo rainforest in Africa. Local people who find better ways to earn money than cutting down trees will be helped with money from a special fund. Their progress will be checked using satellite images of the forest.

723 It was once thought that when a rainforest had gone, it would be gone forever. However, scientists have grown a fresh forest in Borneo to replace one that has been destroyed. Seeds from more than 1300 trees were planted, and the soil was treated with a special fertilizer. Now 30 types of mammal and 116 types of bird have moved in. Local people have been involved with the project, and helped it to succeed.

▶ Workers at an orang-utan orphanage in Borneo care for baby orangs that have lost their parents to hunting or the illegal pet trade.

724 Everyone can make a difference to the future of the rainforests. Shoppers can check they are not buying products that come from rainforest regions, and governments can develop tourism so that local people can earn a living protecting forests, rather than destroying them.

Products that may come from rainforest regions:

* Wood
* Soya
* Beef
* Palm oil

Check labels before buying

725 Rainforests will only be preserved if people respect all of Earth's delicate ecosystems. Everyone who cares about nature hopes that there is still time to halt the damage, and that rainforests will still be around in the centuries to come.

OCEANS

726 Oceans cover more than two-thirds of the Earth's rocky surface. Their total area is about 362 million square kilometres, which means there is more than twice as much ocean as land! Although all the oceans flow into each other, we know them as four different oceans – the Pacific, Atlantic, Indian and Arctic. Our landmasses, the continents, rise out of the oceans.

ARCTIC OCEAN

ATLANTIC OCEAN

PACIFIC OCEAN

ATLANTIC OCEAN

SOUTHE

727 The largest, deepest ocean is the Pacific. It covers nearly half of our planet and is almost as big as the other three oceans put together! In places, the Pacific is so deep that the Earth's tallest mountain, Everest, would sink without a trace.

▶ Mount Everest is the highest point on Earth, rising to 8848 metres. Parts of the Pacific Ocean are deeper than 10,000 metres.

The deepest parts of the Pacific would cover Mount Everest without trace

Light hits the surface of the water

► A cup of sea water appears see-through. It is only when you look at a large area of sea that it has colour.

Scattered blue and green

728 Oceans can look blue, green or grey. This is because of the way light hits the surface. Water soaks up the red parts of light but scatters the blue-green parts, making the sea look different shades of blue or green.

729 Seas can be red or dead. A sea is a small part of an ocean. The Red Sea, for example, is the part of the Indian Ocean between Egypt and Saudi Arabia. Asia's Dead Sea isn't a true sea, but a landlocked lake. We call it a sea because it is a large body of water.

INDIAN OCEAN

EAN

▲ The world's oceans cover most of our planet. Each ocean is made up of smaller bodies of water called seas.

730 There are streams in the oceans. All the water in the oceans is constantly moving, but in some places it flows as currents, which take particular paths. One of these is the warm Gulf Stream, that travels around the edge of the Atlantic Ocean.

I DON'T BELIEVE IT!

Oceans hold 97 percent of the world's water. Just a fraction is in freshwater lakes and rivers.

Ocean features

731 There are plains, mountains and valleys under the oceans, in areas called basins. Each basin has a rim (the flat continental shelf that meets the shore) and sides (the continental slope that drops away from the shelf). In the ocean basin there are flat abyssal plains, steep hills, huge underwater volcanoes called seamounts, and deep valleys called trenches.

▲ Under the oceans there is a landscape similar to that found on land.

Land

Continental shelf

Continental slope

Spreading ridge

Abyssal trench

Abyssal hills

▼ Magma (molten rock) escapes from the seabed to form a ridge. This ridge has collapsed to form a rift valley.

Spreading floor

Ridge

Magma (molten rock)

732 The ocean floor is spreading. Molten (liquid) rock inside the Earth seeps from holes on the seabed. As the rock cools, it forms new sections of floor that creep slowly out. Scientists have proved this fact by looking at layers of rock on the ocean floor. There are matching stripes of rock either side of a ridge. Each pair came from the same hot rock eruption, then slowly spread out.

Sea mount

Volcanic island

Ocean trench

▼ An atoll is a ring-shaped coral reef that encloses a deep lagoon. It can form when a volcanic island sinks underwater.

1. Coral starts to grow

4. Coral atoll is left behind

2. Lagoon appears around volcano

3. Volcano disappears

733 Some islands are swallowed by the ocean. Sometimes, a ring-shaped coral reef called an atoll marks where an island once was. The coral reef built up around the island. After the volcano blew its top, the reef remained.

▶ There are more Hawaiian islands still to come – Loihi is just visible beneath the water's surface.

I DON'T BELIEVE IT!

The world's longest mountain chain is under the ocean. It is the Mid-Ocean range and stretches around the middle of the Earth.

734 New islands are born all the time. When an underwater volcano erupts, its lava cools in the water. Layers of lava build up, and the volcano grows in size. Eventually, it is tall enough to peep above the waves. The Hawaiian islands rose from the sea like this.

Swimming machines

735 **There are over 21,000 different types of fish in the sea.** They range from huge whale sharks to tiny gobies. Almost all are covered in scales and use fins and a muscular tail to power through the water. Like their freshwater cousins, sea fish have slits called gills that take oxygen from the water so they can breathe.

736 The oarfish is bigger than an oar – it is as long as four canoes! It is the longest bony fish and is found in all the world's oceans. Oarfish are handsome creatures – they have a striking red fin along the length of their back.

◄ People once thought oarfish swam horizontally through the water. Now they know they swim upright.

▶ At over 3 metres long, sunfish are the biggest bony fish in the oceans. They feed on plankton.

737 Sunfish like sunbathing! Ocean sunfish are very large, broad fish that can weigh as much as a tonne. They are named after their habit of sunbathing on the surface of the open ocean.

▶ Flying fish feed near the surface so they are easy to find. Their gliding flight helps them escape most hunters.

738 Flying fish cannot really fly. Fish can't survive out of water, but flying fish sometimes leap above the waves when they are travelling at high speeds. They use their wing-like fins to keep them in the air for as long as 30 seconds.

▲ In a large group called a school, fish like these yellow snappers have less chance of being picked off by a predator.

739 Not all fish are the same shape. Cod or mackerel are what we think of as a normal fish shape, but fish come in all shapes and sizes. Flounder and other flatfish have squashed-flat bodies. Eels are so long and thin that the biggest types look like snakes, while tiny garden eels resemble worms! And of course, seahorses and seadragons look nothing like other fish at all!

▶ The flounder's flattened shape and dull colouring help to camouflage (hide) it on the seabed.

QUIZ
1. Which fish like to sunbathe?
2. How many types of fish live in the sea?
3. How does a fish breathe?
4. Can flying fish really fly?

Answers:
1. Sunfish 2. 21,000 3. With its gills 4. No

Shark!

740 Great whites are the scariest sharks in the oceans. These powerful predators have been known to kill people and can speed through the water at 30 kilometres per hour. Unlike most fish, the great white is warm-blooded. This allows its muscles to work well, but also means the shark has to feed on plenty of meat.

▲ Great white sharks are fierce hunters. They will attack and eat almost anything, but prefer to feed on seals.

▼ Basking sharks eat enormous amounts of plankton. They sieve through around 1000 tonnes of water every hour.

741 Most sharks are meat-eaters. Herring are a favourite food for sand tiger and thresher sharks, while a hungry tiger shark will gobble up just about anything! Strangely, some of the biggest sharks take the smallest prey. Whale sharks and basking sharks eat tiny sea creatures called plankton.

SHARK PARTS

Study the labels to learn the shark's special features. Trace the shark without the labels, then see how many parts you can name.

▶ Hammerheads prey on other sharks and rays, bony fish, crabs and lobsters, octopus and squid.

Dorsal fin

Ampullae of Lorenzini (to sense electricity from nearby fish)

Gill

Nostril

Jaw

Pectoral fin

Pelvic fin

Anal fin

Tail fin

742 Hammerhead sharks have a hammer-shaped head! With a nostril and an eye on each end of the 'hammer', they swing their head from side to side. This gives them double the chance to see and sniff out any signs of a tasty catch.

▼ Tiger sharks leave their newborn pups to fend for themselves.

743 Tiger sharks may have as many as 40 pups! The baby sharks develop in eggcases inside their mother's body. Many other sharks also reproduce like this, but it is not the only way. Hammerhead and grey reef shark babies develop inside their mother, not in eggcases. Other sharks, such as dogfish and zebra sharks, lay eggcases straight into the sea, leaving the babies to fend for themselves.

Whales and dolphins

744 The biggest animal on the planet lives in the oceans. It is the blue whale, measuring about 28 metres in length and weighing up to 190 tonnes. It feeds by filtering tiny, shrimp-like creatures called krill from the water – about four tonnes of krill a day! Like other great whales, it has special, sieve-like parts in its mouth called baleen plates.

▲ As the sperm whale surfaces, it pushes out stale air through its blowhole. It fills its lungs with fresh air and dives down again.

745 Whales and dolphins have to come to the surface for air. This is because they are mammals, like we are. Sperm whales hold their breath the longest. They have been known to stay underwater for nearly two hours.

▶ Blue whale calves feed on their mother's rich milk until they are around eight months old.

748 Killer whales play with their food. They especially like to catch baby seals, which they toss into the air before eating. Killer whales are not true whales, but the largest dolphins. They have teeth for chewing, instead of baleen plates.

▲ Killer whales carry the baby seals out to sea before eating them.

▶ The beluga is a type of white whale. It makes a range of noises – whistles, clangs, chirps and moos!

746 Dolphins and whales sing songs to communicate. The noisiest is the humpback whale, whose wailing noises can be heard for hundreds of kilometres. The sweetest is the beluga – nicknamed the 'sea canary'. Songs are used to attract a mate, or just to keep track of each other.

749 Moby Dick was a famous white whale. It starred in a book by Herman Melville about a white sperm whale and a whaler called Captain Ahab.

747 The narwhal has a horn like a unicorn's. This Arctic whale has a long, twirly tooth that spirals out of its head. The males use their tusks as a weapon when they are fighting over females.

▲ The narwhal's 3 metre tusk seems too long for its body.

I DON'T BELIEVE IT!

Barnacles are shellfish. They attach themselves to ships' hulls, or the bodies of grey whales and other large sea animals.

Ocean reptiles

750 Marine iguanas are the most seaworthy lizards. Most lizards prefer life on land, where it is easier to warm up their cold-blooded bodies, but marine iguanas depend on the sea for their food. They dive underwater to graze on the algae and seaweed growing on rocks.

▲ Marine iguanas are found around the Galapagos Islands in the Pacific. When they are not diving for food, they bask on the rocks that dot the island coastlines. The lizards' dark skin helps to absorb the Sun's heat.

751 Turtles come ashore only to lay their eggs. Although they are born on land, turtles head for the sea the minute they hatch. Females return to the beach where they were born to dig their nest. After they have laid their eggs, they go straight back to the water. Hawksbill turtles may lay up to 140 eggs in a clutch, while some green turtle females clock up 800 eggs in a year!

▲ In a single breeding season, a female green turtle may lay as many as ten clutches, each containing up to 80 eggs!

752 There are venomous (poisonous) snakes in the sea. Most stay close to land and come ashore to lay their eggs. Banded sea snakes, for example, cruise around coral reefs in search of their favourite food, eels. But the yellow-bellied sea snake never leaves the water. It gives birth to live babies in the open ocean.

▼ Banded sea snakes use venom (poison) to stun prey, but the yellow-bellied sea snake has a sneakier trick. Once its colourful underside has attracted some fish, it darts back — so the fish are next to its open mouth! The venom of sea snakes is more powerful than that of any land snake.

Banded sea snake

Yellow-bellied
sea snake

MIX AND MATCH

Can you match these sea turtles to their names?
1. Green 2. Hawksbill
3. Leatherback 4. Loggerhead

Answers:
1c 2b 3d 4a

a

b

c

d

▼ Leatherbacks are the biggest turtles in the world and can grow to four metres in length.

753 Leatherbacks dive up to 1200 metres for dinner. These turtles hold the record for being the biggest sea turtles and for making the deepest dives. Leatherbacks feed mostly on jellyfish but their diet also includes molluscs, crabs and lobsters, starfish and sea urchins.

Harvests from the sea

◄ Fishermen attach buoys to their lobster pots, so they can remember where to find them again.

754 Oysters come from beds — and lobsters from pots! The animals in the oceans feed other sea creatures, and they feed us, too! To gather oysters, fishermen raise them on trays or poles in the water. First, they collect oyster larvae, or babies. They attract them by putting out sticks hung with shells. Lobster larvae are too difficult to collect, but the adults are caught in pots filled with fish bait.

755 Some farmers grow seaweed. Seaweed is delicious to eat, and is also a useful ingredient in products such as ice cream and plant fertilizer. In shallow, tropical waters, people grow their own on plots of seabed.

▲ The harvested seaweed can be dried in the sun to preserve it.

► The oil platform's welded-steel legs rest on the seabed. They support the platform around 15 metres above the surface of the water.

Derrick

Crane

Flare

Helicopter landing pad

Oil processing area

756 Sea minerals are useful substances that we mine from the ground. The most valuable are oil and gas. They are pumped from the seabed and piped ashore or transported in huge supertankers. Their use has a negative impact on the environment, however, so scientists are developing better ways to fuel our lifestyles. Salt is another important mineral. In hot, low-lying areas, people build walls to hold shallow pools of sea water. The water dries up in the sun, leaving behind crystals of salt.

757 There are gemstones under the sea. Pearls are made by oysters. If a grain of sand is lodged inside an oyster's shell, it irritates its soft body. The oyster coats the sand with a substance called nacre, which is also used to line the inside of the shell. Over the years, more nacre builds up and the pearl gets bigger.

QUIZ

1. What are the young of lobster called?
2. What substances are pumped from the seabed?
3. Is seaweed edible?
4. Which gemstone is made by oysters?

Answers:
1. Larvae 2. Oil and gas
3. Yes 4. Pearl

► Pearl divers carry an oyster knife for prising open the oyster's shell.

DEEP OCEAN

758 Far down in the dark waters of the deep oceans lies a mysterious wilderness. The deep ocean is a place without light, where the water pressure can crush human bones. Until modern times, people did not believe that anything could live here. Now scientists are discovering new creatures all the time, from colossal squid with huge eyes to giant worms that are 2 metres in length.

▶ Almost 2.5 kilometres below the surface of the ocean, an eelpout fish hides among giant tube worms and crabs at a hydrothermal vent. Only two people have been to the deepest part of the oceans, which is about 11 kilometres below the waves. In contrast, 12 human explorers have walked on the surface of the Moon, which is 384,400 kilometres from Earth.

The ocean zones

ARCTIC OCEAN

PACIFIC OCEAN

759 Oceans are enormous areas of water. They cover more than two-thirds of the Earth's surface. There are five oceans and they make up a giant ecosystem of creatures that depend on seawater to survive.

ARCTIC OCEAN

ATLANTIC OCEAN

PACIFIC OCEAN

PACIFIC OCEAN

INDIAN OCEAN

SOUTHERN OCEAN

ATLANTIC OCEAN

SOUTHERN OCEAN

INDIAN OCEAN

760 At their edges, oceans are shallow and teem with life. These places are called continental shelves. However continental shelves only take up 5 percent of the total area of the oceans. The shelves fall away into deep slopes and from there, the seabed stretches out as dark, enormous plains.

◄▲ There are five oceans. They are all connected and make up one giant mass of water.

► Scientists divide the ocean into five layers, or zones. Different types of animals live in the different zones.

Jellyfish

LIGHT ZONE 0–200 metres

TWILIGHT ZONE 200–1000 metres

DARK ZONE 1000–4000 metres

Sea lily

ABYSSAL ZONE 4000–6000 metres

Tube worms

HADAL ZONE 6000–10,000 metres

DELIGHT IN LIGHT
Find out about the wavelengths of white light. How many colours make up white light, and what are they? Find the answers by searching on the Internet with the keywords 'rainbow' and 'light'.

Coral

Bluefin tuna

Plankton

Octopus

Wolf eel

Hatchet fish

Squid

Gulper eel

Fangtooth

Viperfish

Rattail

Hagfish

Deep-sea angler

Amphipods

Sea cucumber

761 Oceans are deep places. The average depth is 3800 metres, but in some places the seabed lies as deep as 11,000 metres. If all the water in the oceans was removed, a dramatic landscape would be revealed – giant mountains, volcanoes, smooth flat plains and deep trenches.

▲ Sunlight can only pass through the ocean's uppermost layer. Everything below is in perpetual darkness.

762 Sunlight streams through the upper zone of the ocean, giving warmth, light and energy to the creatures that live there. This is called the Light Zone. Light is made up of many colours, and as it passes through water, the colours get absorbed, until only blue light is left. At a depth of around 200 metres, all blue light has disappeared and in the zones below, darkness takes over.

In deep water

763 Living in water is nothing like living in air. The ocean is one of Earth's most remarkable habitats. Ocean water is constantly moving and changing. The creatures that live here have to cope without light, and the weight of many tonnes of water above them.

765 As you travel deeper into the ocean you will feel a great weight on your body. Water is 830 times denser than air, and it is very heavy. It is water's density that helps things to float, or stay buoyant. However, the further down you go, the more pressure the water forces on you.

Cold deep current

Warm surface current

◀ Cold water is denser than warm water, and it sinks to the ocean depths near the polar regions.

Deep water formation

Warm surface current

Cold deep current

◀ Water travels in currents around the world. The largest and deepest of these form a system called the global conveyor.

DEPTH (METRES)

0 — 1 atm

10 — 2 atm

20 — 3 atm

30 — 4 atm

40 — 5 atm

764 At the surface, wind creates waves and the Moon's gravitational pull causes tides. Further down, other forces are in action. Ocean water is continually moving, passing around the globe in giant streams called currents. If you were to get caught in one of these strong, deep currents, after 1000 years you would have journeyed all around the world!

▶ Water pressure is measured in atmospheres (atm). Pressure increases with depth, squashing the molecules of air in this balloon.

766 Although you will soon be cold, you may notice that the temperature of the water around you doesn't change much. Ocean water has great heat capacity, which means that it warms up slowly and cools down slowly too. It can hold on to its temperature about 4000 times better than air can.

▼ Many enormous animals, such as this basking shark, live in the ocean. The dense, salty seawater supports their great weight.

767 The good news is that you won't have to work hard to get food. If you stay still, it will float right past your nose. Because water is dense, tiny creatures and particles of food are suspended in it. Some sea creatures can wave tentacles to catch food, or just open their mouths as they swim!

◄ A magnified view of plankton, tiny animals and plants that float or swim in seawater. They often become food for bigger animals.

MAKING WATER HEAVY

You will need:
two identical cups containing the same amount of water   salt

Add salt to one of the cups and stir. Continue until no more salt will dissolve. Weigh both cups – the salty one should be heavier. Salty water is denser and heavier than fresh water.

▶ A beaker of ocean water may look dirty, but it is full of substances that are food for tiny organisms called phytoplankton.

768 You should never drink seawater. It has lots of minerals, called salts, dissolved in it. A single bath of seawater contains 2.8 kilograms of salts. Most of that is sodium chloride (common salt). Gases, such as oxygen and nitrogen are also dissolved in seawater.

Water 96.5%

Other elements 0.6%

Sodium 1%

Salt 3.5%

Chloride 1.9%

337

The Light Zone

769 The top 200 metres of the ocean is called the Light Zone. At the continental shelf, sunlight can reach all the way to the seabed. However, within 10 metres of the water's surface, nearly all of the red parts of light have been absorbed, which means that many creatures appear dull in colour.

▲ The shiny scales on tuna fish reflect sunlight as they dart from side to side, to confuse their predators.

▶ Green turtles have to visit the surface to breathe air, then they dive to feed on marine plants.

770 Sunlight provides the energy for plants to grow. Marine plants such as seaweed need light in order to make food from carbon dioxide and water, in a process called photosynthesis. Plants also produce oxygen, the gas we breathe, and without it there would be no life in the oceans.

◀ Marine plants, including seaweed (shown here) and phytoplankton, are called algae.

◀ Emperor penguins can stay underwater for up to 20 minutes at a time, hunting for fish.

I DON'T BELIEVE IT!

Six billion tonnes of phytoplankton grow in the Light Zone every year and they produce half of the oxygen in our atmosphere. Without them there would be almost no animal life in the oceans, and few animals on land either.

771 Many marine plants are almost invisible. They are called phytoplankton and are so tiny that they have to be viewed with a microscope. Phytoplankton begin a food web that supports nearly all ocean life. They are eaten by microscopic animals, called zooplankton, and bigger animals too.

772 The Light Zone is bright and full of food, making it a busy habitat. Fish such as anchovies and sardines come to feed on swarms of plankton. In turn larger animals, such as sharks, come to prey upon the fish. Even birds, such as pelicans and penguins, enter this habitat to grab what food they can.

773 Most swimming animals of the Light Zone can move into deeper water to escape from predators. At around a depth of 200 metres almost all sunlight has been absorbed and darkness takes over in the Twilight Zone.

▼ Warm-water corals need sunlight to grow, and they build reefs in the Light Zone.

The Twilight Zone

774 From a depth of 200 to 1000 metres lies the Twilight Zone. Just enough light reaches this zone for animals to see, and be seen by. Predators and prey battle it out in a constant fight for survival.

Siphuncle

Jaws

Brain

Tentacles

Digestive gland

Stomach

Gonad

Funnel

Gills

Heart

775 The nautilus can swim, float and move up and down in the Twilight Zone. It lives in the outermost chamber of its shell, and its inner chambers are filled with gas or liquid. By pushing gas into the chambers, liquid is forced out and the nautilus becomes lighter – and floats up. When the gas is replaced with liquid, the nautilus sinks.

▲ A nautilus fills the chambers in its shell with water or gas by a tube called a siphuncle. Like octopuses and squid, a nautilus propels itself by pushing water out of its funnel.

776 Mighty sperm whales plunge into the Twilight Zone when they are hunting squid. They can dive to depths of 1000 metres and hold their breath for up to 90 minutes at a time. The deepest known dive of any sperm whale was 3000 metres, and the whale swam at a speed of 4 metres a second to get there!

◄ Huge sperm whales are mammals, which means they have to return to the surface to breathe.

777 It is hard to see if your eyes are deep inside your head. Barreleye fish don't mind because they have see-through heads. They swim with their big, green eyes peering upwards. When the fish sees its prey, it flips its body upright and rotates its eyes in its head. This allows the fish to keep its prey in view while swimming up to grab it.

Eye

Mouth

Nostril

◄ A barreleye fish's eyes are very sensitive, which help it to spot its prey in low light.

778 There are few hard surfaces to attach to, so animals in the Twilight Zone are mostly floaters and swimmers. Many have unusual shapes and their bodies are often soft and watery. Comb jellies are soft-bodied animals, but they can turn hard by contracting muscles. Some have long, sticky tentacles to grab prey.

▼ Comb jellies swim by beating rows of comb-like plates, which bend light rays to make colourful shimmers.

▼ Sea pens anchor themselves to the seafloor in the Twilight Zone. They feed on plankton by catching it in their feathery branches.

TRUE OR FALSE?

1. Barreleye fish have see-through heads.
2. Sperm whales can breathe underwater.
3. Nautiluses swim using fins.
4. The Twilight Zone is pitch black.

Answers:
1. True 2. False 3. False 4. False

341

Monster of the deep

779 **Giant squid are monsters of the deep.** They can grow to 15 metres in length, including tentacles, which alone can grow to 12 metres. Their eyes are thought to be the largest of any animal. Each one is up to 40 centimetres in diameter!

780 Little is known about these mysterious animals because they live in the Twilight Zone. Giant squid can swim well, and with their good eyesight they can spot fishing nets and move swiftly away. Very few have ever been caught, and what is known about them has been revealed from dead specimens, or remains that have been found in the stomachs of sperm whales.

▶ Giant squid have a reputation as fearsome monsters. In fact, they are more likely to be gentle giants of the deep.

ANIMAL GIANTS

Put these animal giants in order of size, from largest to smallest:

African elephant
Hercules beetle
Blue whale   Giant squid

Answer:
Blue whale, giant squid, African elephant, Hercules beetle

Teeth

Sucker

Tentacle

Eye

Beak

Arm

781 People have known about giant squid for hundreds of years. The first one to be recorded was found in Iceland in 1639, and the stories and myths began. People feared that these creatures could sink ships or grab people on deck. When sperm whales were discovered with scars caused by giant squid suckers, people realized that these predators battle with large whales.

782 Giant squid are predators. No one knows for sure how they live, but like other squid they probably hunt fish, octopuses and smaller squid. Their muscular tentacles are equipped with giant, toothed suckers that can grab hold of wriggly prey.

▶ The eye of a giant squid has a diameter bigger than a person's head.

The Dark Zone

783 Below 1000 metres absolutely no light can penetrate. So far from the Sun's rays, this habitat is intensely cold, and there is bone-crushing pressure from the enormous weight of water above. It is called the Dark Zone, and it extends to 4000 metres below the ocean's surface.

784 It snows in the Dark Zone! Billions of particles fall down towards the seabed, and this is called marine snow. This 'snow' is made up of droppings from animals above, and animals and plants that have died. Small flakes often collect together to become larger and heavier, drifting down up to 200 metres a day. Marine snow is an important source of food for billions of deep-sea creatures.

▲ Fierce-looking fangtooth fish can swim to depths of around 5000 metres, into the Abyssal Zone, when they follow their prey.

I DON'T BELIEVE IT!

The orange roughy lives in deep water where its colour appears black if any light reaches it. This is believed to be one of the longest living fish – one individual allegedly reached 149 years of age.

785 A fangtooth fish may have enormous teeth, but at only 15 centimetres in length, these fish are not as scary as they sound. Fangtooths have poor eyesight, and in the Dark Zone other senses are just as valuable. These fish can detect tiny movements in the surrounding water, which they follow to find their prey.

786
Greenland sharks live under the Arctic ice at depths of up to 2000 metres. Not much is known about how these giant fish live because of their unusual habitat. Nearly all Greenland sharks are blind because of parasites, tiny creatures that damage their eyes. However, they have a good sense of smell, which they use to sniff out the rotting flesh of other dead animals to eat. They also prey on seals and other sharks.

▲ Greenland sharks can grow to 6 metres long. They live in the Arctic and often swim close to shore, but pose little threat to humans.

▼ Giant isopods are crustaceans that live in the Dark Zone. They are related to crabs, shrimps, lobsters and woodlice, and can reach a length of 35 centimetres. Isopods have long antennae that help them feel their way in the dark.

787
Giant isopods are peculiar crawling creatures that look like huge woodlice. Their bodies are protected by tough plates, and they can roll themselves up into a ball when they come under attack. Isopods live on the seabed, searching for soft-bodied animals to eat.

The Abyssal Zone

Continental shelf

Continental slope

Abyssal plain

Underwater volcano

▼ The Abyssal Zone is an enormous seascape of mountains, volcanoes, trenches and muddy plains.

Ocean ridge

Deep-sea trench

Sea mount

ABYSSAL ZONE

788 Below the Dark Zone is the Abyssal Zone, or abyss, which reaches from 4000 to 6000 metres. Where the continental slope ends, the sea floor stretches out in a giant plain. Around one-third of the seabed is in the Abyssal Zone.

789 The abyssal plains have mountains (called sea mounts), trenches and valleys. Many sea mounts are drowned volcanoes, and there may be 30,000 of them in the world's oceans. The sides of the mounts are sheer, which causes water to flow upwards in a process called upwelling. This flow of water brings nutrients to the area, and many animals live in these habitats.

790 Most waters of the Abyssal Zone contain little food. Animals rely on finding marine snow, which may take several months to fall from the surface, or hunting other deep-sea creatures. Many are scavengers, which means they only feed when they find food, such as the remains of other animals that have died. With a shortage of food, creatures here move around very little to save energy.

◀ Basket stars can survive in the abyss. Each arm is branched into many smaller parts to catch particles of marine snow.

▼ There are around 60 types of hagfish. They have eel-like bodies with four hearts, but no bones.

791 An Atlantic hagfish is a slimy, fish-like animal of the abyss with disgusting eating habits. It is nearly blind but has a good sense of smell, which helps it to find prey. A hagfish has tentacles and hooks around its mouth to grab hold of its victim's flesh. Then it burrows into the prey's body, eating its insides. A hagfish can survive for many months without feeding again.

792 The most common fish in the Abyssal Zone are called rattails, or grenadiers. There are around 300 different types of rattails in the world and scientists estimate that there are at least 20 billion of just one type – that's more than three times the number of humans!

▼ Rattails are slow movers so they probably creep up on their prey to catch them. They are also scavengers, eating anything they can find on the seabed. Here, they swarm around a bait cage and the submersible *Mir I*.

347

793 One of the world's strongest types of glass is made by a creature of the abyss. The Venus' flower basket is a type of glass sponge that has a strong skeleton. Glass sponges build their structures from strands of silica, the material used to make glass.

▶ The Venus' flower basket lives at depths of 5000 metres in the ocean waters of Southeast Asia.

794 Sponges are the simplest of all animals. Most sponges live in oceans and they are attached to solid surfaces. Since they can't move to find food, sponges create water currents that move through their bodies so they can filter out any particles of food.

Osculum

Flow of water

Spicules
(strands of silica)

Pore

▶ Special cells near the pores have tail-like parts, that move in a beating motion. This sucks water into the sponge, and out through the osculum.

795 Sponges don't have normal body parts, tissues or organs. They are more like an organized collection of cells. Their bodies lack bones, so they are supported by a structure made from tough materials, such as silica. Engineers examine creatures and plants that build tough structures to help them design better buildings.

◄ The Venus' flower basket is strong because it has a lattice structure. The Eiffel Tower in France has a similar structure.

797 The Venus' flower basket glows with bright colours around its base. In the darkness, the lights and colours may attract tiny, curious creatures, which are swept into the sponge by water currents and eaten.

796 The Venus' flower basket builds its structure by 'gluing' together needles of silica, each no thicker than a human hair. The construction follows a beautiful pattern, which gives the sponge great strength to withstand the water pressure at depths of 5000 metres or more.

▶ Cloud sponges are another type of deep-living glass sponge. They can provide a safe living area for other small animals.

The Hadal Zone

798 The oceans plunge to depths greater than 6000 metres in only a few places, called trenches. This is called the Hadal Zone, named after the Greek word 'hades', which means 'unseen'. It's the perfect name for the most mysterious habitat on Earth.

Mariana Trench 11,034 metres
Tonga Trench 10,882 metres
Philippine Trench 10,540 metres
Kuril-Kamchatka Trench 10,500 metres
Kermadec Trench 10,047 metres
Bonin Trench 9994 metres
New Britain Trench 9940 metres
Izu Trench 9780 metres

Mount Everest 8848 metres

▲ Earth's largest mountain, Everest, could fit into eight of the world's deepest trenches.

799 The deepest of all trenches is the Mariana Trench in the Pacific Ocean, which plunges to 11,034 metres. It is 2550 kilometres long and about 70 kilometres wide. This trench was created when two massive plates in the Earth's crust collided millions of years ago.

800 Scientists know very little about animals that live in the Hadal Zone. Collecting live animals from this depth causes great problems because their bodies are suited to high water pressure. When they are brought to the surface the pressure drops, and they die.

► Snailfish thrive in the ocean's deepest waters and have been found at depths of more than 7000 metres. They have large heads and bodies that taper to slender tails.

HADAL ZONE

Propeller

Snorkel

TRIESTE

Tunnel

Water ballast
tanks

▶ *Trieste* is a deep-sea
submarine that was built
in Italy and launched in
1953. The scientists sat
inside the crew sphere,
which hangs below the
large gasoline tank.

Gasoline
tanks

Iron pellet ballast
hopper

Crew
sphere

Window

▼ Walsh (left) and Picard
(centre) spent 20 minutes in
the Mariana Trench before
returning to the surface.

801 A submersible, called the *Trieste*,
was built in the 1950s, which could dive to the
Hadal Zone. In 1960, explorers Don Walsh and Jacques
Piccard climbed aboard and began one of the most
dangerous journeys ever undertaken. It took five hours
to descend to 10,911 metres in the Mariana Trench
and here they saw the deepest-known crustacean – a
red shrimp. Other similar creatures called amphipods
have been collected at depths of 10,500 metres.

CURIOUS CREATURES

Draw a picture of your own
Hadal Zone creature. It should
probably be dark-coloured,
with tiny eyes, or none at all,
and very ugly. Body parts that
help it feel its way around a
dark habitat would be helpful.

802 The deepest-living fish are believed
to belong to a family called *Abyssobrotula*.
One fish, *Abyssobrotula galatheae*, was
captured in 1970 at a depth of
8370 metres. It was found by explorers
in the Puerto Rico Trench. Scientists
tried to bring the fish to the surface,
but it did not survive the journey.

Muds and oozes

803 **The remains of all marine creatures eventually get eaten or drift down to the seabed.** These remains, which are mostly marine snow, become deep-sea sediments. They form layers of muddy ooze that can be up to 450 metres thick.

804 Most creatures that live on the seafloor are scavengers. A dead whale can provide food for millions of other animals, including shrimp-like amphipods and copepods, worms, rattails and hagfish.

Rattails

Greenland shark

Amphipods

Hagfish

Crab

KEY
1. Crabs, hagfish, amphipods, rattails and sharks strip the flesh from the fresh body.
2. Next, worms are the main colonizers, living off the enriched sediments.
3. Finally, the whale's bones produce sulphides – chemicals that bacteria, mussels and clams feast on.

805 **The muddy layer of the abyssal plain may look smooth, but close up there are tiny trails and holes.** Every handful of mud contains millions of microscopic animals. Foraminifera and radiolarians are tiny shelled single-celled organisms that live in the sediments. When they die, their shells dissolve into the muddy ooze.

806 The abyssal plains are home to many types of sea cucumbers.

These sausage-shaped animals are common in this habitat. Some burrow in the mud, while others can swim. Most move over the seafloor, picking up any bits of food they can find.

▼ It can take up to 100 years for a whale carcass to be devoured. More than 30,000 different types of animal feed and live off the carcass at different stages.

Mussels and clams

③

Bacterial mat

②

Squat lobster

Polychaete worms

I DON'T BELIEVE IT!

The seabed of the Antarctic Ocean has some mega-sized animals. Scientists found giant spiders and worms, and fish with huge eyes and body parts that scientists described as 'dangly bits'!

▼ Tripod fish stand still for hours at a time, facing the water currents, and wait for food to drift towards them.

807 Tripod fish have very long spines, called rays, on their fins.

They use these to stand on the muddy seabed without sinking as they wait for prey to drift by. They are almost blind but can sense vibrations made by other animals nearby.

Deep heat

808 The deep ocean floor is mainly a cold place, where animals struggle to survive. However, there are some extraordinary areas where the water is heated to temperatures of 400°C and living things thrive.

▼ The minerals in the water produce dark clouds that look like smoke, and these vents are called 'black smokers'. Over time, they build up rocky structures called chimneys, which can grow to the height of a 15-storey building.

809 Below the Earth's surface is a layer of hot, semi-liquid rock, called **magma**. In places, magma is close to the ocean floor. Water seeps into cracks in rocks, called hydrothermal vents, and is heated. The water dissolves minerals from the rocks as it travels up towards the ocean floor, and bursts through a vent like a fountain.

810 The first hydrothermal vents were discovered in the Pacific Ocean in the 1970s. Since then, others have been found in the Atlantic, Indian and Arctic Oceans. The largest known region of hydrothermal vents lies near the Mid-Atlantic Ridge and is the size of a football pitch.

KEY
1. Vent mussel
2. Ratfish
3. Vent crab
4. Vent octopus
5. Chimney
6. Sea spider
7. Tube worms

811 Some hydrothermal vents do not support much life, other than microscopic creatures.

Others support colonies of limpets, shrimps, starfish and tube worms, which survive without any sunlight. They are able to live and grow due to the minerals in the super-heated water from the vents.

▲ Hydrothermal vents known as 'white smokers' release cooler water and plumes of different minerals to black smokers.

812 Vent tube worms can grow to 2 metres long and they live without eating anything.

Each worm is attached to the seabed and is protected by the tube it lives in. A red plume at the top collects seawater, which is rich in minerals. These minerals are passed to bacteria in the worm's body, and are then turned into nutrients.

Plume

Blood vessel

◄ Bacteria that live inside the tube worm turn the minerals into food, which the worm needs to survive.

Heart

Bacteria

Tube

UNDER PRESSURE

You will need:

milk carton   sticky tape

With an adult's help, make four holes on one side of an old milk carton, one above the other. Put sticky tape over the holes and fill the carton with water. Hold it over a bowl while you pull the tape off. Water will pour out fastest from the bottom hole because it has the most pressure on it.

Deep-sea coral

813 Tiny creatures called coral polyps build large reefs in the cold, deep ocean. Coral reefs are often found in warm, shallow waters, and they attract a wide variety of life. Cold-water reefs are not such varied habitats, but there may be more cold-water reefs than warm-water ones.

814 Coral polyps have tube-shaped bodies and tentacles around their mouths. All polyps feed by filtering food particles from the water, and they have thousands of tiny stingers to stun bigger prey.

815 Coral polyps produce a hard substance called calcium carbonate, which forms a protective cup around them. Over time, the stony cups collect and grow into a reef, held together by a cement of sand, mud and other particles.

I DON'T BELIEVE IT!

Air pollution from carbon dioxide causes the oceans to become more acidic. This stops polyps, especially cold-water ones, from being able to grow their stony skeletons.

Bubble gum coral

Flytrap anemone

Lophelia pertusa

Squat lobster

▲ A specimen of bamboo coral is carefully lifted from the deep sea in a collection box that is attached to a submersible.

▼ Cold–water coral creates a special habitat where other animals can live, find food and shelter. A group of living things that depend on one habitat like this is called an ecosystem.

816 A type of cold–water coral polyp called *Lophelia* is the most common reef builder in the Atlantic Ocean. One reef can cover 2000 square kilometres and is home to animals such as squat lobsters, long-legged crabs, and fish – especially babies called larvae.

817 Other cold–water communities have been found in the deep oceans. Engineers drilling for oil in the Gulf of Mexico found cold seeps (places where gases leak out of cracks in the rocks) and animal life thrived nearby. The gases are an energy source for bacteria that feed there. Animals that feed on the bacteria are in turn eaten by crabs, corals, worms and fish.

Brittle stars

Alfonsino fish

Gorgonian sea fan

On the move

818 Travelling in the ocean is different from travelling in air. Animals can simply float or drift along because they weigh 50 times less in water than they do in air. Currents help too. They can bring food to animals that are attached to the seabed, or they can carry animals towards food.

◀ Little sea butterflies are a type of sea snail. They can swim slowly through the water by flapping their 'wings', or they float in the currents.

▼ For this tube anemone, being attached to the seabed means it is impossible to make a quick getaway from the giant nudibranch that is attacking it (bottom).

819 Animals caught in deep–sea currents have to go with the flow, unless they are strong swimmers. Swimming takes 830 times as much energy as staying still because water is dense and heavy. Tiny zooplankton are weak swimmers, so when they get caught in currents, they drift along until they become free.

820 Many marine animals cannot move from one place to another. They are attached to the seabed and stay there, waiting for food to come to them. These animals, such as sea lilies and tube anemones, have feathery tentacles that they use to filter the seawater and collect particles of food.

821 **Billions of animals undertake a journey every night.** They travel up from the Twilight and Dark Zones into the Light Zone to feed, and return to deeper water in the morning. This mass movement is called a vertical migration and it represents the largest migration, or animal journey, on Earth.

822 **Lantern fish are mighty movers of the ocean.** The champion is called *Ceratoscopelus warmingii* and it lives at a depth of 1800 metres in the day. At night it swims upwards to depths of 100 metres to feed and avoid predators, and then it swims back. This feat is like a person running three marathons in a day!

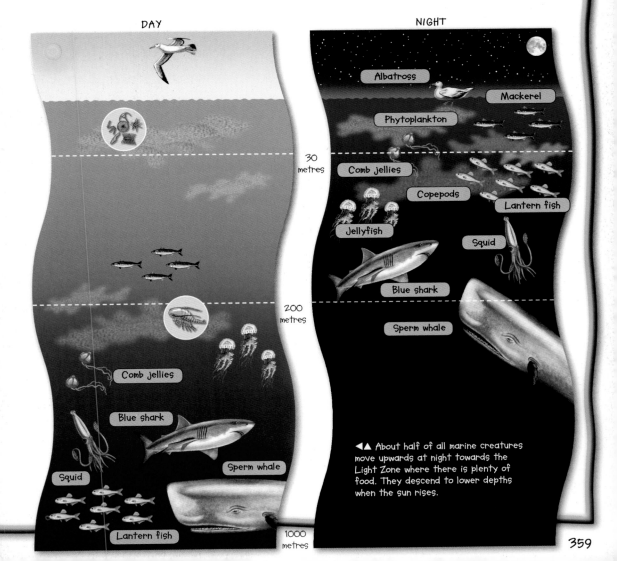

DAY

NIGHT

Albatross

Mackerel

Phytoplankton

30 metres

Comb jellies

Copepods

Lantern fish

Jellyfish

Squid

Blue shark

200 metres

Sperm whale

Comb jellies

Blue shark

Squid

Sperm whale

Lantern fish

1000 metres

◄▲ About half of all marine creatures move upwards at night towards the Light Zone where there is plenty of food. They descend to lower depths when the sun rises.

Breathing and diving

Gill slits

823 Animals need to take a gas called oxygen into their bodies to release energy from food. Taking in oxygen is called breathing, and the process of using it to release energy is called respiration. Most marine animals are specially adapted to take in dissolved oxygen from seawater.

▲ As a shark swims, water enters its mouth, passes over its gills where oxygen is absorbed, and then leaves through the gill slits.

MAKE A SWIM BLADDER

Blow up a balloon. It is now filled with gas, like a swim bladder. Put the balloon in a bowl or bath of water and try to make it sink. Now fill the balloon with water, and see if it will float.

824 Fish breathe using gills. Like our lungs take oxygen from air, gills take in oxygen from water. Most fish also have a swim bladder, which helps them to cope with the changing pressure as they swim deeper. A swim bladder is a gas-filled sac that expands as a fish moves upwards, and shrinks as it descends. All deep-sea fish have gills, but they do not have swim bladders because the immense pressure would crush them.

Blowhole

◀ Whales, such as this killer whale, come to the surface to breathe. They have one or two blowholes on the top of their heads. These are like nostrils, and this is where air enters the body. When air is breathed out of a blowhole it creates a water spout.

As a sperm whale dives, its ribs and lungs contract (shrink). They expand again when the whale surfaces.

The whale's heartbeat slows by half so less oxygen is needed.

The spermaceti organ is a huge mass of oil. It probably helps the whale to dive deep by changing its ability to float.

The nasal passages fill with cool water to help the whale sink.

▲ The sperm whale is adapted for diving in very deep water. It can stay underwater for up to 90 minutes while hunting for giant squid.

825 Seals, dolphins and whales are air-breathing mammals, but their bodies are adapted to life in water. The sperm whale can store oxygen in its blood and muscles, which allows it to descend to over 1000 metres to hunt. Its flexible ribcage allows the whale's lungs to shrink during a dive.

826 Super-speedy pilot whales are called 'cheetahs of the deep'. During the day, these predators swim at depths of around 300 metres, but at night they plunge to 1000 metres in search of prey. Pilot whales can plummet 9 metres a second at top swimming speed. They need to be fast to catch their prey of large squid, but also because they need to get back to the surface to breathe.

▼ Most marine worms have feathery gills that absorb oxygen from the water. However, some do not have gills and absorb oxygen through their skin.

827 Simple creatures do not have special body parts for breathing. They can absorb oxygen from the water directly through their skins. The amount of oxygen in the water falls from the surface to a depth of around 1000 metres, but it increases again at greater depths.

828 Animals of the deep create their own light to attract prey, a mate or to confuse predators. This is called bioluminescence and it takes place in organs called photophores. These usually produce blue light, but some animals can glow with green, red or yellow light.

Bioluminescent lure used to attract prey

◄ A shortnose greeneye fish produces its own light. In the dark, it glows green, especially its eyes.

Under white light

In the dark

Light rays

Lens

Skin

► The special cells inside a photophore that produce light are called photocytes.

Colour filter

Photocytes (light-producing cells)

Reflector

829 Hatchet fish are deceivers of the Twilight Zone. Photophores on their bellies produce light and disguise the fishes' outlines when seen from below, against the faint light. Hatchet fish can also adjust the light to match the brightness of any light from above.

◄ The viperfish has rows of photophores along its underside. These help to hide it from predators below.

830 Spotted lantern fish use their photophores to attract mates.
They are one of the brightest deep-sea fish, with brilliant displays of bioluminescence along their sides and bellies. The photophores are arranged in different patterns depending on whether the fish is male or female, and what type of lantern fish it is. This helps the fish to find the right mate.

831 It is not just fish that can glow in the dark.
Mauve stinger jellyfish emit a beautiful violet-blue colour when they are disturbed. Firefly squid not only cover their bodies with lights, they can also produce a cloud of glowing particles that distracts predators while they make a quick getaway.

▶ Mauve stinger jellyfish produce quick flashes of light when they sense movement in the water. They even flash when waves pass over them at the ocean's surface.

832 Tiny vampire squid have enormous eyes and can produce light all over their bodies whenever they want to.
These squid are able to control their bioluminescence, producing dazzling displays of patterned light that can be dimmed or brightened, probably to scare off predators. When a vampire squid is hunting it does not light up. This means it can surprise its prey.

BIG WORD, LITTLE WORD
Use the word 'bioluminescence' to create as many as new words as you can by rearranging the letters. Each word must be at least two letters long. Use a dictionary to check the spelling of your words.

363

Deep-sea food

833 The ocean food chain begins in the Light Zone. Phytoplankton use the Sun's energy to grow. In turn, they are eaten by other creatures, passing on energy and nutrients. It takes a long time for energy and nutrients to filter down to the sea floor, so many deep-sea animals scavenge food, eating whatever they find, while others hunt.

▼ Nearly all energy used by marine life comes from the Light Zone. Phytoplankton begin the nutrient cycle, and upward-flowing water currents complete it by bringing nutrients back to the surface.

Sun

Phytoplankton

Zooplankton

Upwelling of nutrients

Carnivores

Faeces and animal remains fall as marine snow

Bacteria and bottom feeders such a sea cucumbers process marine snow, releasing nutrients

834 Copepods and krill (zooplankton) may be small but they play a big role in the deep-ocean ecosystem. These tiny, plant-eating crustaceans exist in their billions. They swim up to the surface every evening to try to avoid being eaten. In the morning they swim back down into the deep, dark waters. Krill can live to depths of 2000 metres.

I DON'T BELIEVE IT!

One krill is not much bigger than a paperclip, but the total weight of all the krill in the world is greater than the total weight of all the people on the planet!

◄ Goblin sharks have soft, flabby bodies and long, strange-looking snouts. They are pinkish white in colour.

835 Large predators, such as sharks, seals and whales, may reach the Dark Zone, but few go deeper. Goblin sharks swim slowly in the Dark Zone and they have snouts that may help them to find food. Their huge jaws can snap forwards to grab prey such as small fish and squid.

▼ Gulper eels can grown to 2 metres in length. They have pink photophores on their tails to attract prey.

837 Fangtooth fish are also known as ogrefish. They use their unusually sharp, long teeth to grab hold of squid and fish. Food is scarce in the deep ocean, but with such large jaws, fangtooths attempt to eat almost any prey that comes along, even animals that are larger than themselves.

► This soft-bodied animal called a predatory tunicate lives in the Twilight Zone. When an animal swims into its hood-like mouth it closes shut like a Venus flytrap.

836 Gulper eels are all mouth. These predators of the Dark Zone have enormous mouths, but small teeth. It may be that gulper eels use their big mouths for catching lots of small prey at a time, rather than one large, meaty prey.

365

Anglerfish

838 If you cannot find food in the dark, make it come to you! Anglerfish have long growths on their heads that work like fishing rods, and the tips are coated in glowing bacteria. Other animals are attracted to the glowing light, called a lure, and are quickly snapped up by the anglerfish.

▲ In the 2003 Disney Pixar movie *Finding Nemo*, Marlin and Dory narrowly escape the jaws of an anglerfish.

839 There are many different types of anglerfish and all look very strange. The hairy anglerfish is one of the strangest and it lives at depths of up to 1500 metres. It gets its name from its fins, which have long spikes, and the sensitive hairs that cover its body.

Tassel-chinned angler

Long-rod angler

Deep-sea angler

— Males —

► Two tiny males are attached to this female Regan's anglerfish. These anglerfish are sometimes called phantom anglerfish.

840 Finding a mate in the dark can be tough, so some male anglerfish stay attached to a female! The males are much smaller than the females, so they can grab hold and hitch a lift that lasts for life. While scientists have found many types of female anglerfish they are still searching for some of their tiny male relations!

842 A dragonfish also lures prey to its death. When a dragonfish spies a shrimp to eat it produces a red spotlight made by photophores below its eyes. The shrimp can't see red, so it is unaware it is being hunted. The dragonfish then snaps up its prey in its large mouth, full of ultra-sharp teeth.

▼ Monkfish are so well camouflaged that they are almost impossible to spot when lying on the ocean floor.

841 Anglers are types of anglerfish that lie on the seafloor. Their wide, flat bodies are covered in soft, fleshy growths that help them to blend in with the mud where they hide. Anglers use their fins to shuffle along, flicking their lures as they go. They are often caught and sold as food, and also better known as monkfish.

Hide and seek

843 Throughout the animal kingdom, creatures use colours and patterns to hide from predators or prey. In the deep oceans, colours appear different because of the way light is absorbed by water. Colours, other than black and red, are not very useful for camouflage. Deep-sea creatures have developed special ways to avoid being detected.

▲ Deep-sea glass squid are mostly transparent, apart from some brightly coloured polka dots on their bodies.

844 Some deep-sea animals are well adapted for hiding and seeking. Glass squid are almost completely transparent, so light passes through their bodies, helping them go unnoticed. A thin body can help too, because it is hard to see from certain angles. With little light around, enormous eyes are useful. Big eyes can collect more light and turn it into hazy images.

▲ Spookfish have enormous eyes, giving them very good vision.

845 Silvery scales on a fish's back are perfect for reflecting light and confusing a predator. When shimmering scales are seen against dim rays of light in the Twilight Zone, the outline of a fish's body becomes less obvious, and it fades into the background or even disappears.

Silvery, reflective scales

Light-producing photophores

846 When there is no light, animals rely on senses other than sight. Many deep-sea animals can feel vibrations in the water. Shrimp have sensory organs all over their bodies, including their antennae, which can detect movements nearby. Many fish can also sense the small electrical fields generated by other living things.

▲ By using their photophores to produce light and their silvery scales to reflect light, hatchet fish become almost invisible to predators.

▶ The snipe eel's jaws curve away from each other so they never fully close.

847 Snipe eels have long, ribbon-like bodies, and jaws that look like a bird's bill. They live at depths of up to 1800 metres and can grown to 1.5 metres in length. As males mature their jaws shrink, but their nostrils grow longer. This probably improves their sense of smell and helps them to find females.

ODD ONE OUT

Which of these animals uses colour and pattern to scare other animals, rather than to hide?
Zebra Wasp Tiger
Leaf insect
Arctic fox

Answer:
Wasp

369

Searching the deep

▼ This timeline shows how technology has developed, improving ways of exploring the deep ocean.

1775 The *Turtle* was an early, one-man submarine

1837 The waterproof Siebe diving suit was developed

1872 HMS *Challenger* set sail for a four-year study of the deep ocean

1882 The USS *Albatross* continued this important research

1925 *Meteor* began mapping the seafloor

1934 William Beebe and Otis Barton used a bathysphere to make the first deep-ocean dive

848 Early ocean explorers had to overcome many problems. Divers needed a supply of air and to be able to cope with the water pressure. If divers ascend too quickly, the sudden change in pressure can cause the bends – a life-threatening sickness.

849 The first diving suit was invented in the 1830s. It was made of waterproof canvas and rubber, and allowed divers to descend to around 60 metres. About 40 years later a ship called the HMS *Challenger* explored the deeper oceans.

Thruster

Oxygen supply

Boat cable

▲ Newt Suits have joints, so divers can move their arms and legs.

Pincer

850 Today's deep-diving suits are made of metal. These Newt Suits allow divers to work at a depth of 300 metres. Suits have thrusters to help divers move underwater, communication systems to link to the boat at the surface, and video cameras.

851 *Alvin* was the first submersible that could take explorers deep into the Dark Zone. It has made more than 4500 dives, and it was on one of these that hydrothermal vents were first discovered. A programme of modernization means *Alvin* will be able to reach depths exceeding 6000 metres.

853 There are other ways to find out the secrets of the deep, including taking pictures from space. Satellite images provide information about deep water currents and the undersea landscape. Sonar is a method that maps the ocean floor by bouncing sound signals off the seabed.

1960 *Trieste* dived to the Mariana Trench

1964 Deep-sea submarine *Alvin* was built

1984 The *Nautile* can carry up to three people to depths of 6000 metres

1987 The Newt Suit was developed

1988 *Jason*, an underwater ROV, was launched

1990s Satellites were used to map the seafloor

852 One of the safest ways to explore the deep is using a Remotely Operated Vehicle, or ROV. These unmanned submersibles are lowered to the seabed by cables and are operated by the crew of a ship on the surface. In future, ROVs will be able to operate without cables, so they will be able to move around more freely.

▶ The Monterey Bay Aquarium Research Institute has developed a deep-sea robot called the Benthic Rover. It is helping scientists discover more about the effects of global warming on the oceans.

KEY
1 Video camera
2 Water current meter
3 Respirometer measures gases in the sediments

Sea changes

854 Billions of years ago, life began in the oceans — and this environment is still home to most living things. Every part of the ocean matters, from the shallow seashores to the deepest trenches. It not only provides habitats for marine animals and plants, it also provides us with food and greatly affects our atmosphere and climate.

▶ Robot submersibles are used to gather valuable information about the deep ocean. They can deploy bait cages to attract animals for observation and research, and collect samples to take back to the surface for further study.

855 Overfishing threatens all sea life. Krill, for example, are an important source of energy for billions of ocean creatures, but they are now being harvested in huge amounts, especially in the Antarctic. There is a danger that if too much krill is taken for humans to eat, there will not be enough left to support the ocean ecosystems, including deep-ocean life.

856 Pollution is a major problem — rubbish is dumped in the oceans, tankers leak oil and the crisis of carbon dioxide pollution looms. This is caused by burning fossil fuels, which pollutes ocean water and causes the climate to heat up. A new plan is to use the deep oceans to store carbon dioxide. This gas would be collected from power stations and buried deep in the seabed, in a process called carbon capture and storage.

857 The precious deep-ocean habitat is being destroyed by humans faster than we can uncover its mysteries. However, in recent times, people have begun to understand how important it is to respect the oceans and protect their wildlife. Hopefully there is time for nations to work together to avoid further damage, and uncover new secrets of the deep.

I DON'T BELIEVE IT!

If you could take all living things on Earth and fill a giant box with them, ocean life would take up 99.5% of it. The leftover space could hold everything that lives on land!

Index

Entries in **bold** refer to main subject entries. Entries in *italics* refer to illustrations.

A

abyssal plain 320, 352
abyssal zone *334*, **346–347**
acid rain 171
African plate *69*
African rainforests **294–295**, 314, 316
agouti 284, *284*
air 12, 116, 117
 lightning 52
 oxygen 22
 rain 50, 118
 tornado 58
 underwater exploration 0
 weather 108
 wind 126
air pressure 117, 126, 142, *144*, 145, 146, 147
albatross 258, *258*
algae, lakes 21
alligators 287
Alps *19*, 163, *163*
aluminium 179, *179*, 182
Alvin 371, *371*
Amazon rainforest **286–289**, 314, 315
 people **288–289**
Amazonia 282, *286–287*
amber 168, 204, *204*
amethyst 187, *187*
ammonites 196, *196*, *202*, 210, 211, *229*
amphibians 287
Amundsen, Roald 45, 268, 271, *271*
Andes mountains *19*, 27, 43, 71

anemone *358*
 fossils 206
 Southern Ocean 256, *256*
Angel Falls 33, *33*
anglerfish **366–367**
animals,
 adaptations **136–137**
 drought 64
 earthquakes 39
 fossils 168, *168*, 192, 194, 196
 mummification 204
 polar **244–247**, **254–257**, 272
 rainforest 278, **302–303**, **306–309**
 twilight zone **342–343**
ankylosaurs *226*
Anning, Mary 214, *214*
Antarctic Circle 239
Antarctic plate *69*
Antarctica 45, *45*, 47, 124, *125*, **242–243**
 animals **254–257**, 260
 expeditions **270–271**
 ozone hole 273
 South Pole 237, *237*
ants 309, *309*
Archaeopteryx 217, 231, *231*
Archaeoraptor 229
Arctic Circle 239
Arctic foxes 44, *246*
Arctic hares 44, 240, 245
Arctic Ocean 44, **240–241**, 318, *334*
 animals **244–247**, 264
 expeditions **268–269**
 metamorphic rock 165
 North Pole 237, *237*

Arctic Ocean (*cont.*)
 people **262–267**
 pollution 273
 protection 274
Arctic tern 252, *252*
ash (volcanic) *28*, 29, *29*, 66, *67*, 74, 75, **78–79**, 102, *156*
 dangers 84, 85, *85*
 Mount Pinatubo 97, *97*
 Mount Vesuvius 98
Asian rainforests **296–297**
asteroids 166, *166*
Atacama Desert 43
Atlantic Ocean 318, 319, *334*
atmosphere 12, **116–117**
 deforestation 315
 meteoroids 166
 volcanoes *14*, *15*, 102
 water cycle *119*
 weather 108, 144, 146, *146*
atoll 321, *321*
aurora 135, *135*, 239
Australia *42*, 290, 291
autumn *110*, 111, *111*, 137
avalanche 56, *56*, 57, 125, *125*
Azores 71

B

bacteria 22, 49
 fossils 194, 212
 hydrothermal vents 355, *355*
 ocean food chain *364*
 thermal pools 31
barreleye fish 341, *341*
basalt 77, 155, 156
Basilosaurus 217

basket stars *346*
basking shark 324, *324*, *337*
Bates, Henry 286, 308
bats 23, *195*, 217, 302
bauxite 179, *179*
beaches 191
bears 205, 241, 282, *282*
Beaufort Scale 127, *127*
belemnites 197, *197*
biodiversity 278
bioluminescence **362–363**
birds 23, 339
 Antarctica **258–259**
 Archaeopteryx 231
 rainforest 279, **304–305**
birds of paradise 304, 305, *305*
blizzard 56, 57
blubber 247, 248, *251*, 264
blue-green algae 212
bones 184, 194, 195, 200, *201*, 226
boreal forests 241
brazil-nut tree **284–285**
British Museum 215
bronze 179, *179*
Burgess Shale 207, *207*
bush vipers *283*
butterflies *306*, 308

C

cactuses 43
calcite 161, 164, 172, *174*, 175, 185, *185*
caldera 73, *73*, 105
Cambrian Period *169*, *207*, *208*, *209*
camels 136
Canadian Shield 212

carbon 213, *213*
carbon dioxide,
  climate change *44*,
    149, *149*
  plants 300
  volcanoes 90
caribou (reindeer) *240*,
  241, 264, **266–267**
Caspian Sea 34, *34*
cassowaries *283*, 291
cave painting 176
cave salamander 37
caves 24, **36–37**, *151*,
  161
  fossil-hunting 219
Celsius, Anders 143
Centigrade scale 143,
  143
chalk,
  calcite 175, 184
  Cretaceous Period
    209
  fossils 202, *211*
  pigment 176
  sedimentary rock
    160, *160*
Challenger Deep 48,
  49
chameleons 292, *307*
chimps 313, *313*
cliffs 27
  fossil-hunting 219
  rock strata 191
climate 108, 115, 315
climate change
  148–149
  dinosaurs 167
  polar regions 273,
    274
  rainforests 280
cloud forests *281*,
  281, 283, 290, 296,
  298–299
clouds **118–121**, 120,
  120
  atmosphere 116
  hurricane 60

clouds (*cont.*)
  lightning 52, *52*
  monsoons 112
  rain 50, *50*, 118
  snow 124
  thunderstorms 128,
    128
  tornado 58
  water cycle *51*, *119*
  weather forecasting
    145
coal,
  acid rain 171
  fossils fuel 183, *183*
  polar lands 263, 272,
    274
  sedimentary rock
    159
cock-of-the-rock 304,
  304
cockatoo 312
coelacanth 230, *230*
cold-water coral reefs
  356–357
Colorado River 33,
  33, 158, *159*, 210
Columbus, Christopher
  310
comb jellies 341, *341*
comets 166, *166*
Compsognathus 217
conifer trees 241, 280,
  282
continental drift 68,
  68
continental plates 18,
  19, *71*
continental shelf *49*,
  320, *320*, 334, 338
Cope, Edward Drinker
  215, *215*
copper *178*
  alloys 179
  body minerals 185
  fireworks 182, *182*
  pigments 177, *177*
coprolites 231

coral reefs 356
  atolls 321, *321*
  deep ocean **356–357**
  light zone *339*
core, Earth's 68, 152,
  152
craters 15, 21, 73, *73*,
  97, 166, *166*
Cretaceous Period
  208, 209
crevasses *46*, *242*
crocodiles 216, 217
crops 64, 65, 115, 149
crust, Earth's,
  earthquakes 38
  metamorphic rock
    162
  mountain formation
    18, 19, 26, *27*
  oceanic *48*
  plate boundaries 70
  rock cycle 152, *152*
  volcanoes 28, 66, 68,
    72
crystals 174, *174*
  calcite *185*
  cleavage 175
  gemstones 186
  gypsum 37
  Hutton 191
  ice *57*, 124, *124*
  igneous rock 154,
    155
  magma *153*
  metamorphic rock
    162, 163, *163*
  minerals 172, *172*,
    173, 174
currents,
  animals 358
  erosion 171
  ocean 319, 336,
    336
Cuvier, Georges 168,
  198, *198*
cyanobacteria 212
cyclones 60, 130

D
dams 93
dark zone *334*,
  344–345, 359, *359*,
  365, 371
Darwin, Charles 199,
  199, 286
dating fossils **210–211**,
  212
day 16, 111
Dead Sea 34, *35*
deep ocean 48,
  332–333, 335
  animals **362–363**,
    368, 369
  coral **356–357**
  exploration **370–371**
  trench *48*
deer 23, 205, 282
deforestation 280,
  314–315
delta 20, *20*
deserts 24, **42–43**, 114,
  114
  animals 136, *136*
  drought 64
  erosion 171
  flash floods 112, 122,
    122
  sand storm *133*
  tornado 59
diamonds 163, 174,
  175, *186*, 187, *187*,
  188–189
dinosaurs 209
  eggs *223*, 229
  feathers 233, *233*
  fossil sites 216, *216*,
    217, *217*
  fossils 166, 168, 169,
    197, 199, *224*, 225
  mummified 204
  reconstructions
    226
Diprotodon 217
diving suits 370, *370*
doldrums *126*

Index

dolphins 251, **326–327**, 361
dragonfish 367
drought **64–65**, 115, 149
Dust Bowl 65, *65*, 115, *115*
dust devils 59, 133
dust storms 64, 65, *65*, *115*

E
eagle 297, *297*
Earth **12–13**, *13*
  age of 191
  continents *14*
  day and night 111
  formation of **14–15**
  geology **190–191**
  life **22–23**
  magnetic field 211, *211*
  Poles 236
  seasons 110, 238
  spin **16–17**, 44, 238
  temperature **24–25**
earthquakes 24, **38–39**
  tsunamis 38, 41, *41*
  volcanoes 91, 96
earthworms 23
easterlies *126*
echinoids 211
ecosystem 285
  ocean 334, 364
eels 369, *369*
El Niño 64, *64*, 115
electricity,
  generation 88, 127, *127*
  lightning 52, 53, 128
elements 172, 178, 180
elephant birds 312
elephant seals 254, 255, *255*
elephants 23, 198, *198*, 217, *294*

elk 245, *245*
emeralds *186*, 187, *187*
emergent layer 279, *279*
emperor penguins *45*, **260–261**, *274*, *339*
eons 208
epiphytes 299, *299*
epochs 208
Equator 50, 108, *108*, 113, *113*, 126, 280, 282
erosion *151*, **170–171**
  fossil-hunting 219
  rock cycle 152, *152*, 153
  sedimentary rock 158
eruptions **80–81**, 92, 102
  Mount Pinatubo **96–97**
  Mount St Helens **94–95**
  Mount Vesuvius **98–99**
estuaries 20
Eurasian plate *69*
evaporation 50, *51*, *119*
evergreen trees *111*, 282
evolution 233
  fossils 168, 198, 199, 207

F
Fahrenheit scale 143, *143*
fangtooth fish 344, *344*, 365
feathers 227, 244, *260*, 304, 305
feldspar 172, 175
ferns 281, 290
fireworks 182

fish **322–323**
  bioluminescence 362, *362*
  fossil *203*, 214, 216, 217
  gills 360, *360*
  light zone 339
  polar regions 256, 257, *257*, 272, 274
fishermen 330
  polar people 262, *262*
flatfish 323, *323*
flint 160, *160*
floods **62–63**, **122–123**
  climate change 273
  hurricanes 60, 61
  mangrove forest 312
  rain *51*
  volcanoes 86, 87
fluorite *174*, 182, *182*
flying fish 323, *323*
food chain **364–365**
fools gold 181, *181*
forest floor 279, *279*
fossil fuels 183
fossil-hunting 190, 191, **214–215**, **218–221**
fossil sites **216–217**
fossilization **200–201**
fossils **168–169**, **192–195**, **198–199**
  Burgess Shale 207, *207*
  cleaning **222–223**
  Cretaceous Period 208, 209
  dating **210–213**
  displaying **224–225**
  excavation *193*
  famous **230–231**
  formation **200–201**
  geological time scale 208
  living 230
  moulds and casts **202–203**

fossils (*cont.*)
  myths and legends **196–197**
  reconstructions **226–227**
  sedimentary rock 158
  soft-bodied creatures **206–207**
  study **208–209**, **232–233**
  trace 205
  trade **228–229**
Franklin, Benjamin 53
freshwater 34, 35, 42, *43*, *286*
frogs *204*, 216, 279, 287, 289
fronts, weather *144*
frost 141, 170
fulgurites 53, *53*
fumaroles 30, 82, 83, *83*, *90*
fungi 279, 306, *306–307*
fur 227, 244, 245, 247, 248, 264

G
gas (fossil fuel) 183, 190, 272, 274, 331
gases,
  atmosphere 12, 50
  Earth's formation 14, *14*
  fumeroles 83, 90, *90*
  volcanoes 14, 28, 29, *29*, 74, *74*, 75, 78, 80, 81, 97, 102
geckos 136, 303
geese 252, 253
Geiger counter *213*
gemstones **186–189**, 190, 217
geological maps 218
geological time scale **208–209**

geology **190–191**
geothermal energy *82,*
  88, *88*
geysers **30–31**, 82, 83,
  83, 105
giant isopods 345, *345*
giant sloth *199*
giant squid **342–343**
giant titan lily 300,
  300
giant tubeworms 49
gills 322, 360, *360,*
  361
glaciers **46–47**
  Arctic Ocean 240
  erosion 170
  lakes 21
  polar ice caps *242*
  tourism *263*
global warming 44, *44*
  drought 65
  flooding 63
  hurricanes 61
  polar regions 273
  rising sea levels 49
  underwater
    exploration *371*
gneiss 163
goblin sharks 365, *365*
gold 178, 179,
  180–181, 312
Gondwana 290
gorillas *298*, 313
Grand Canyon 33,
  33, 158, *159, 210*
granite 154, 156, 157,
  172
gravity 117, 170
great white shark 324,
  324
greenhouse effect *149,*
  273
Greenland sharks 345,
  345
grenadiers 347
ground squirrels 245,
  245

groundhogs 140, *140*
Gryphea 196
guide fossils 211
Gulf Stream 319
gulper eels 365, *365*
gypsum 37, 159, 160,
  161, 174, 182

H

habitats,
  oceans **336–337**, 339
  rainforest 278, 285
hadal zone *334,*
  350–351
hagfish 347, *347,* 352
hailstones **54–55**, 129,
  129
hammerhead sharks
  325, *325*
hardness 174, *185,* 188
hardwood trees 295
hatchet fish 362, *369*
Hawaiian islands 69,
  69, 101, *101,* 107,
  321, *321*
Hendrickson, Sue 228
Hercules beetle *286*
hibernation *245*
high pressure *117,* 126
Hillary, Edmund 26,
  26
Himalayan Mountains
  18, *19,* 26, 27, 46,
  51
hippos 217
HMS *Challenger* 370,
  370
hot spots 69, 100, *101*
hot springs 30, *31,* 49,
  82, *82*
Howard, Luke *120*
human fossils *219,* 231
humidity 146
hummingbirds 305
hurricanes **60–61**, 127,
  130–131
  climate change 149

hurricanes (*cont.*)
  floods 122
  weather satellites
    147, *147*
Hutton, John 191, *191*
hydrothermal vent 49,
  332, **354–355**

I

ice 46
  Antarctica 45, *45,*
    242, *242,* 243
  Arctic *237,* 240, 248
  erosion 219
  glaciers *242*
  hailstones 54
  lightning 52
  melting 49, 272,
    272, 273
  polar regions 44,
    125, 234, 256, 272,
    272, 273
  preservation 205,
    205
Ice Age 47, 49
ice crystals *57,* 124,
  124, 128
ice storm **56–57**
icebergs 47, 240, 241,
  243, 260, *263*
icebreaker ships *235,*
  262
ichthyosaurs *200,*
  214
igloos *264,* 265
igneous rock 76,
  154–157
  basalt 155, 156
  dolerite 154
  Earth's magnetic
    field 211
  fossils 202
  gold 180
  granite 154, 156,
    157
  Moon rock 167
  pumice 156, *156*

igneous rock (*cont.*)
  rock cycle 152, 153,
    153
  silver 178
iguanas 136, *287,* 328,
  328
Iguanodon 199
Indian Ocean 41, 318,
  319, *334*
Indo Australian plate
  69
inner core, Earth's 68,
  152, *152*
insects,
  fossils 216, *216,* 217,
    225
  rainforests 278, 279
Inuit people 165, *165,*
  262
iron 17, 236
  body minerals 184,
    185
  meteorites 166
  pigments 177
  rock cycle 152, *152*
isobars *144,* 145

J

jaguars *303,* 309
jellyfish 256, *256*
  bioluminescence 363,
    363
  fossil sites 206, *206,*
    207, *207,* 217
jungles 280, 296
Jupiter 104

K

K2 mountain 26
Kalahari Desert *42*
Khan, Genghis 131,
  131
Kilauea *80,* 101,
  107
killer whales 251, 327,
  327
Kobe earthquake *39*

Index

Krakatoa 41, 87, *87*, *100*, 103, *103*
krill 248, 254, 274, 364

L

lahars 86, *86*
lakes **20–21**, **34–35**
  fossilization 200
  volcano 73, *73*
  water cycle *119*
lantern fish 359, 363
lapis lazuli 177, *177*
Lascaux cave paintings 176
lava 28, *29*, 66, *67*, 73, 74, 75, **76–77**, 80, *80*, 81
  diverting 92, 93
  fossils 202
  hazards 84, *84*
  igneous rock 154, *154*, 155
  Mount Vesuvius 99
  pillow 100
  pumice 156
leeches 287
lemmings 245
lemurs 292, *292*, 293
light zone *334*, 335, **338–339**, 364, *364*
lightning **52–53**, **128–129**, 138, *138*
limestone 158, 160, 161, 172
  calcite 175, 185
  caves 36
  fossils 202, 218
  Santana Formation 216
  Solnhofen 217
liverworts 281
lizards 136, 279, 287, 290, *291*
lobsters 330, *330*
logging 289, 310

low pressure 117, *117*, 126, 130
Lucy **231**

M

macaws 307, *307*
Madagascar **292–293**, 312
magma 28, *29*, 66, 68, *68*, 69, 72, 74, *74*, 75, 81
  diamonds 188
  fumeroles 83
  hydrothermal vents 354
  igneous rock 154
  metamorphic rock 162
  minerals 172
  ocean floor *320*
  plate boundaries 70
  rock cycle 152, 153, *153*
magma chamber 72, *72*, *74*, *154*
magnetism,
  Aurora 239
  dating fossils 211, *211*
  Earth 17, *17*, 236
  minerals 174
malachite 177, *177*
mammoths 205, *205*, 213, *220*, 225
mangroves 281, *281*, 312, *312*
Mantell, Gideon 199
mantle 68, 69
  metamorphic rock 163
  plate boundaries 71
  rock cycle 152, *152*, 153
  volcanoes 72, *101*
marble *151*, 164, 185
Mariana Trench 48, 350

Mars 105, *105*
Marsh, Othniel Charles 215, *215*
Mauna Kea 101
Megatherium 199
Mercury *12*
metals **178–179**, 190, 236, 274
metamorphic rock **162–165**
  rock cycle 152, 153, *153*
meteorites 15, 21, 148, *148*, 166, 167
Microraptor 233
Mid-Atlantic Ridge 70, 71, 354
mid-ocean ridge 321
migrations,
  Arctic animals 241, 250, **252–253**, 266
  ocean animals 254, 359, *359*
minerals 150, **172–175**
  aluminium 179
  Arctic 263, 274
  azurite 177, *177*
  body **184–185**
  calcite 172, 175
  Dead Sea 34
  diamonds **188–189**
  erosion 171
  feldspar 172, 175
  fireworks **182**
  fossil fuels 183
  fossils 168, *168*, 201, 202, 203
  galena 175, 177
  gemstones 186
  geology **190–191**
  gold **180–181**
  granite 156
  graphite 189
  hardness 174
  hot springs *82*
  hydrothermal vents 49, 354, 355, *355*

minerals (*cont.*)
  kaolinite 183
  lakes 21
  lapis lazuli 177, *177*
  malachite 177, *177*
  mercury sulphide 176
  metals **178–179**
  metamorphic rock 162, 163, *163*, 164
  mica 172, 175, *175*
  oceans 331
  pigments **176–177**
  quartz 172, 175, *175*
  sea 337
  sedimentary rock 159, 160
  stalactites 161
  volcanic water 89
mining 173, *173*
  Arctic 274
  coal *183*
  diamonds 188
  metals 178
  rainforests 289, 312
  salt 184
mirage 115, *115*
Mohs scale *174*
molecules 117, *172*
monkeys 279, 303, 313
  fossils 217
monkfish 367, *367*
monsoon 51, *51*, 112
Moon 135, *135*, 141
  craters 15, *15*, *166*
  rocks 167, *167*
  tides 336
moose 245, *245*
mosasaur *215*
mosses 279, 281, 290
moths *283*, *293*
mould fossils 168
Mount Aconcagua 27
Mount Broma *69*
Mount Cook *19*, *26*
Mount Etna 93, *93*

Mount Everest 18, 26, 26, *318*
Mount Fuji 106, *107*
Mount Irazu *81*
Mount Kilimanjaro 26, *69*
Mount Mazama *73*
Mount McKinley *27*
Mount Pelée *85*
Mount Pinatubo **96–97**
Mount Rainier *69*
Mount Ruapehu *86*
Mount Spurr *90*
Mount St Helens *28*, *78*, **94–95**, 102
Mount Tambora 29
Mount Thor 27
Mount Unzen 85, *85*
Mount Vesuvius **98–99**, 102, 156
mountain lions 282
mountains 24, **26–27**
  Antarctica 242
  avalanches 56, *56*
  formation **18–19**, *27*, 72
  cloud forests 283
  clouds 118, *118*
  erosion 191
  glaciers 46, 47
  Mauna Kea 101
  ocean floor *49*, 320, 335, 346
  rainforests 281
  rivers 20, *20*
  rock cycle 152, 153
  snow 125
  volcanoes 28, 72
muddy ooze **352–353**
mudflows 84, 86, *86*, 87, 92, 93, 95, *95*, 97, *97*, 123, *123*
mudstone 206
mummification 204, *204*
musk oxen 245, *247*, 264

N
Namib Desert *42*
Nansen, Fridtjof 268, *268*
narwhal **250–251**, 264, 327, *327*
Natural History Museum *224*
nautilus 340, *340*
Neanderthal people 203
New Guinea rainforests 290, 291
New Zealand 31, 290, 291
Niagara Falls 33
night 16, 111
nocturnal animals 302
Norgay, Tenzing 26, *26*
North American plate *69*
North Pole 16, 17, 24, **44–45**, 236, *237*
  day and night 111, *111*
  explorers **268–269**
  seasons 110, *238*, 239
  snow 125
Northern Lights *239*
nutrients 185, 254, 364, *364*
nuts 311

O
oarfish 322, *322*
oases 42, *43*
ocean floor *48*, **320–321**
Oceania rainforests **290–291**
oceanic plate *48*, 71
oceans 12, **48–49**, 147, **318–319**
  deep **332–333**, 335
  drought 64, *64*

oceans (*cont.*)
  formation 15
  habitat **336–337**
  hurricanes 60, 61
  products **330–331**
  rock cycle 152, 153
oil (fossil fuel) 183
  geology 190
  polar regions 263, 272, 274
  seabed 331
  spills 273
Old Faithful geyser 31, *105*
Olduvai Gorge *219*
ooze, seabed **352–353**
opals 187, *187*, 217
orang-utans 296, *296*, 314, *317*
orbit, Earth's *17*, 110, 238
orca 251
orchid bees 285, *285*
ores **178–179**, *178*
Ötzi the Iceman 57
outer core, Earth's *68*, 152, *152*
overfishing 372
Oviraptor 232, *232*
oxbow lakes 20, *20*
oxygen 22, 117, *117*
  fish 322
  fossilization 206
  oceans 337, 338, 339
  plants 300
  respiration 360, 361
oysters 330, 331
ozone hole 273

P
Pacific Ocean 48, 318, *334*
  drought 64, *64*
  Mariana Trench 350
  Mauna Kea 101
Pacific plate 101
pack ice 240

Panderichthys 233, *233*
Pangaea 69
parrots 291, *294*
pearls *186*, *187*, 331, *331*
Peary, Robert 45, 268, *268*
penguins 45, *45*, 47, 237, **260–261**, 273, *273*, *274*, *339*
permafrost 241
permineralization 201
petrels 258
photosynthesis 338
Piccard, Jacques 48, 351
pigments **176–177**
Piltdown Man 231, *231*
piranha fish *282*, 287
pitcher plants 301, *301*
plains, seabed *49*, 320, 334, 335, 346
planets 14, 105
plankton 22, 254, *337*, 339, 364, *364*
plants 22, 185
  deserts 43
  fossils 168, *168*, 192, 194, 196, 211, 216
  ocean 338, 339
  rainforests 278, 279, **300–301**
plate boundaries 69, **70–71**, 80
platinum 179
plesiosaurs 35, 214
poison-dart frogs 289, *289*, *306*
polar bears 44, 137, *137*, **246–247**, 273
polar climate 108, *109*, 137
polar regions **234–235**, **272–275**
people **262–267**

Index

Poles 16, 46, 47, 49,
    108, *109, 110*, 238
Amazonia *289*
coral reefs 356
erosion 171
global warming 44,
    44
oceans 373
polar regions 273,
    274
Pompeii 98, 156, *156*
porcelain 183
potassium 184, *185*,
    213
prehistoric life 192,
    201
ptarmigan 244, *244*
pterosaurs 209, 214,
    216, 217
pumice 78, *78, 79*, 98,
    101, 156, *156*
pyroclastic flow *74*,
    75, 79, *79*, 81, 84,
    85, *85, 87*
    Mount Pinatubo *96*,
    97
    Mount St Helens 95,
    95

Q

quartz 156, 172, 175,
    175, 180
quetzal 299, *299*

R

rafflesia flower 301,
    301
rain 20, 24, **50–51**,
    108, **118–119**
    clouds 60, 120
    deserts 42
    drought 64
    Earth's formation 15
    floods 62, 63, 122
    hot springs *31*
    hurricanes 60, 130,
    131

rain (*cont.*)
    ice storm 56
    monsoons 112
    Mount Pinatubo 97
    rainforests 278
    rivers 32
    thunderstorms 129
    water cycle *51*
    weathering 170
rainbows 134, 135
rainforests 24, 113,
    276–281
    Africa **294–295**
    Amazon **286–289**
    animals **302–303**,
    306–309
    Asia **296–297**
    birds **304–305**
    climate change 149,
    149
    deforestation
    314–315
    endangered **312–313**
    Madagascar
    292–293
    Oceania **290–291**
    people 291
    plants **300–301**
    products **310–311**
    conservation
    316–317
    rain 50
rats, fossil 217
rattails 347, *347*, 352
redwoods 280, *281*
reindeer (caribou) *240*,
    241, 264, **266–267**
reptiles 216, 287,
    328–329
respiration **360–361**
rhinoceros, fossil *193*,
    217
Rhyniognatha 225
Richter scale 39, *39*
Ring of Fire 69
River Amazon 32, *32*,
    286, *286*

River Nile 32, *62*, 123
rivers **20–21**, **32–33**
    erosion 170, 191
    floods 62, 122
    fossilization 200
    water cycle *119*
rock cycle **152–153**
Rockies *19*
Ross, James Clark 270
rosy periwinkle 293,
    293
ROVs 371
rubber 311, 314
rubies 186, *186*, 187,
    187

S

sabre-toothed cat 205,
    229
sago palm trees 297
Sahara desert 42, *42*,
    114, 126
salt 159, 184, *184*, 331
salt water 34
sand 53, 171, *171*,
    194
sand devils 59
sand dunes *42, 43*,
    431
sandstone 158, 160,
    202
sapphires 186, *186*,
    187, *187*
satellites 147, *147*,
    219, *219*, 371
schist 163
Scott, Robert 45, 271
sea butterfly *358*
sea cucumbers 347,
    353, *364*
sea levels 49, 63
sea mounts 346
sea snakes 329, *329*
sea spiders 49
sea urchins 211
seabed *49*, 334, 346,
    352–353

seals 44, 361
    climate change 273
    ocean food chain
    365
    polar regions
    248–249, 254, 256,
    264, 272
seamounts 100, 320,
    321
seas 12, 319, *319*
    erosion 171
    floods 62
    formation 15
    fossilization 200
    tornado 59
    volcanoes **100–101**
    water cycle 50, *51*,
    118, *119*
    fossil-hunting 219
seasons **110–114**,
    238–239
    products 330, *330*
    weather forecasting
    140, *141*
sedimentary rock
    158–161, 210
    chalk 160, *160*
    coal 159
    evaporites 159
    fossils 201, 202, 206,
    218
    geological time scale
    208
    gold 180
    limestone 158, 160,
    161
    rock cycle 152, *152*,
    153
    salt 184
    sandstone 158, 160
sediments,
    fossils 168, *168*, 194,
    200, 201, *201*, 202
    rock cycle 152, *152*,
    153, 158
Shackleton, Ernest
    270, *270*

shale 162, *162*, 163, 202, 206, 207
sharks **324–325**, 339, *360*, 365
    fossils 198, *198*, 217
    fossil 209, 216, 217
shells, fossil 195, *196*, 227
shooting stars 166, *166*
shrimps 207, 355
silver 178
skuas 259, *259*
slate 162, *162*, 163, 165, *165*, 202
sloths 298, *298*
smelting 178, *178*
snails 217
snakes 279, 287
snow **56–57**, 108, **124–125**
    clouds 120
    glacier *242*
    igloos *264*
    polar regions 234
snowshoe hare 245
snowy owls 44, 244, *244*
solar power 316, *316*
solar wind 239
Solnhofen 217, *217*, 231
South American plate *69*
South Pole 16, 17, 24, **44–45**, 236, 237, *237*, *273*
    expeditions 268, **270–271**
    seasons 110, 239
    snow 125
Southern Lights 239
Southern Ocean *47*, 242, **254–257**, 274, *334*
space rocks **166–167**

sperm whale 253, 326, *326*, 340, *340*, 343, 361, *361*
sponges **348–349**
spring *110*
squid 256, 272, 274
    bioluminescence 363, *363*
    camouflage 368, *368*
stalactite 161, *161*
starfish 355
Stegosaurus 215
Steno, Nicolas 198, *198*
stick insects 306, *306*
Stone Age people 160
strangler figs 284
stratosphere 116
subduction 71
submersibles 371, *372*
sugarcane *310*, 311
sulphur 89, *89*, 182
sulphur dioxide 83, 90
summer 110, *110*, 238, *238*, 239, 242
Sun **114–115**
    atmosphere 117
    day and night 16, 111, *111*
    erosion 179, 219
    halo 135, *135*
    ocean food chain 364
    rain 50, 118
    seasons 110, *110*, 238, 239
sunfish 322, *322*
Surtsey 29, *29*, 101

T
taiga 241
talc 174, *174*
tapir *278*
tar pits 205
tarantula spider 308
tectonic plates 38, *38*, **68–71**, *101*

teeth 184, 194, *194*, 195, 198, 199, 200, *201*
temperate climate 108, *109*, 137
temperate forests 280, 282
termites 309, *309*
thermometer 143, *143*
thunderclouds 54, *54*, 58, *59*, 133
thunderstorms 52, *52*, **128–129**, 132
tides 336
tiger sharks 325, *325*
time periods 208
toads 135, 287, *308*
toco toucan *278*
Toricelli, Evangelista *142*
tornadoes 51, **58–59**, **132–133**, 149
trace fossils 169, 205
trade winds 126
tree frog *279*
tree kangaroos *290*
trees 111, 230, *230*, 241, 278, 280
trenches *48, 49*, 320, 335, 346, 350
Triceratops 229
Trieste 48, 48, 351, *351*
trilobites 211, *211*
tripod fish 353, *353*
tropics 282
    climate 108, *108*
    cyclones 60, 61
    forests 282
    hurricanes 60
    rain 50
    rainforests 113, 280, 282, 284
    seasons 112, 113, *113*
    storms 122, 130
    wind 126

troposphere 116, 117, 120
tsunamis 38, **40–41**, 62
    mangrove forest 312
    volcanoes 86, 87
tubeworms *195*, 355, *355*
tuna fish *338*
tundra 240, *240*, 241, 245, 253, 266
tunicates *365*
turtles 328, *328*, 329, *329*
    fossils 216, 217
tussock bird 259, *259*
twilight zone *334*, **340–343**, 359, *359*, 365
twisters 58, 132
typhoons 60, 97, 130, 131
Tyrannosaurus rex 194, 228

U
Uluru 158
uranium 182, 213

V
valleys,
    Antarctica 242
    fossil-hunting 219
    glaciers 47
    ocean floor 320, 346
    weathering 170
Venus *12*, 105
Venus flower basket **348–349**
vertical migration 359, *359*
vine snakes 302, *302*
vines 279
viperfish *362*
volcanic bombs *74*, 77, *77*

Index

volcanoes 24, **28–29**,
   **66–69, 72–77,
   80–81, 102–105**,
   191
   Antarctica 242
   ash **78–79**, *156*
   atmosphere *14*, 15,
      15
   climate change 149
   diamonds *188*
   effects **86–87**
   fossils 202
   hazards **84–85**
   igneous rock 154,
      154
   lake 21, *21*
   landscape features
      82–83
   Mauna Kea 101
   metamorphic rock
      163
   Mount Pinatubo
      96–97
   Mount St Helens
      94–95
   Mount Vesuvius
      98–99
   mountains *18, 27*
   myths and legends
      106–107
   ocean floor *48*,
      100–101, 320, 321,
      321, 335, 346
   people **88–89**
   plate boundaries 70,
      71, *71*
   rock cycle 152, 153
   thermal pools 31
   VEI scale 102, *102*,
      104, 105
voles 245
volcanology **90–91**

W

Wallace, Alfred 286
walruses 249, *249*, 264
Walsh, Don 48, 351

waste pollution 274
water,
   caves 36, *36*
   deserts 43
   drought *64*
   Earth 12
   eruption 74
   floods 62, 63
   fossilization 200,
      200, 201, 202
   fumeroles 83
   hardness 185
   hot springs **30–31**
   ice 46
   life 22
   minerals 172
   oceans 319
   rivers 32
   snow 124
   thunder 52, 128
   tsunamis 40
   volcanic 89
   weathering 170
water cycle *51*, 118,
   119
water lilies 287
water pressure 48
water vapour 118,
   119, *119*, 121
waterfalls 20, **32–33**
waterspouts 59, 133,
   133
waves 24, *25*, 336
   earthquakes *38*
   erosion 171, 219,
      424
   hurricanes 131, *131*
   tsunamis 40, *40*
weather 24, **108–109**,
   116
   air pressure 117, *117*
   animal adaptations
      136–137
   El Niño 115
   forecasting **140–147**
   fossil-hunting 219
   hail 54

weather (*cont.*)
   measurement 146, *146*
   myths **138–139**
   patterns 64, 65, 108,
      144
   rain 50
   thunderstorms 128
weathering *152*, 158,
   170–171
westerlies *126*
whale shark 22, *22*
whales **326–327**
   breathing *360*, 361
   fossils 217, *217*, 225
   ocean food chain
      365
   polar regions
      250–251, 253, 254,
      256, 264
   conservation 274
   whaling 272
Williamsonia 194
wind chill 262
wind vane 142
winds **126–127**, *145*,
   147
   Dust Bowl *115*
   eruptions 102
   hurricanes 130
   mackerel skies 121
   monsoons 112
   sand dunes *43*
   snow *124*
   tornadoes 58, 132
   weathering 170, 171,
      171, 219
winter 110, *110*, 238,
   239, 242
wolves 205, 245, 247,
   247
wood 310, 314
woodpeckers 137, *137*
woolly mammoth 57,
   57, 198, 213
worms 206, 207, 352,
   361, *361*

Y

Yanomani people 288,
   288
year *17*, 110, 238
Yellowstone National
   Park 31, 105, *105*

Z

zinc 184, *185*
zone fossils 211

Acknowledgements

All artworks are from the Miles Kelly Artwork Bank
Cover Emma Jayne, The Bright Agency

The publishers would like to thank the following sources for the use of their photographs:
(t = top, b = bottom, l = left, r = right, c = centre)

Alamy 162 nagelestock.com; 213 sciencephotos; 262 Bryan & Cherry Alexander Photography; 267(t) Bryan & Cherry Alexander Photography; 316(b) BrazilPhotos.com

Ardea 348–349 Pat Morris

Corbis 24 Gary Braasch; 29 Yann Arthus-Bertrand; 30 David Samuel Robbins; 33(r) Pablo Corral V; 36(t) Robert Dowling; 40 Jeremy Horner; 43(b) Frans Lemmens/Zefa; 44(t) Tim Davis, (b) Rick Price; 47(t) Paul A. Souders; 50 Image Source; 57 Reuters; 58 Eric Nguyen; 60 Warren Faidley; 70 Yann Arthus-Bertrand; 79(t) Jean du Boisberranger/Hemis; 80 Douglas Peebles; 81 Bettmann; 85(t) Michael S. Yamashita, (b) James Andanson/Sygma; 87 Jacques Langevin/Sygma; 93(t) Vittoriano Rastelli, (b) Roger Ressmeyer; 94 Bettmann; 96 Alberto Garcia; 97(b); 99 Bettmann; 106 R.CREATION/amanaimages; 154–155 Jim Sugar; 155 Micha Pawlitzki/zefa; 156(t) Roger Ressmeyer; 157(t) Reuters; 161 David Muench; 163 Frank Lukasseck; 165 Ric Ergenbright; 171 Paul A. Souders; 180 Michael Yamashita; 183(br) Jason Hawkes; 184 Anthony Bannister, Gallo Images; 188(t) Anthony Bannister, Gallo Images; 189(b) Bettmann; 190 George Steinmetz; 191(t) Roger Ressmeyer, (b)Corbis; 192 Annie Griffiths Belt; 194 Layne Kennedy; 204 Michael Amendolia; 217 Mike Nelson; 218 Martin Schutt; 219(t) Paul A. Souders; 220 Ted Soqui; 221(t) Reuters; 222 Michael S. Yamashita; 224 Bill Varie; 228 Ladislav Janicek/Zefa; 229(t) Louie Psihoyos; 231(c) Bettmann; 232(b) Louie Psihoyos; 238 Rob Howard; 242 Tom Bean; 258 Wolfgang Kaehler; 259(b) Paul A. Souders; 263(t) Jack Jackson/Robert Harding World Imagery, (b) Patrick Robert; 265(t) Galen Rowell; 268 Stapleton Collection; 269 Jason Roberts/Push Pictures/Handout/epa; 271 Van Hasselt John/Sygma; 272 Paul Souders; 280(l) Owen Franken; 281 Frans Lanting, (tr) Demetrio Carrasco/JAI; 295(tr) Martin Harvey; 311(br) George Steinmetz; 314 Frans Lanting; 347 Ralph White

Dreamstime.com 294(t) Sloth92; 311(tc) Braendan; 338(t) Tommy Schultz

Ecoscene 53(l) Nick Hawkes

FLPA 54(t) Jim Reed; 92 S Jonasson; 150 Michael Krabs/Imagebroker/FLPA; 158–159 Tim Fitzharris/Minden Pictures; 170 Tim Fitzharris/Minden Pictures; 214 Martin B Withers; 239 Matthias Breiter/Minden Pictures; 240–241 Michio Hoshino/Minden Pictures; 241(br) Patricio Robles Gil/Sierra Madre/Minden Pictures; 246(t) Michio Hoshino/Minden Pictures; 246–247(b) Jim Brandenburg/Minden Pictures; 249 Michio Hoshino/Minden Pictures; 252(t) Michael Quinton/Minden Pictures; 252–253(b) Fritz Polking; 256–257 Norbert Wu/Minden Pictures; 274–275 Colin Monteath/Minden Pictures; 289(tr) Mark Moffett/Minden Pictures; 295(b) Frans Lanting; 296(bl) Jeffrey Oonk/Minden Pictures; 310–311 ImageBroker

Fotolia.com 26(r) QiangBa DanZhen; 33(l) Albo; 56(t) flucas; 83 Marko Heuver; 172(t) Cornelius; 176(t) Domen Colja, (cl) Graça Victoria; 219(t) sharply_done, (bl) Mark huls, (r) Bruno Bernier; 182(t) Andreas Meyer; 183 (inset) A Marcynuk; 185(t, l–r) NiDerLander, Maksim Shebeko, (tr) Darren Hester; 186–187(bg) martreya; 280(r) urosr; 282(bl) amaet; 283(r) Impala; 294(b) fivespots; 306(tc) Michael Luckett; 311(tl) Shariff Che'Lah, (tr) Uros Petrovic; 338(c) Tommy Schultz; 339 Desertdiver; 340–341 cornelius; 360(t) zebra0209

Fredrik Fransson 100(b); 101(b)

GeoEye satellite image 95(t); 100

Getty Images 36(b) Stephen Alvarez; 39(b) Paul Chesley; 55 AFP; 56(m) Aurora; 62(b) Mike Goldwater; 86 AFP; 88–89 Philippe Bourseiller; 89 AFP; 91 Philippe Bourseiller; 104 Jonathan S. Blair/National Geographic; 186–187(t); 276–277 Siegfried Layda; 292–293(t) Roy Toft; 316(tr) Matthias Clamer; 346(b) Jean Tresfon; 367(t) Neil Bromhall; 372–373 Emory Kristof/National Geographic

iStockphoto.com 338(b) tswinner; 338–339 MiguelAngeloSilva; 360(b) sethakan

Monterey Bay Aquarium Research Institute 371(b) c. 2007 MBARI